D1063217

Memories Are Like Clouds

by
Diana J. Dell

Writers Club Press
San Jose New York Lincoln Shanghai

Memories Are Like Clouds

All Rights Reserved © 2000 by Diana J. Dell

No part of this book may be reproduced or transmitted in any form or by any means, graphic, electronic, or mechanical, including photocopying, recording, taping, or by any information storage or retrieval system, without the permission in writing from the publisher.

Published by Writers Club Press
an imprint of iUniverse.com, Inc.

For information address:
iUniverse.com, Inc.
620 North 48th Street
Suite 201
Lincoln, NE 68504-3467
www.iuniverse.com

ISBN: 0-595-00141-6

Printed in the United States of America

Dedicated to Daddy, Mom, Jimmy, Ruth, Barbara, Kenny, and Ricky

Contents

Kenny

Kenny died in Vietnam on November 5, 1968, a date etched forever in my memory. While walking point on his final day, my brother moved a platoon through a heavily mined area and disarmed several booby traps. His scout dog tripped a well-concealed land mine; and the fragments from the explosion killed Kenny and his dog instantly, or so the Army informed our family, obviously, to lessen the pain.

Before flying off to war 10 months earlier, he talked into the nights of returning a hero with medals to prove it. And that he did. Kenny came home with numerous decorations, including the posthumously awarded Bronze Star with first oak leaf cluster. The citation, by direction of President Lyndon Baines Johnson, stated that Kenny "distinguished himself by exceptional heroism in connection with ground operations against an armed hostile force in the Republic of Vietnam while assigned to the 49th Infantry Platoon (Scout Dog), 199th Light Infantry Brigade. Sergeant Dell's valorous actions and devotion to duty, at the cost of his own life, were in keeping with the highest traditions of the military service and reflected great credit upon himself, the 199th Light Infantry Brigade, and the United States Army."

It is still agonizingly painful to remember the funeral. I stared in a daze as the seven uniformed reservists, safe from combat but not its destruction, stood at attention, aimed their rifles at Heaven, and fired three times with precision. The 21-gun salute sounded like three single shots. Taps drifted throughout the cemetery and touched the souls of those congregated, even the people who did not know Kenny, 21 for eternity, lying in the flag-draped coffin. The young men cried the hardest; many openly wept for perhaps the first time in their adult lives. More than for Kenny, they seemed to grieve for themselves, for their own generation, for their own useless war. The remaining tearless women could not hold back any longer when they heard the angry boys sobbing uncontrollably.

Exhausted with sorrow, I could not shed a tear. I resented the obvious response taps was meant to evoke. Losing Kenny forever was unthinkable.

Because being at that grave site was unbearable, my only means of escape was the past. From Kenny's final resting place, I stared down at our little town in the valley and let my thoughts float like the clouds above the cemetery back in time to childhood.

Memories are like clouds. They drift in and out of our minds in no particular order. One minute we are completely in the present, then some thought will catapult us into the past.

One of my earliest memories was of climbing into my former crib to check out the baby. When Kenny was born, I forfeited that initial bed along with my position of preeminence within the family. When he arrived on October 30, 1947, I was 20 months old. Gabbing away for five months, I tried in vain to teach him important words. "Pepsi Cola hits the spot. Twelve full ounces, that's a lot. Twice as much for a nickel too. Pepsi Cola is the drink for you! Nickel, nickel, nickel, nickel. Trickle, trickle, trickle, trickle."

The year Kenny entered the world, Al Capone departed it, not with a bang but a whimper. Jackie Robinson shattered racial barriers, while Maria Callas brought down the curtain to thunderous applause at her debut in Verona. People sighted flying saucers everywhere, except at the wedding of Princess Elizabeth and her charming prince. Blanche Dubois's and Stanley Kowalski's smoldering passions helped Tennessee Williams win the Pulitzer, and Anne Frank's attic memories touched the heart of the world.

When Kenny joined our family, big brother Jimmy was seven and, similar to every other boy in America, thought Joe DiMaggio was a hero.

Harry Truman was president. There were many firsts that year. Chuck Yeager sped into history books with supersonic flight. Groucho Marx zinged America on "You Bet Your Life"; "The Jack Paar Show" premiered on radio; and Lassie trotted into the studio and barked his way into America's homes.

Mommy, looking like a teenager at 26, was then a mother of four. While listening to favorite radio programs in the maternity ward, she learned that more doctors smoked Camels than any other cigarette.

What a year to be born! Edwin Land sped up photography with the one-minute picture; Redi Whip topped off desserts without any mess in the kitchen, not counting a few ceilings accidentally decorated by either too eager or too clumsy kids; and "made in Japan" usually meant junk until Sony hit the world scene in 1947.

"Zip-a-dee-do-dah" was a fairly easy song for elder sister Barbara to sing when she was a precocious five-year-old.

The new Tony Awards recognized quality on Broadway, and film-makers around the world showcased their celluloid creations at the brand-nouveau Cannes Film Festival. While Kenny strengthened his lungs with wails for milk or bellows to be held, Ethel Merman belted out "There's No Business Like Show Business" to cheering theatergoers.

World War II veteran Daddy was 31 going on 16 with his zest for life. Although he had planted his feet solidly in the family, his head remained floating in the clouds. He often dreamed of the first million he hoped to make in his two-year-old wholesale candy business.

Kenny's birth fulfilled Daddy's other wish for another son. In grati-tude to the hospital staff, he proudly passed out boxes of chocolates to doctors, nurses, and aides that wonderful fall morning when he felt like a millionaire.

Small World

Our home at 241 Quay Street, East Vandergrift, Pennsylvania, had a roll-up green awning and a swing on the red-bricked front porch. Kenny and I swung there with Mommy on many peaceful afternoons and rainy evenings, listening to her stories as the '40s drifted into the '50s. Always more entertaining and informative than the radio, she vividly recollected the Roaring '20s, the Great Depression, and World War II, events she lived through and wanted so much to share. Not only did the two of us follow her around the house like baby ducks, but also we hung onto her every word, fascinated by her many anecdotes. Kenny and I were her captive and rapt audience. Our world revolved around our mother.

Grownups admired us, and our heads received more pats in months than some pampered cats acquire in their entire nine lives. Kenny and I started conversations with just about everyone, and the outcome rarely disappointed us. Older people loved to talk; we loved to listen. The more interest we showed, the more stories we heard. Besides Mommy, neighbors were another source of valuable knowledge we absorbed during daily walks in the neighborhood.

Mrs. Trotaskovich, a widow who lived directly across the street, worried about bowel movements. For some reason, she called her bowels "barrels" and constantly fretted about people she knew moving theirs.

Kenny could not understand the connection between daily bodily functions, or "going pu pu" as he dubbed it, and people hurling over Niagara Falls in barrels. I couldn't explain, because at that point in our lives I was still trying to figure out the nuances of the English language.

Words that sounded the same had different meanings, such as "salary" and "celery," and other words had shades of differences. Babies drank milk from bottles, yet Daddy called Mommy his baby. Weird. All I knew about Mrs. Trotaskovich's barrels was that if she did not move them every morning, she was unbearable to be near. That woman ate more prunes than anyone alive: stewed prunes, prune juice, prune pastry, and prunes straight out of the box. Her tongue was perpetually purple. When we saw her on her porch grinning and singing Slovak hymns early in the morning, we knew those barrels of hers had moved (to where? we wondered), and all was right with the world.

John and Mildred Pinchek and their two daughters resided to the right of our house. Mary Pinchek, the younger sister, was soft-spoken and could have been a model for the poster of the righteous Catholic girl—angelic, chaste, and full of grace. Her older sister was another matter entirely. A few years after graduating from high school, Maggie, the elder Pinchek daughter, had a baby out of wedlock. Everybody in town was polite to her face-to-face but behind her back labeled her a "bad girl." The father of the passion child was already married and denied participation in the sordid deed. Fat chance he was telling the truth. From the time their son was six months old, he was a spitting image of the father. Possessing plenty of guts, Maggie named the baby after her paramour and repeatedly told the boy who his father was. In a small community that rarely had more than 2002 inhabitants, neither keeping a secret nor avoiding someone was hardly possible. Little Archie and Big Archie saw each other daily without ever speaking. When the son stared at the father, he appeared to be gazing into a mirror of the future.

Kenny and I adored babies, legal or otherwise, and cultivated Maggie's friendship to get to spend time with Little Archie. (Townsfolk consistently called the boy "Little Archie" and the man "Big Archie." The relatives of the alleged father also used those two terms, even though they denied any relationship whatsoever, so help them God.)

Listening to Maggie, who peppered her sentences with lots of naughty expressions, we acquired new and exotic words when she spoke of Big Archie. Oh, we heard other grownups swear once in a while: "Damn it, Jim, the kids' teeth are going to rot out if you keep giving them all that candy." However, our parents never, ever uttered the F-word; it was the ultimate bad word, although we didn't have an inkling what it meant. It sure was great when Maggie got angry or had too many highballs. Wow! Could that woman cuss up a storm!

Old folks treated young 'uns like dumbbells. The big people assumed for some reason that children had no ears or did not understand the spoken language. Then, after a while, adults started the spelling routine: "Maggie made so much noise at 3:00 a.m. when she came home stinking d-r-u-n-k as usual, she could have awakened the dead." While most tots were learning how to spell c-a-t and d-o-g, Kenny and I were memorizing, but not letting on that we knew, words such as t-r-a-m-p and d-i-s-g-r-a-c-e.

Adam Adamchik and his widowed mother lived next door to the Pincheks. Exempted from the draft because he worked in the steel mill, Adam was the sole support of his mom. Mother and dutiful son were gentle-hearted and kind to children—perfect neighbors, and their house was a great Halloween stop.

The Adamchiks' neighbors were Kathy Vazshinyak, a single woman, and her widowed mother, a crabby old lady. Kathy and Adam were the same age, late-20s, and neither dated, yet people called him a carefree bachelor and pitied her, a washed-up spinster approaching 30. Fun-loving Daddy used to tease each about the other, but the only response he got from either of them was a blush or an excuse that something was boiling over on the stove.

Beside the house of Miss Vazshinyak and her demanding, grouchy mother was the Lazinski home. Mr. Lazinski, a grade school dropout, was 6-foot tall and blond. Mrs. Lazinski, also a grade school dropout, was the same height with coal-black hair. Both parents were serene and graceful. Neither walked; each glided along without a care in the world.

The oldest Lazinski boy, a blond, was ambitious and athletic, the town hero throughout his high school years, captaining and starring on the football team. Off the playing field, he was president of the student body and every club that begged him to join. Eagle-eyed scouts from the Big Ten thrust athletic scholarships at him, but he chose a scholastic one offered by Yale. While in New Haven, he made the people of East Vandergrift proud as he continued his pigskin prowess in the Ivy League.

The Lazinski second-born was a spitting image of her mother down to the glide. Following a lackluster high school education, she got pregnant, quickly married, and settled up the street from her family home.

The third-born resembled the father and, upon being told for the millionth time how beautiful she was, hit the fashion scene in New York for a successful modeling career.

The juvenile delinquent of the Lazinski clan was the fourth child, born with dark, brooding looks. When a window was broken, tires slashed, or other prank committed by unknown assailants, he was one of the first of those rounded up for questioning, along with the other usual suspects of mischievous deeds.

If someone knocked on the Lazinski door with good news or bad news, it was safe to ask what honor the blond, fifth child had received and what trouble the sixth and dark-haired one had gotten into.

When baby Eddie (our brother Jimmy's classmate and pal) started sprouting light hair, the relatives breathed a sigh of relief, knowing that he would turn out great.

Perched on the corner of Quay and Reed Streets, the Lazinski house was across from the 85 steps that led up to Vandergrift Lane, the only road out of town. The Haitkus family lived at the bottom to the right of the steps. Mr. Haitkus's hobby was coin collecting, which he started as a youngster in the 1920s. As an enterprising kid, he volunteered to roll coins at the banks uptown in Vandergrift. Spotting one needed for his collection, he replaced it with a comparable one—a dime for a dime, a penny for a penny. By the time the 1950s rolled around, the collection was valued at $50,000, or so he bragged to Kenny and me while proudly displaying his treasure.

His son did not find numismatics exciting enough. The Haitkus boy instead saved, laminated, and hoarded baseball cards, while Jimmy and his boyfriends attached their waxed cards to the spokes of bikes, pretending they were driving motorcycles.

A widow, who lived alone but was visited often by her three daughters from convents and two sons who were priests, owned the house next to the Haitkus family. There was a lifelike Blessed Virgin Mary statue in her postage-stamp yard, as well as holy pictures and crucifixes in every room of the house; moreover, the frail lady sat on the porch all day long praying the rosary. If ever a miracle were going to occur, it would have been right there.

On a cloudy Sunday afternoon when the kids in their black garb were home for a visitation, one of the nuns spotted Kenny and me playing with Jimmy's Lincoln Logs on our porch, and over she came for a hug. As Kenny nestled in her lap, and I settled beside them listening to her soothing voice recite a religious fable, it started to thunder and lightning. As usual, I began to cry. Kenny joined in. It's curious how people remember first times, no matter how long ago; but as she held us tightly, I do recall how she remarked that thunder was merely God's moving furniture. That made perfect sense. It may not have taken our fear away, but at least someone had given a reasonable explanation for the frightening clamor.

Next to the holy dwelling was our family's former rental home, which had no front or back yard; instead, it had a side yard. The Dell family moved to Quay Street shortly after Daddy returned from the war. At that time, he rented a house from Mrs. Berostek, whose two soldier-sons were in Japan helping MacArthur with postwar reorganization.

The price was $35 a month, but our generous father insisted on paying $10 more because Mrs. Berostek was a widow.

The candy business was doing well, and Mommy was pregnant with Kenny, thanks to the failed Catholic Church rhythm-method our parents were practicing. Surprised, yet delighted, they decided it was time to have a place of their own and bought the property across and down the street a few yards for $7500 with $500 down.

The five of us—Daddy, Mommy, Jimmy, Barbara, and I—walked across Quay Street in the summer of 1947, a few months before Kenny was born. By the time he was carried across the threshold, the rest of the family was settled into the coal-heated, three-bedroom, one-bath, two-story white house with a front and back porch. There were French doors between the dining room and hallway and built-in wooden bookcases in the living room. Too old-fashioned for our mom, she had the fancy doors and solid oak bookcases removed by the only carpenter in town. Watching him hammer and saw, Kenny and I sat silently. His was the first profession my kid brother wanted to follow when he heard that Jesus, too, was a carpenter.

The bathroom had a tub with claw feet where Kenny and I bathed together. Barbara hid her slacks underneath the bathtub, where she thought Mommy wouldn't find them. Why? Miss Barbara Ann Dell preferred wearing dresses so that the neighbors, who claimed our hammy sister resembled Shirley Temple, could admire her frilly panties when she twirled.

Mrs. Berostek owned the two lots across the street. One lot was where our family earlier lived, and the other had a second house in the back and a large yard. There, Widow Berostek planted a victory garden during WW II and since war's end, added flowers along with a statue of the Blessed Virgin. Holy Mary, Mother of God, stood 5 feet tall with her arms outstretched at the front of the property line, inches from the sidewalk. When people passed by, they involuntarily crossed themselves and bowed their heads.

The double-decker on the back plot was where Mrs. Berostek lived alone ever since her two sons went off to war weeks after Pearl Harbor. She resided on the second floor and rented out the first. Behind the house were her chicken coop, outhouse, and grape vine, then the road, Vandergrift Lane, the only way to get in or to get out of town.

Next to the Berostek properties lived an elderly widower and his two grown sons. The older boy, Lefty, had an anchor tattoo on his arm from his Navy days and toiled in the steel mill as the breadwinner of the household. His kid brother Cazzy was unemployed because of a heart condition. As a result, he used up his time gossiping with housewives and trading curses with Mrs. Trotaskovich, his next-door neighbor, whenever she had not moved her "barrels."

Butch Kilouskas and his family lived to the left of us. He didn't own real estate, but we labeled it "Butch's house." Kenny and I constantly heard Jimmy yelling, "Mom! I'm going over to Butch's house!"

His older sister Betty baby-sat Kenny and me before Barbara was old enough to do the honors. Our sis was by far stricter than Betty Kilouskas, who generally went home crying that she did not know how in the world six pillows became split open or why the slats on the bed in the boys' room got broken in half. How could she hear the bouncing on beds during pillow fights with the radio in the living room blasting? Besides the deafening music that rendered her clueless to antics upstairs, she gabbed on the phone to her girlfriends from the second our parents walked out the front door till five minutes before their expected return.

Butch and Betty's mom was sociable whether chatting with neighbors while sweeping their porches or assisting a customer. She waited patiently as Kenny decided to either purchase the licorice penny candy nicknamed "nigger babies" or blow the whole nickel on a Clark Bar at her family's combination candy store-pool hall a short stroll up the alley behind Eddie Lazinski's house. "Mom! I'm going to Eddie's house!"

The pool hall faced the alley, and the candy store fronted McKinley Avenue, the longest street in town. A purple curtain separated the two worlds. When a big boy eager to get another Coke parted the divider, after finishing a game, we caught a glimpse into the forbidden territory. We spotted Jimmy in there often, but a big-brother nickel flipped to Kenny kept our mouths shut any time Mommy, who believed bad boys played pool, asked his whereabouts. If what she thought were true, then every adolescent male in town must have been a bad boy. Kenny and I encountered them all there at one time or another while we pondered selections through the glass-enclosed candy case.

Mr. Kilouskas allowed anyone, with or without parental permission, to hang out in the back room. Because he worked part-time for a housing contractor, it was rumored he stole a brick a day for years until he had enough to build the store. It's hard to imagine his having that much patience, since he seemed to always lose his temper over the most trivial concerns. No one could waste time deciding which sweet to buy when he ran the store. The split second kids opened the door and saw him, they either ran back outside or blurted out the first choices that came to mind after he asked in a booming voice, "Watta younse want? Make it snappy, I'm a busy man." When the penny transactions were completed, he parted the purple curtain and roared, "No loafin' allowed. Pay and rack 'em or get da hell outta here. Dis ain't no playground." Why Mrs. Kilouskas chose him as her life's mate was anyone's guess. He was as rotten and mean to her as he was to the paying clientele.

Restless with boredom one summer night, Jimmy and his buddies decided to sneak into the pool hall to shoot a few free games. Getting in was a piece of cake. They knew that Mr. Kilouskas did not always lock the back door when he closed for the day. Being amateurs at breaking and entering, the boys turned all the lights on and made such a racket that some irate woman who lived a block away called Mrs. Kilouskas to gripe. Butch's mom wasn't on the phone more than three seconds before her worse-half grabbed the phone, cut the old lady off, and contacted our cop. Within minutes, the town's sole policeman and Mr. Kilouskas burst into the pool hall swinging baseball bats and hurling curses at the frightened boys who were racing out the back.

I do not know where they thought they were going to hide, because the cop and the charm school flunky went from one boy's house to another's, informing the parents of what their sons had done. The angry families convened a meeting at our house and decided to let the lone lawman take the kids to jail for the night to teach them a lesson.

Before sending her firstborn to the slammer, Mommy ordered Daddy to give Jimmy a licking. After dramatically yanking off his belt, towering father led whimpering son to the cellar and shut the door behind them. Then, after giving Jimmy a big bear hug to calm him down, Daddy whispered in his ear to begin screaming. Meanwhile, what we heard upstairs sounded like a flogging. The cracks of a belt followed by Jimmy's wails were accompanied by wretched sobs from Barbara, Kenny, and me.

Moments after the fake whipping, Jimmy fell in line with the other juvenile delinquents, who were already weeping and marching in single file two blocks to incarceration. Word around town spread fast. While the lads sniffled throughout the night in the only cell, their grandmothers brought them cookies and hot cocoa. The next day each young man swore on a Bible that he would never be bad again, because, so the warning went, reform school would be the next punishment.

Oh my, the gossip in town over that escapade was unbelievable. While old biddies shook their heads in disgust and shrieked Polish, Lithuanian, and Slovak curses at the guys, younger brothers exalted them as though they were the Jesse James' gang, and girls their age gawked at them with fresh, admiring eyes.Mommy, on the other hand, watched Jimmy like a hawk. He had to report his every move to her from morning till night. To make sure he understood the seriousness of the crime, she grounded him for two months. That meant Jimmy could go outside only to school and to church, where he could and better repent for his sins by being a pious altar boy.

"You brought shame to our family," Mommy declared daily for a very long time thereafter.

Convinced it would take years before they could walk down the street without adults viewing them as terrible criminals, those humiliated boys suffered greatly. It did not take long, however, for their offense to be put on the back burner. Within a few months, two unmarried young women got pregnant and became the talk of the town. In a wink of an eye, Jimmy and his cohorts became old news. Also, because he sorely missed the money the boys spent in the pool hall, Mr. Kilouskas admitted them back in. The big billiard B and E, mentioned now and then over the years, became part of our town's notorious folklore.

Barbara and her girlfriends chose not to conduct business there even before the burglary. For one thing, the Kilouskas's shop did not have any place for patrons to sit. Instead of standing, the girls sipped pop in the booths and listened to the juke box at Joe Stemplensky's candy-variety store across the street.

Joe's was the only place in the world that sold a chocolate-malted ice cream treat called a "cho cho," which he made himself, then put in a waxed-paper container with a stick. You pushed the stick up and the cylinder down as you gobbled up the frozen ice cream.

The big girls lingered in a wooden booth devouring cho chos, listening to romantic Nat King Cole singles, and giggling while they observed boys they had crushes on play the pinball machine.

Green with envy, Kenny and I desperately wanted to slide in beside them, feast on cho chos, sing along with the records, and watch them watch boys they were sweet on. Later we would mimic them until they chased us away. Sadly, though, before all that fun began, we couldn't get across the main street by ourselves, and Barbara did not intend to accommodate us. No matter how much we begged, badgered, and bawled, it was useless. She and her friends fiercely protected their privacy from prying younger siblings' eyes and ears by simply ignoring our theatrics.

McKinley Avenue was the castle moat, and the imaginary drawbridge would not be lowered until Kenny was potty-trained. Eager to hurry along the event, I ordered him to hold on until we could make it home whenever a strained expression appeared on his face. The toilet training was completed once he understood that no more diapers meant we could cross McKinley Avenue to pester Barbara at Joe's candy store. Kenny became goal-oriented from an early age, and Mommy bragged for years afterwards how her baby boy toilet trained himself. Right.

Butch Kilouskas was 10 years my senior, played the accordion, and knew I had a mad crush on him. He practiced daily on his front porch while Kenny and I sat on the swing on ours heeding his every sweet note. I was convinced he was serenading me. Because I was never skillful at acting coy, everyone in the neighborhood knew of my feelings. It was hopeless trying to resist his blond crewcut, soft baby-blues, and that huge smile he flashed in my direction. What a dreamboat! Violins and the strumming of Gypsy guitars may bewitch many women, but I will warmly remember my earliest sweetheart whenever I hear an accordion solo of "The Beer Barrel Polka." Butch performed at dances and weddings and was paid as well as the older musicians. Being in love with a celebrity, I practically swooned when the blond hunk waved to me from the bandstand at functions our family attended.

In the 1940s and 1950s, it seemed as though we went to a wedding every Saturday, many of them s-h-o-t-g-u-n. Large, loud, and loads of fun, they started in the afternoon and continued through the wee small hours of the morning.

Immediately following the High and very lengthy Mass, the guests trooped to the Polish, Slovak, or Lithuanian club for the reception. Relatives of the couple and churchwomen cooked up a storm. The buffet tables were brimming with scrumptious Eastern European dishes: pickled herrings, Warsaw salad, kielbasa, pierogis, ham hocks in sauerkraut, stuffed cabbage, duck's blood soup, dumplings, Hunter's stew, Polish links, fried potatoes with sausage (getting hungry, yet?), cauliflower ala Poland, pickled eggs, tongue and potato salad, baba au rum, almond tortes, nut rolls, poppyseed rolls, and plenty more. The only store-bought food was the wedding cake that no one ate anyway. Single girls took individual slices home and tenderly placed them under their pillows as a good-luck gesture in the diligent pursuit of snagging a good provider.

The father of the bride paid for the shindig, which included an open bar. Boy, how the wedding guests drank! And danced! Outnumbering adults five to one, little kids polkaed with each other as well as with the bride and groom. Those Slovaks also had a tradition that Mommy thought was vulgar of paying to dance with the bride. Men encircled the lucky young woman and waited their turn to pay for the privilege of whirling the bride. While her dad stood to the side holding a large hat, the men forming the circle clapped their hands and stomped their feet to the music. During this raucous ritual, my mom usually had her hands covering her face in embarrassment at the spectacle that she found barbaric. After the tired bride and the overheated men plopped down, old ladies got up to dance, fast and slow, with each other. Weddings were always grand celebrations that did not end until the last person left at dawn.

Butch's family owned a house behind the one they lived in. The renters were Mr. and Mrs. Paschis and their son, who was Barbara's age. When they bought a home of their own and moved, Kenny and I felt a tremendous loss. Their new residence across the railroad tracks was a cheerful, yellow house near the Kiskiminetas River. Deciding to visit them one day, Kenny and I ventured across the rails, knowing we were doing something that was forbidden. Mrs. Paschis was shocked when she came to the door and saw us standing there, looking guilty but glad to see her friendly face. This was not the first time we sat in her new living room, but it was the first time we ever came without our parents.

Gracious as ever, Mrs. Paschis brought out cookies and couldn't have been nicer, even when Kenny accidentally knocked over and broke a lamp. We were terrified she would tell on us for not only crossing the tracks but also for wrecking her property. After soothing away our tears, she walked with us as far as Joe's candy store. There, she kissed us and said, "If you two promise never to cross the railroad tracks again, I won't squeal on you." Bless her soul. Mrs. Paschis never breathed a word about our misadventure that fall day in 1949.

Mrs. Bober and Ronny, her change-of-life baby, lived next to Butch's house. (Mr. Bober had died of black lung disease a few weeks before his only child was born.)Ronny was Jimmy's age, and he spent as much time at our house as Kenny and I did at his. Mrs. Bober narrated amazing stories of Lithuania, her and her dearly departed husband's birthplace. Since Daddy's parents were born in Lithuania, she filled our minds and hearts with information about our cultural heritage. Those peanut butter cookies with chocolate icing were another compelling reason to pay a visit. Every Tuesday, Mrs. Bober baked those most extraordinary, stick-to-the-roof-of-your-mouth goodies.

Skipping over to her house, Kenny and I caught up on tales, such as what happened after the pagan duke, Jogalio, married the Queen of Poland, Jadwiga, converted to Christianity, and then ruled in the 14th Century as Wladyslaw IV, King of Poland and Lithuania. While we sat in the kitchen listening to antiquity lectures, Mrs. Bober insisted that we help ourselves to a few more cookies to make sure they were good enough for Ronny's later consumption, as if we were court tasters or something. We didn't mind, though, helping her out by sampling baked delights. I mean, what are neighbors for, anyway? While in pursuit of some sugary treat, we picked up a history lesson here and there. Before either of us could read, we knew that Lithuanian, with origins in Sanskrit, is the oldest language in Europe.

The two of us, babies of the family, would have made excellent Indian scouts. During strolls through the neighborhood, we knew who was baking what by tilting our heads back and sniffing the air.

Calling on Maggie Pinchek, we played with Little Archie and always tried some of the apple pie she had recently pulled out of the oven. Oh, those dazzling aromas—baked apples, cinnamon, and baby powder! Surely parts of Heaven must smell like that.

While cutting a gigantic slice of one-hour-old chocolate-layered cake, Mrs. Trotaskovich recounted accounts of the magnificent period of statehood in the Great Moravian Empire for Slovaks before those horrid Hungarians crushed her ancestors in the 10th Century. When she dropped her voice to a whisper and searched furtively around the room, as if she were going to catch someone hiding near the icebox, Kenny and I knew we were going to hear more current history. Some stories Mrs. Trotaskovich divulged were so scandalous that they could have curled anyone's hair, and we usually hung on to every bit of tantalizing news.

Even today, it is difficult to imagine Mrs. Berostek, our former landlady, as a brazen hussy flapper (as Mrs. Trotaskovich described her) during the 1920s. She looked like every other grandmother in East Vandergrift. We could not picture old lady Berostek (the one in the size-18 housedress and polka-dotted babushka securely tied over her gray hair, who seemed to always have a kettle on for tea) drinking bathtub gin during Prohibition and coming home at dawn with her underwear in her pocketbook.

We learned, however, that things were different in those days. For one thing, almost half the people in town made moonshine. The place reeked like a gigantic saloon. Since the federal marshal could not be everywhere at once, East Vandergrift, as every other small town in Western Pennsylvania, had an appointed local official patrolling for violations concerning the Prohibition law. It was one great opportunity for a small-time, lowly paid public official to procure some extra money on the side. People paid Mr. Mijorsky protection money and were happy with the good luck of having a dishonest cop on their side. Almost everybody broke the law and drank, or so the recitals went.

With descriptions of Prohibition forming mental pictures of something out of the Wild West, Kenny wished with all his might that he had been alive back then, instead of during the boring post-World War II years.

You could tell who produced moonshine, the neighborhood storytellers told Kenny and me, because of the odor when you passed the lawbreakers' houses. Some people brewed it for their own use; others made a business out of it. A few, besides Mr. Mijorsky, became rich, invested in the stock market, then lost everything in the crash of '29.

Once a neighbor didn't want to pay Mr. Mijorsky for the moonshine she made and sold, and he called in the feds. When the violator heard the fuzz were coming, she asked our maternal grandmother, Bupchie, to hide 15 gallons in her house on McKinley Avenue. Obliging Bupchie hid the booze in the coal cellar until the agents searched the house next door and, finding nothing, left.

Practically everybody made beer, but Mr. Mijorsky didn't care. Controlling the whole town by himself was impossible; he just could not outrun the kids who were racing down the streets warning people he was coming.

Our preschool imaginations were fueled further whenever Widow Berostek lowered her speech to a hiss and looked conspiratorially around the kitchen. With eyes twinkling, she conveyed more about those wild, devil-may-care, eat, drink till dawn, and be merry, for tomorrow may never come, Prohibition days, whilst Republican Presidents Harding, Coolidge, and Hoover snoozed in the White House. To our delight, Mrs. Berostek regularly treated us to some juicy gossip concerning one of the neighbors.

Mrs. Sorbanski, the widow who moved into the house where the Paschis family once lived behind Butch's house, was at one time a very wealthy individual whose husband had been the biggest moonshiner in town. The couple owned a race track in Apollo, across the river, (along with a string of horses) and lived high off the hog. Wearing diamonds and furs, she turned her nose up as she rode through the then unpaved streets in her chauffeur-driven Model-T. The Depression and the repeal of the Volstead Act brought her and her wheeler-dealer spouse crashing to Earth. They lost everything. Twenty long and hard years later, there she was, surviving in a two-room bungalow rented and paid for by her children, long gone from town, sick of hearing about the illustrious past. Mrs. Berostek's choice comment at the end of a Mrs. Sorbanski story was, "The bigger they are, the harder they fall."

Generally, though, Mrs. Berostek knifed Mrs. Trotaskovich in the back more than she did anyone else. I don't think it was really meant to be malicious, just enlightening to Kenny and me, two very inquisitive kids and extremely good listeners. Mrs. Berostek told stories about plenty of people we knew, saw often, or liked. The two little squirts, as big Daddy nicknamed us, knew the skeletons in every neighbor's on the block closet as well as strangers' not-so-secret past lives two streets away.

A boy could grow up to be a bishop (or a cardinal like Adam Maida), dedicate his life to God's good works, and take care of his mother until her final breath, but never would it be forgotten that the cleric was caught stealing a pie from his neighbor's windowsill when he was nine. No one's slate was ever wiped clean. Evil deeds from the past followed a person for the rest of his life and beyond in East Vandergrift.

Mrs. Berostek's tea kettle whistled away while we listened to her warm and comforting voice. She spoke in the same way adults talked to each other, which Kenny and I appreciated. The facts were presented plain and simple as she sipped her tea, passed the plate of cookies, and began another yarn of her younger days.

"No beating around the bushes," she began the day's civics lesson, "Mr. Mijorsky was a man of low morals. The drunk and skirt-chaser didn't have no respect for his wife or family." Mrs. Berostek's hands flew to her colossal breasts at the mere thought of such depravity. With a smile that could melt an iceberg crossing her wrinkled face, she then continued. "While he lay dying—may God strike me dead if I'm lying— he confessed to the Slovak priest, the one who left town in 1936 under very mysterious surroundings. But that's another story. Anywho, Mr. Mijorsky confessed that he killed a man." Stopping long enough to chuckle, she proceeded. "And then, he didn't die after all. Serves him right, the no-good son of a bitch and not very nice man. He was so evil he cursed in front of innocent children." To emphasize this shocking remark, she shook her head from side to side in total disbelief of his corrupting ways, oblivious to her own swearwords while telling the story to two innocent children.

The time was pre-Communion days, which meant Kenny and I did not know beans about the Roman Catholic Church or any other place of worship for that matter. We never questioned how anybody found out about Mr. Mijorsky's deathbed confession that was supposed to be a secret the priest carried to the grave. Believing everything we heard, there were never any interruptions in the story with questions or debates concerning the sanctity of the sacrament of penance.

Without having to stop or backtrack with unnecessary explanations, Mrs. Berostek wove her yarns and made the characters remarkably daring. Bribable civil servant Mr. Mijorsky, the guy we knew as a daffy old geezer slouched in a rocking chair on his daughter's porch, was notorious as the Polish Mafia chieftain during those glorious Prohibition days when gangsters and flappers strutted their stuff. Husky, tough, immoral, and handsome, Mr. Mijorsky had the eyes for no one else but Mrs. Trotaskovich. Many people, including Mrs. Trotaskovich herself, claimed she was some looker back then.

Bogart and Bacall. Tracy and Hepburn. Gable and Lombard. Wallace and David. They came later; but in the jazzy '20s in East Vandergrift, Mijorsky and Trotaskovich were the beautiful twosome. The captivating couple drank and danced in public, while Mijorsky's helpmate stayed at home and took care of the children. The cad spent more time and money on sexy Mrs. Trotaskovich than he did on his saintly spouse and adorable, well-behaved Mijorsky offspring.

Once upon a time when Mrs. Trotaskovich still had her own teeth, she was entertaining another man at her home. (The same house across the street from ours, no less.)In walked Mr. Mijorsky drunk as a skunk and fit to be tied to see her in the arms of the married mayor. Insane with jealousy (remember, Mrs. Trotaskovich was quite the vamp), Mr. Mijorsky pushed the also-on-the-take city official down the cellar steps and broke his neck. It was not clear to anybody which came first, the broken neck or the shove, even though the mercurial love team of Mijorsky and Trotaskovich swore on a Bible that the VIP fell down the steps while they were innocently lounging in the parlor having a cup of coffee. Sure. The case of the mayor's murder was dropped until Mr. Mijorsky's dying words years later, but even then the priest could not take the stand.

Pretty heady stuff for three- and four-year-olds. Our adrenaline pumped when we meandered by Mr. Mijorsky, perched on his daughter's front porch, drooling onto his shirt. Mrs. Trotaskovich, too, became less of a one-dimensional character. She might have looked like a frumpy, flour-smelling grandmother before we heard the murder account, but afterwards she took on a new aura. The old woman constantly baking, devouring prunes, and worrying about her barrels was a person with a shady past. When she sent Kenny to the basement for another sack of flour, I tagged along. Our pulses raced with the excitement and terror of being at the actual homicide scene. With ghoulish delight, we feared and yet loved being alone with Mrs. Trotaskovich, the town's mystery woman.

Stupid bureaucrats run the CIA. If they really wanted to obtain secrets, all the spooks would have to do is hire preschoolers, dress them in overalls and scruffy shoes, keep them skinny so that every mother and grandmother within a hundred miles would ply them with food to fatten them, and send the tots off to gather intelligence. Merely tell the kiddies to keep their mouths shut and all the secrets of the universe would be whispered into their ears.

Kenny and I had easy access to neighbors' unlocked houses, just as everyone had easy access to ours. After pushing open back doors, we stuck our heads in and shouted, "Yoo hoo! Anyone home?"

Figaro, Figaro, Figaro

The women of East Vandergrift did not bake much in July and August. During those sweltering, pre-air-conditioned days, the only cooking was done on top of the stove. Relief from the muggy weather was provided by breezes from open windows, screen doors, an occasional fan, and welcome rain showers. Nonetheless, there was no deprivation from scarcity of baked goods.

Every other day in the late morning, Kenny's ears perked up the moment he heard peculiar but familiar music floating toward our house. A small red truck, no bigger than a station wagon, with the sides and rear partially exposed, slowly made its way up the street. From the loudspeaker attached to the roof, we caught people singing in Italian or German. Often it sounded as though they had recently lost their best friends and were about to die of broken hearts. Very sad music indeed. Then at other times, they were quite silly repeating the same word over and over and over again.

The driver, an itinerant baker, was also an opera singer on the radio. During the early hours, he trekked from town to town delivering baked goods. After hustling cakes in the morning, he spent the afternoon at a small AM station taping his show and cutting records, while his wife stayed home preparing products for the next day. The poor woman. Her kitchen must have been as hot as h-e-l-l.

The traveling pastry pusher, whose show immediately followed the famous Metropolitan Opera broadcast every Saturday, had a wind-up Victrola on the passenger seat that was hooked somehow to the loud speaker on the truck top. Robert Merrill, Patrice Munsel, or another famous vocalist announced his arrival in plenty of time for Mommy to get a dollar from her purse and send Kenny outside to stop the fire engine-colored vehicle. Sporting a thick German accent and a large handlebar mustache, the cookie salesman had a soft baritone voice. Kenny and I did not care much for his taste in music; however, his desserts were not only delicious but also were delightful to look at as well.

Finally, when we were brave enough to try a new and different treat, Boston cream pie became our favorite selection. How we envied people in Massachusetts who got to eat them all the time, while we enjoyed them only in the summer.

Herr Fromer, as he called himself, was very formal, never using our first names, although he heard them hundreds of times over the years. Kenny was "Herr," and I was "Fraulein." What's more, he never once patted our heads or admired us in the same way other grownups did, as though we were the cutest kids who ever came down the pike. Once, to get his attention, we discussed giving the "Heil, Hitler" salute but somehow knew that was not a wise thing to do.

The music varied, but the scene was the same. Instantly recognizing the exiting section of "The Toreadors" in *Carmen*, Kenny raced outside and flagged down the miniature red van by jumping up and down and flailing his arms like a shipwrecked soul stranded on a desert island viewing a vessel on the horizon. Meanwhile, I grabbed the money from Mommy, darted outside, and stood beside Kenny at curbside. Herr Fromer braked the truck, turned off the record, handed Kenny the Boston cream pie before we had a chance to tell him what we wanted, took the money, and continued up Quay Street. The guy really knew his customers well. Yet, we always were slightly disappointed that he never asked for a squeeze as everyone else did.

It's not that he was unfriendly; on the contrary, he was extremely pleasant but rather reserved. Since he sang on the radio, which made him a star in our eyes, we were on our best behavior in front of him. But as soon as his confectionery-filled vehicle reached Eddie Lazinski's house at the end of the block, Kenny and I started singing tunes more to our taste. "If I knew you were comin' I'd've baked a cake," we bellowed off-key at the top of our lungs. Marching up the front steps heading into the house, I held open the screen door, and Kenny slowly shuffled in past me while precariously balancing the Boston delicacy on his head.

Mommy and Herr Fromer were formal with each other whenever she personally came outside to place an extra order for company. Tipping his hat, he greeted her with a warm smile and a friendly "Guten Morgan, Frau." All women he called "Frau," not their last names, just "Frau." Kenny guessed that he didn't have children of his own, because he treated us as he did adults, with the same prim and proper politeness.

Opera was rarely heard in our home, except for the few times the radio was tuned in to the Metropolitan Opera during a rain shower or snow storm. On those occasions when the family listened in, we patiently waited for Herr Fromer's show immediately afterwards. Singing selections from the music that preceded him, the cream puff peddler then explained in English what the pieces were about. It was obvious that Herr Fromer loved opera, and Daddy declared it to be the world's greatest music. To Kenny and me, however, it was simply a lyrical alert that our Boston cream pie was only a block away.

Aunt Veronica

Even today when I hear opera music it makes me think of pastry, just as the big band sound brings back happy memories of Aunt Veronica, our mother's baby sister. Barely out of her teens when we were kids, she told Kenny and me scary stories until we cried. Fibbing to Mommy, our auntie then claimed that she didn't know why in the world we were so upset, the whole time laughing and calling us babies as our tender and affectionate mother hugged away our fears and tears. The second those crocodile tears dried and her sister walked out of the room, she swiftly turned to us and asked, "Want to hear another scary story, kiddies?" The answer was always "Yes!"

Frequently it was obvious when she was joshing, but every once in a while we weren't quite sure. For years I believed her story that I was adopted after being dumped at the front door in a basket one snowy night. The minute Aunt Veronica tried the same pitch on Kenny, the truth became evident. I clearly remembered when he was brought home from the hospital. On that crisp fall day, Aunt Veronica appeared at the front door, cuddling the new addition to our family wrapped in a blue blanket. Without saying a word, she came over to the rocking chair where I was sitting shyly, placed the soft, fresh-smelling bundle of brother in my lap, and introduced me to Kenny. This was the first time I ever heard that word.

Aunt Veronica still lived at home on McKinley Avenue with her mother, stepfather, and bachelor brothers. Bupchie, our Polish grandmother, was old-fashioned, strict, and suspicious of the ways of America. Mommy's mother actually believed that high school boys and girls swam nude together in gym class; as a result, she vehemently refused to let Aunt Veronica, her youngest and only child to graduate, take the class. Mommy, on the other hand, was as modern as Bupchie was old-world, and Aunt Veronica knew she was darn lucky to have our mother as a sister. The warmth for her older sibling was passed along to us kids, oftentimes in the form of teasing.

Daddy had hired her as his bookkeeper-secretary-confidante when he opened the candy business after returning from the war. Their offices on Grant Street uptown in Vandergrift were filled with boxes of sweets and the swinging sounds of Harry James, Benny Goodman, and Dizzy Gillespie. In between jitterbug numbers, Frank Sinatra, her heartthrob, crooned her favorites, "You'd Be So Nice To Come Home To," "Night and Day," and "I'll Never Smile Again." Aunt Veronica loved to listen to music and to sing whenever possible during every waking moment. Upon seeing Kenny and me run in her direction, she predictably broke into a chorus of our all-time favorite, "I Love You a Bushel and a Peck." Aunt Veronica got and gave oodles of hugs around the neck.

When not singing, teasing, scaring, hugging, or laughing, she was giving us reject candy or telling traditional fairy tales, but with a modern twist. For instance, at Cinderella's ball the guests danced to Glenn Miller, and the pumpkin was changed into a Cadillac convertible. The wicked stepmother looked exactly like Mrs. Trotaskovich, the widow across the street, when she hadn't moved her barrels. Prince Charming was a dead ringer for Aunt Veronica's latest flame. The Fairy Godmother could have been Mommy's twin. And last by not least, Cinderella was 5' 9", fashionably shapely, had gorgeous brown hair and fabulous dark eyes, and was the very best aunt in the whole wide world. Surprise. Surprise. Goldilocks and Snow White fit the same description.

Our house on Quay Street was her home away from home; she slept over whenever she had a date, because Bupchie made her return at ten o'clock. Understanding Mommy, however, let her stay out as late as she wanted and even bought her stylish outfits and the newest perfume to make sure her baby sis not only had fun, but also looked and smelled nice.

Her dates had to pass inspection, or "muster" as our ex-soldier dad termed it, and invariably did once they handed the appropriate nickels to Kenny and me.

Resembling a glamour puss in the contemporary full skirt with crinolines to accentuate her tiny waist and wearing spiked heels with pointed toes, Aunt Veronica pirouetted once or twice then bent down to pick up Kenny for a goodnight air-kiss. The performance was repeated for my benefit and, I suspect, to highlight her svelte figure for the hat-in-hand, nervously grinning escort.

Many evenings before television invaded the house, Mommy, Daddy, Aunt Veronica, and one of her suitors turned on the radio or put records on the hi fi and jitterbugged in the living room. Those hep cats knew the popular dances like the mambo and sometimes to show off in front of us kids did the Charleston as they had seen at the movies when they were kids themselves.

Tall and lanky, Aunt Veronica was constantly out for a good time. Sousha, her best girlfriend, and she were quite popular and had a ball in high school during World War II, a time when the whole country, to hear them tell it, was in the same mood. They became freshmen that September before America entered the war and graduated a few months before the end in 1945. During those four years they, like other young Americans not quite sure what the next day had in store, had a swing-time mentality. The two teenyboppers dated lots of boys who later enlisted and were shipped overseas, some never to return.

While baby-sitting Jimmy and Barbara, Aunt Veronica was the first to read the telegram that tersely confirmed Uncle Stanley's death in the Black Forest. A decade earlier she was a tiny first-grader when widowed Bupchie married widower Ju Ju, our Polish grandfather. Stanley, one of Ju Ju's three young sons, or "Stush" as everyone fondly called him, became as much her real brother as though they were linked by blood, not just marriage.

Before Stanley shipped overseas, he cried and confided to Aunt Veronica that he knew he would not return. His body was buried in Europe, but his Silver Star and other medals were sent home to Bupchie and Ju Ju on McKinley Avenue. Aunt Veronica also tore open the Western Union telegram concerning another brother, our Uncle Caz. With relief she read that he was wounded, not dead.

Similar to other homefront citizens, Aunt Veronica participated in scrap metal drives and rationing. On her way to school each day, she passed the Gold Stars proudly displayed in windows and comforted worried friends waiting for news or letters from brothers and boyfriends in the service.

"The Western Union boy had the worst job during the war," she recounted often when referring to those days.

While Daddy was overseas and Mommy worked as a waitress, Aunt Veronica took care of Jimmy and Barbara. That's when she honed her craft of scary storytelling for Kenny and me, two children still only gleams in our soldier-father's eyes.

America was either laughing or crying; when not attending funerals, the country threw parties. Asked to sum up the early '40s, Aunt Veronica proclaimed they were jiving and swinging, even though her favorite beau had died in the Battle of the Bulge. Many years later, any time the nostalgic and melancholy ballad, "I'll Be Seeing You," came on the radio, her stiff upper lip quivered, and she left the room abruptly. Returning moments later dabbing her eyes with a wadded handkerchief, she announced too loudly that she was probably coming down with a cold.

The blood-red lipstick and matching fingernail polish looked as elegant on Kenny and me as it did on her. What a sport! After discovering that we had been in her purse helping ourselves to makeup, she applied another layer of lipstick to her already well-glossed mouth and covered our faces with red lip marks. Then, after making us squeal with delight from kisses, she pulled up our undershirts and planted a big smackeroo on my inny and Kenny's outty.

Nothing we did ever made Aunt Veronica angry. When she was warned by her older sister not to frighten us, we could tell by the mischievous sparkle in her eyes as Mommy left the room that we were going to be terrified out of our wits by another one of her fairy tales involving a little boy named "Kenny" and a little girl called "Diana" who looked exactly like us. Aunt Veronica saved happy endings for Mommy's benefit; however, when we were alone with her, the two kids who resembled us to a T were always eaten by monsters, kidnapped by Gypsies, or turned into toads.

Mutsy Futsy

The first time Kenny was steady enough for me to take him for a walk, I clutched his hand and led him across the street to call on our former next-door neighbors. They lived on the first floor of the Berostek double-decker behind our former rental house.

Mrs. Berostek resided on the second floor, and Martha Mitski and her brother Martin, or "Mutsy Futsy" as kids nicknamed him, lived below. Their parents had died within a week of each other during the war when Martha was only 19, and Martin became the sole responsibility of his sister. Miss Mitski deserved much more out of life.

A year younger than Jimmy, Mutsy Futsy was a pain in the *dupa*—Bupchie's best-liked Polish word. None of the kids played with him, because he was a crybaby and a tattletale. Yet, Martha never saw his disagreeable side and used to brag how he helped out by collecting pop bottles for the deposits.

No one could stand Mutsy Futsy, but everyone felt sorry for his uncomplaining sister, a seamstress at a clothing store uptown who made enough money for the essentials. Wanting to aid her in any way they could, housewives placed empty bottles on their porches every night for Mutsy Futsy to pick up in the morning before school. Having an established and impressive route, he also had as customers families with boys who would have loved the extra money in their own pockets from the returns. Martha was such a saint that folks put up with Mutsy Futsy's whining and complaining about women not rinsing out the bottles to his satisfaction.

A first-class putz and bully, he grabbed candy out of little kids' hands while knocking them off their tricycles; yet, boy, did he hightail it out of there the instant elder brothers, like the cavalry, showed up to defend younger siblings. Then, Mutsy Futsy would run home sobbing, and the heroic siblings were punished for picking on the poor orphan. Martha was a softy with him, and he was like the bad seed, wicked when adults were not watching and a mama's, or sister's, perfect darling when they were. Everything about him was obnoxious, from his stupid-sounding snicker that came out "tee hee hee" to his greasy, orange hair, green teeth, and chunky hips.

Kenny and I loved Martha, one of the dearest persons alive, who welcomed us with open arms into her cozy kitchen. Even as toddlers, though, we were wise enough to time our social calls when Mutsy Futsy wasn't home alone. Tots, too, know that pulling wings off flies is not a nice thing to do.

Once we went to visit, thinking Martha was home when we saw a light on in the kitchen. As it turned out, the big bully was home sick, and Martha was at work. The second we opened the door and saw him, we beat a hasty retreat, but he blocked the exit and began taunting. To my surprise and uneasiness, he picked me up, placed me on the living room floor, and laid his body on top of mine. I certainly did not enjoy this game and started punching him. Kenny, thinking Mutsy Futsy was hurting me, began crying and whacking the bully's head. Angry, the fat jerk shrieked at us to go home because we were bad and he was going to tattle on us if we repeated to anyone what he had done. We didn't understand what happened but wanted to get out of there as fast as possible. After that, Kenny and I made a point to stay far away from Mutsy Futsy.

The Five-and-Ten
Cent Store

Barbara and Jimmy bonded during World War II, and Kenny and I formed our partnership during those postwar years before beginning school. We watched enviously as Jimmy and Barbara departed for the third and first grades. They seemed old and wise, while we felt like the babies left behind.

Actually, staying at home wasn't all that bad. Once a week we went to work with Daddy at the candy business. Aunt Veronica supervised our counting candy bars, changing records on the turntable, and killing flies with big swatters in the summer. After a hard day at the salt mine, Daddy took us to the five-and-ten cent store.

A trip to the five-and-ten then was today's equivalent of going to Disneyland. Three swinging doors opened onto a magical kingdom. One side door swung into the record section, where the latest 45's by Patti Page, Doris Day, and Rosemary Clooney played. The middle and largest door was the most popular. When shoved open, it lured children with the aroma of fresh-popped popcorn and the sugary scent of candy. Our favorite entrance faced the fish tank, bird cages, and school supplies. The goldfish and other aquatic creatures greeted us when Kenny and I went shopping with Daddy. Before going in, we loved guessing how many fish would be floating dead then viewed with morbid fascination the other fish gobbling up deceased brethren.

If possible, our pushover pop would have happily beheld our glee as he paid the fish clerk in the blue smock who netted goldfish and put them in white plastic containers with metal handles. Daddy's eyes conveyed that he truly wanted to buy us those fish, but recollections of his wife's constant warning as we left the house of "Jim, don't you dare bring home any goldfish!" stopped him every time he almost weakened to our whiny pleas.

The same was true at Easter with the yellow, purple, and pink baby chicks. Our mother, we heard often enough, had already gone through too many tormenting burials in the back yard with Barbara and Jimmy. She did not want to observe two more kids with broken hearts crying over pastel baby chicks that never had a chance of surviving past Easter Monday. And furthermore, Mommy had witnessed one goldfish too many fed to death out of careless, uninformed love.

Still, it was fun viewing the fish bump into each other as they swam and trying to count them in the tank. It was comparable to assessing the exact number of jellybeans in a large bowl. They were really packed in there.

The birds next to the fish tank smelled awful and scared us when they flapped their wings against the cages. It was impossible to comprehend why anyone in his right mind wanted to put a bird in a cage. We were accustomed to observing birds perched on the telephone lines, and the first robin seen after winter suggested spring was rounding the corner. That red-breasted bird signaled that the Easter Bunny was hopping our way with baskets of goodies. Birds outdoors seemed much friendlier than those squawking canaries at the five-and-ten, and it was not difficult for our young minds to understand their bitterness at lost freedom of flight.

After being shooed away by the female clerk in the water-stained blue smock, Kenny and I ambled around to check out pencil boxes, crayons, and colored construction paper. Loving pencils, we wrote on any piece of paper we could find at home. Well, it wasn't exactly writing, more like X's and other letters Barbara taught us.

Wise Mom hid every pencil in the house after Kenny and I ruined Jimmy's homework and left our marks on hundreds of family pictures we discovered hidden in the back of a closet. Sniffing out a shred of paper, no matter where it was, was a constant challenge, and nothing was safe from our scribbling fingers. Checkbooks, newspapers, napkins, books, envelopes, hat boxes—you name it, we doodled on it.

Dawdling in the stationery department reminded us that playing school was another especially liked activity. Barbara was the teacher; Kenny and I were her naughty pupils who had to scrub the blackboard after class for being bad. Trying not to appear overjoyed at the daily punishment, we hoped she would not catch on that we absolutely adored cleaning her toy blackboard. Besides, we knew thanks to Jimmy that in real school the best students like Barbara were rewarded with that task. Yet, how odd it was that if our mother asked her to wash a window, our big sister professed that she had a mountain of homework, with not a minute to spare. The other school activity Kenny and I were crazy about was dusting the erasers and watching chalk dust fly in the air. How fun it was being covered with a white powdery film that transformed us into aged-albino midgets!

While Daddy browsed for boring household junk (kitchen curtains and rods), Kenny and I wandered up and down the aisles of the five-and-ten, eventually making our way over to the toy section. Obeying Daddy's strict order of staying together, we held hands while examining every single plaything on the shelves. Every trip, Daddy bought us one trinket each, so we had to comparison shop carefully.

The week between five-and-ten visits was an eternity. People now tend to remember how back then there was more snow in the winter or how much hotter the summers were. I'm not so sure if those recollections are true, but I absolutely believe that time was slower. Minutes then were more like today's hours, and yesteryear's hours seemed as long as current days. Because we focused solely on the present, seven days lasted forever. On the bright side, since Kenny and I played together, we enjoyed not only our own but also each other's toys.

Goldfish, both dead and alive, and pencil boxes quickly disappeared from our thoughts as we inspected miniature dump trucks, decks of old maid cards, coloring books, and the extensive baby doll selection.

I never really cared for baby dolls. By the time I was old enough to have the desire for one, Kenny was born. His tears were real, and he was warm to the touch. Who needed a doll? Teddy bears were cute, and bride imitations were beautiful; but dolls that were supposed to resemble babies seemed fake. They were no comparison to the real McCoy. Kenny cried without pulling a string or flipping him over, and he drank from a bottle. When Mommy changed his diaper, it had for-real, smelly ca ca in it. I never met a baby doll who could achieve that.

Baby dolls were very low on my toy wish list, and Kenny could not stand the sight of them. He said they made him gag. Barbara, on the other hand, always preferred her dollies to Kenny and me any day. Unlike us when we were infants, they didn't stink to high Heaven when she changed their spotless diapers. But most of all, she fancied the make-believe world of plastic, obedient children to her obstreperous (her word) younger brother and sister.

Although I didn't want to own one, I still relished staring at the baby dolls with adorable dresses, colorful bows, and synthetic curls crowning plastic faces.

One day, while Kenny was shooting at the dolls on the top row with an unloaded cap gun, I spotted one that did not resemble any I had ever seen before. The exquisite, colored baby doll on the middle row was a black-velvet contrast next to the rosy-cheeked, yellow-haired white ones. Her dramatic face, framed with coal-black hair, was dark brown. The chubby arms and legs were darker still. In comparison, the other dolls surrounding her were pasty-pale.

Kenny had selected his toy, a milk truck, and tried to talk me into choosing the cap gun with 50 years' supply of caps. But my mind was set on the exotic-colored baby doll the instant our eyes met. From another world, she was similar to those people who lived across the bridge in

North Vandergrift. Riding through their community on the way to the drive-in movie and viewing their faces flash past the car window at twilight, I wondered what it was like to be a Negro. What would it be like to be dark and mysterious and different from the people in my world?

Annoyed at my fascination with the new object of my affection, Kenny aimed the cap gun and shot her. He maintained that he killed her because, he flatly stated, the imaginary bullet hit her right between the eyes. Now that she was dead, he suggested I tell Daddy that I wanted either the milk truck or the cap gun. Smarty-pants would then choose the other and end up playing with both. He thought he could talk me into anything, when in fact I always gave in to him because I delighted in seeing him happy. It sure as heck beat the alternative—his bawling. By the way he was acting, I could tell he was jealous of the attention I was paying the Negro doll, sitting cutely in the middle row. I could read him like a book, as Daddy used to say.

Unable to wait any longer, I grabbed Kenny's hand and went to find Daddy. There he was in the boring paint department recounting a joke that originated with our parish priest, Father Shezocki. Three men clerks, not in blue smocks I noticed, were laughing. Daddy was regaling them about some traveling salesman and a farmer's daughter. The second the audience (wearing white shirts and ties) saw Kenny and me approaching, they shushed Daddy, who upon spotting us clammed up. It was obvious they did not want Kenny and me to hear the story, the same one we heard bits and pieces of all day. What I caught was as humorous as Kenny's favorite dirty joke of the pig falling in the mud. Little Snookums on the radio, now she was hilarious.

After some gentle coaxing, Daddy let us lead him by the hands to the toy department to see our choices. Proud as a peacock, Kenny showed him the truck. Daddy smiled as he reached for it. It was my turn. I could not wait to take home the doll, the first one I ever wanted. When I pointed to her, my father laughed. It wasn't the same reaction I got whenever I said something cute. Ordinarily I was aware when that happened. Instead, it seemed as if he were chuckling at my expense. Without meaning to do so, Daddy bruised my feelings. I felt dumb in front of him, the smartest person in the world.

Not wanting to be left out of a good thing, Kenny did not help matters, or my feelings, by joining in with one of his imitation grownup laughs. I hated it when he guffawed and ho ho hoed like some scrawny Santa Claus out of costume. Their laughter attracted attention. Customers and clerks turned their heads to stare in our direction. Upon hearing a woman close by ask her husband what was so amusing, I wanted to die on the spot. What was so funny? All I knew was that I felt stupid. Sizing up the situation, I quickly snatched the cap gun out of Kenny's paw and announced I had changed my mind. The silver gun was what I wanted instead.

Just as soon as he stopped snickering, Daddy asked me repeatedly in the kindest voice, "Are you sure you don't want the Negro baby doll?"

My head shook "yes" while my heart cried "no," but I assured him in my best adult-like voice that I was just kidding about the baby doll. Ha. Ha. I wanted the cap gun the whole time and was just making a joke. "Wasn't it funny?"

I kicked Kenny in the shin when he said I was lying and really, truly desired a baby doll. Adding insult to injury, he insisted that playing with a baby doll instead of him was the stupidest thing he ever did hear. He then went into his gagging routine to the amusement of a throng of onlookers.

I searched for the colored baby doll the next trip to the five-and-ten cent store, but she was gone. Trying to be the benevolent older sister, Barbara assured me that she went to live with another little girl across the bridge and now had a home with her own kind of people.

Words and Deeds

Kenny, Mommy, and I rested on the front porch swing often and discussed how remarkable Eleanor Roosevelt, our mom's idol, was for standing up for the rights of the less fortunate, especially minorities and people of color.

Kenny and I thought "Amos 'n Andy" was a scream, but our mother made sure we knew that Negroes—as people called African-Americans then—were as good as white folk, sometimes better. After shuddering at the horrible mental image of colored men beaten and lynched in the South for merely glancing at white women, Kenny and I heard plenty more stories of the injustices against Negroes. Yet, we never personally knew any blacks.

Settled by immigrants from Eastern Europe, East Vandergrift was as segregated as any redneck town in Georgia or Mississippi. The only time we got close to a Negro was when the family went swimming and picnicking at Crooked Creek Park, a few miles away. There, blacks had their own section of the manmade beach. Park officials didn't post signs for whites and coloreds; but the two races didn't socialize.

While Barbara and Jimmy frolicked in the water and our parents set up lunch on the blanket, Kenny and I strolled along the water's edge in the area where the black people sunned. Clutching hands while circling back to our family's spot on the beach, we initiated small talk with and accepted cookies from colored parents preparing picnics for their kids. There is no doubt in my mind that more than one dark-skinned mother turned to her husband after a sociable chitchat and commented on how adorable white children were.

The palefaced short people, including us, may have been as cute as June bugs, but they were also as stupid. Without thinking, kids rattled off "Eenie, meenie, minie moe; catch a nigger by the toe; if he hollers, let him go; and out goes Y-O-U!" countless times a day, without ever hearing the words they were saying.

Sweet Daddy

Our candy truck was a white van that Jimmy, Barbara, Kenny, and I loved to ride in and proudly pose beside for the camera. Greater joy cannot be bestowed on a child than to have a father own a candy business. Such a pushover, Daddy placed a rigged vending machine in the cellar. Money did not have to be inserted to get out chocolate bars. Heavenly days! Because of generous Daddy, our house was the favorite Halloween stop for every kid in East Vandergrift.

Rituals

"Now I lay me down to sleep. I pray the Lord my soul to keep." Kneeling beside our beds with hands folded and eyes closed in deep concentration (Barbara and I in our room, Kenny and Jimmy in theirs), we said our prayers in unison every night. "If I should die before I wake, I pray the Lord my soul to take."

The Dell kids may have fallen asleep with quiet thoughts of dying, but we awoke to the noisy roar of the vacuum cleaner. Before Barbara and Jimmy left for school, our energetic mother began cleaning. Saving the upstairs till last, she didn't want to rouse Kenny and me too early since we both hated getting up in the mornings.

After vacuuming the downstairs, Mom charged up the steps to her and Daddy's bedroom then dashed down the hallway to where the girls slept. The middle area was last. Having all the privileges of the baby of the family, Kenny was allowed to doze the longest, but he rarely got a chance to enjoy that indulgence.

Whenever Mommy reached the girls' room, I quickly jumped out of bed, scurried to Kenny's bed, climbed in with him, and anxiously waited for the whirring Hoover upright to approach its final destination. Hearing it make its way down the hall, we leaped onto the floor, stuffed the pillows under the blanket and bedspread, and hid in the closet. Then the vacuum cleaner turned off.

In a melodious voice, Mommy sang out in the general direction of the bed, "I know where you're hiding. And I'm going to get you." With the mild warning out of the way, she pounced on the bed and hugged the pillows.

Stepping out of Jimmy's size-ten shoes in the dark closet, we both pushed the door open and hollered, "Boo! We fooled you." It was amazing how clever Daddy's two little shrimps were to trick her every day for years.

Daisy

After eating the piping hot farina layered with brown sugar, Kenny and I ran outside. "Get plenty of fresh air, and don't forget to pick me some daisies," was our mom's customary farewell. Out the kitchen door we flew, eager to play hide-and-seek, collect rocks, and visit neighbors for chats and snacks.

One special spring morning a pleasant surprise was awaiting as we skipped past the garbage cans and stepped into the dirt alley. The Bielak's chickens were pecking and clucking, so we bounded over to their coop to harass them into squawking even louder. When Kenny cock-a-doodle-doed, flailed his arms, and stuck out his tongue, they started scampering in circles and flapping their wings in excitement. Boy, were they mad. Not causing quite enough chaos for our satisfaction, we continued the ruckus with other animal imitations.

Predictably, Mrs. Bielak banged open her screen door and shrilled, "Don't scare my chickens, or you'll regret you ever were born. Get away from them, or I'll tell your mother you were bad. Shoo!" Emphatically slamming the door, she disappeared into her clean-as-a-whistle kitchen. The nerve, her hollering like that, just for poking fun. What a crab.

Reluctantly obeying, we darted in separate directions, like movie outlaws desperate to shake the posse off their trail. Kenny and I sympathized with the guys wearing the black hats and the Indians encircling the covered wagons. There was something tragic about the underdogs that we both found appealing.

Kenny wedged his tiny frame into the small space between the Bielak shanty (where Mr. Bielak stored garden tools) and their neighbor's one-car garage. A no-man's land of 12 inches separated the two properties. Meanwhile, I raced down the alley and hid behind old lady Poleski's garbage cans. That exact spot was the half-way mark from our house to the baseball field at the end of the alley.

After a few dust-settling moments, I tiptoed back and found Kenny crouched down with his spine pressing against the garage and his knees touching the shanty. In his hands was the tiniest kitten in the world. Similar to the way grownups reacted to kids, he was patting the kitten's little head and murmuring baby talk to it. Geez, and I thought big people had the exclusive on stupidity. Not wanting to be left out, I squatted beside him and joined in the petting.

Deciding to feed it, I scampered into the house, poured some milk into a chipped soup bowl, and carefully carried it out. Lying on our stomachs, Kenny and I observed it lap the milk as though it had not eaten in a week. The kitty must have been starving, because its tongue darted in and out of its mouth at least a zillion times. The baby feline let us pat it as it drank every drop, licking the bowl clean.

The rest of the morning was spent watching the kitten nap, play with string, paw at our fingers, wash itself, and spin in circles trying to catch its tail. After an exhausting few hours, we finally worked up the courage to tell our pet-hating mom about the kitten and ask, even beg, if we could keep it. The strategy was to remind her of the farm our family lived on before Daddy went off to war. Before Kenny and I were born, Barbara and Jimmy had a calf, two dogs, 12 baby chicks, 16 rabbits, and (best of all) a scarecrow to play with. Yet, we deprived younger kids never once had a single pet. The logic was in place. If it did not work, we would tap tears as a last resort.

During the discussion of who should say what, Mommy surprised us, appearing out of nowhere. We three gulped audibly as Kenny and I stared up at her and she focused down on the kitten by the soup bowl. What happened next is still a puzzle. Our mother's gushy reaction toward the furry, diminutive creature was unexpected but evidence enough that we finally had a pet of our own.

Kneeling in the alley between us with the baby cat in her arms, sentimental Mommy named it "Daisy" after showing us how to differentiate between a male and female. The floral name was chosen for our daily chore of picking flowers, which was forgotten once Kenny found the kitten.

Daisy captured our attention and graced the neighborhood on Quay Street for a few months until the day she followed Barbara and Jimmy down the field, where Jimmy was off to pitch a baseball game. Barbara and her girlfriends tagged along to watch the boys they had crushes on. When the gang finally reached the diamond, they turned around and realized that Daisy was nowhere in sight. Later, after shedding buckets of tears, bereft Barbara said, "At the time I assumed the kitten had gone back home." Boo Hoo.

For two days everyone in the family hunted all over town for Daisy, but she had disappeared into thin air. Daddy even notified the village policeman to conduct a search, but no trace could be found of the kitty's whereabouts. Poof! She was gone.

Kenny cried so hard that Daddy carried him to the five-and-ten cent store and bought him two goldfish and a bowl with a plastic mermaid stuck in pebbles at the bottom. Talk about dull. All they did was swim in circles, eat, and poop. Day and night they swam in circles, ate, and pooped. It became monotonous and predictable, and sure enough they (like their cousins at the five-and-ten) were spotted doing the dead-man's float.

"Moooommmm, the goldfish are dead," Barbara hollered then shifted to the book she was reading.

No one else in the household seemed too upset regarding their demise. Since no emotional attachment existed, Kenny thought Jimmy's idea of flushing them down the toilet was an excellent one, a sort of burial at sea. Big brother explained that the toilet flushed into our town's river, the Kiskiminetas, which flowed into the Allegheny River, which swept into the Atlantic Ocean, where millions of sunken pirate ships with buried treasures awaited discovery. Wow! Jimmy sure knew his geography.

The only tears shed at Bess and Harry's funeral were Kenny's. Flushing the toilet too quickly, our speedy mom robbed him of the chance of doing the honors himself. The fish tank at the five-and-ten cent store completely bored us after that.

Ole Man River

Oh, the mighty Kiskiminetas—our river—that golden Bess and Harry flushed into, along with the town sewage, coursed all the way to the Atlantic Ocean, exactly as Jimmy had described. Long before its waters were used to dump waste from homes and steel mills, the Indians and white settlers used it as a link between the mountains to the east and the Allegheny River.

"In 1791 it became an official highway," Barbara learned in school and repeated to an enthralled audience at supper.

Before the bridge was built uptown in Vandergrift, the Kiskiminetas was part of the Pennsylvania Canal. Railroads drove the canals out of business a couple of decades before the first house was constructed in East Vandergrift.

The Kiskiminetas River may not have been as well known as the majestic Mississippi, but famous people traveled on it when it functioned as a canal. Charles Dickens plied its waters in 1842, and in his *American Notes* mentioned the coarse life in backwoods USA. Observations along the Kiskiminetas may not have thrilled the English author, but Zachary Taylor had no complaints when he sent his war horse east by way of this route following the Mexican War.

Before it became contaminated, a variety of fish (bass, pike, salmon, catfish, perch) swam in the Kiskiminetas. After hearing stories from very old old-timers about the big ones that got away, Jimmy, Kenny, and other boys in town wished they could have caught fish in it, too; but the river had been contaminated from the dumping of "pickle liquor," a sulfuric acid, into the water from the Johnstown Mines. By following suit and making matters even worse, the steel mills disposed of their waste products 24 hours a day into the river. On top of that, sewage from homes flushed its way to the waters when indoor plumbing replaced outhouses.

Over the years, those few individuals who complained about the pollution were labeled "troublemakers" by the owners of the mills. The choice was simple: jobs or sport fishing. Some things never change.

Jimmy and his boyfriends erected a shack on the banks of the river. In it, they smoked cigarettes, peeked at girlie magazines, and yearned about how wonderful it would be to see a naked woman in the flesh. Nicknamed "The Termite," the shed consisted of Chequita banana and orange crates that the boys had scrounged from Hovanik's grocery store's garbage pile in the alley next to Kilouskas's pool hall. Inside their hideout, they played poker on a table someone had thrown away. This home away from home was near the ice house, where folks said bad girls went to do naughty things with boys.

The Termite was within spitting distance of a pier built from old railroad ties, discarded tires, and junk. Jutting into the river, the jetty had boards missing, and it looked as though one good breeze would knock over the whole contraption. But kids still tempted fate and walked on the pier all the time. Besides the great view of the water, the pier, and the ice house, the shack was within proximity to the main sewer that channeled the town's toilet contents into the river.

When Jimmy had to baby-sit Kenny, he took him to The Termite. Afterwards, Kenny told me that they swore a lot there and posted dirty pictures on the walls. I couldn't see with my own eyes, because no girls were allowed inside, not even kid sisters.

Jimmy's second abode was set afire by Mommy and the other mothers after they found out that their sons had been drinking beer there. Exactly how much beer do you suppose? A case? A keg? Hardly. The truth: Danny Zalenski had stolen two bottles of brewski (as the guys called it) from his parent's beer garden, and six kids split them. As they tried to destroy the evidence by tossing the empties into the river, Jimmy and Danny were spotted by some old lady walking her dog nearby. The enraged teetotaler immediately contacted Mrs. Zalenski, who called Mrs. Dell, who spoke to the other mothers. Similar to the villagers in a Frankenstein movie, the raging moms marched to the shack, dragged out the boys, and burned The Termite to the ground. They rationalized that any youngster drinking beer at 12 would be robbing banks at 16. None of them wanted a juvenile delinquent for a son. You could put money on it.

Without a doubt, fish in the Kiskiminetas River would have been wonderful. Nonetheless, even with its filth, boys and girls had enormous fun swimming, ice skating, and rowing boats in it, as well as building forts, trapping muskrats, roasting weenies, climbing trees, picking berries, and discovering Indian arrowheads and prehistoric fossils along its shores. The rest of the time kids simply stared at the cloudy water and daydreamed while the Kiskiminetas River slowly flowed through our little corner of the world to the ocean.

A Rose by
Any Other Name

Born before World War II, Jimmy and his pals had secret nicknames for use only among themselves, forbidden to anyone outside their group. Big secret. Let's see, the guys were Jughead, Beaner, Fudd, Gardenia, Dinky, Gummy, Flash, Chicky, Tank, Gooch, Stretch, and—of course—Digger, alias Jimmy Dell.

Have You Heard
the Latest?

Life seemed simple back then. Inevitable routines made up each day, beginning at the crack of dawn. Roosters crowed at sunrise; the milk man delivered dairy products at 7:30 a.m.; and when Daddy drove his candy truck up Vandergrift Lane to work, Cazzy Petrouski (bearing the latest gossip) sauntered across the street for a cup of coffee.

Never having a job in his entire life, Cazzy lived in a rundown house next door to Mrs. Trotaskovich with his widower father and brother Lefty, a worker in the steel mill. Upon being informed from a school nurse that young Cazzy had a heart murmur, his mother refused to let him out of her maternal sight even to play with the other boys. Predictably, he became a sissy. After Mrs. Petrouski died, he went to hell in a handbag, spending his work-free days strolling from house to house and gabbing with housewives.

Cazzy's stiffest competitor was Sousha, Aunt Veronica's high school girlfriend. A year after graduating, Sousha got married and gained 110 pounds. The transformation from slim, popular coed to fat, nosy busybody was astonishing. Huffing and puffing, she began her daily rounds of gossiping at the other end of town and wended her way over to Quay Street.

Close to the time the iceman made his delivery for our icebox, early-riser Cazzy was beginning his daily rounds as well, spreading bad news from house to house and trying desperately to avoid Sousha at all costs.

Sallying forth from our home, Cazzy meandered to the section where his rival had started.

They were quite a sight to behold. Cazzy swished around town in dirty old blue jeans, and Sousha waddled along in a flowered house-dress. Both tried frantically to beat each other with the news along their daily routes. It was a scene right out of a Marx Brothers' film.

Our "it's not polite to gossip" mother barely tolerated either of them. Their tattling went in one ear and out the other, as she liked to say.

Pretending to be playing under the dining room table while they gabbed, Kenny and I caught it all: who got stinking drunk the night before, which PG young woman had to get married PDQ, which dead-beat's car was repossessed.

One positive aspect of Sousha was that she walked in the kitchen door, delivered the reports quick and dirty, and abruptly left. In contrast, with nothing else to do, Cazzy lingered around the house, following Mom from room to room. Upstairs and downstairs, he daintily sipped coffee with his pinkie finger extended and chain smoked.

Mom vacuumed, dusted, mopped, and washed the kitchen floor on her hands and knees every single day. Daddy daily remarked that it was clean enough to eat from. Whenever food dropped on it, we kids felt it was safe to pick it up and pop it into our mouths. That's true, unless the pieces were detestable like lima beans which then had to be tossed away because of all the germs on the kitchen floor.

East Vandergrift had loads of other blabbermouths besides Cazzy and Sousha. Those two were unquestionably in the major league, but plenty of bush leaguers competed. One of Kenny's favorites was Mabel Rechnousky, who always wore her hair in pin curls. Walking behind the butcher counter at Hovanik's grocery store to make sure honest-as-the-day-is-long Mr. Hovanik didn't put his thumb on the scale, trading tantalizing tidbits with Sousha or Cazzy at the post office, chasing her kids down the alley swinging a menacing broom above her head, piously exiting the Confessional, or lounging in our kitchen while chugging a fifth cup of coffee in 15 minutes, wherever and at whatever time of day or night, Mabel's locks were bound in bobbypins as though she were preparing to get all dolled up for a prom or wedding.

Tall and rail thin with a pockmarked face from childhood chicken pox worsened by teenage acne, this character constantly had an unfiltered cigarette dangling from her lips. The butt was removed only long enough to cough. Gabby but good-hearted, Mabel was the first person to show up after a death in the family. Bearing a tuna casserole or marble cake, she was prepared to pitch in and assist anyone in need. With rolled-up sleeves and tightly wound wisps of thin hair, she served food, brewed coffee, cleared the table, washed dishes, and gossiped with the mourners.

Our attractive mother never let anyone, even Cazzy, see her in curlers. When an unexpected guest or delivery person rang the door bell, she darted upstairs to comb out her hair before answering the door. Continually concerned about her appearance, she even applied another layer of lipstick before climbing in bed next to her mate for the night.

Not Mabel. Why should she? Her hubby was either at the steel mill working or at one of the clubs drinking. Mabel, who Kenny and Jimmy thought would have made an excellent antenna for a television with weak reception, was perpetually getting ready to look her very best in case her husband decided to take her dancing or socializing. Fat chance that was ever going to happen, but at least she was ready in case it did.

The Radio

It was amazing how thoroughly and quickly Mommy cleaned the house. When the Polish, Lithuanian, and Slovak church bells tolled at noon, she was finished. After sending Kenny and me to Hovanik's grocery store for fresh lunch meat, she lit up her first cigarette of the day, flipped on the radio in the living room, sipped a cup of black Maxwell House coffee, and puffed away on the unfiltered Lucky Strike. L.S.M.F.T. "Lucky Strikes Mean Fine Tobacco," the friendly announcers notified her and the other housewives in America after a busy morning of housecleaning before the kids came home from school for lunch.

Mommy loved listening to the radio ever since the first time she had as an eight-year-old. Back then in the 1920s, her girlfriend's parents had a small table model. The father and Mommy tuned in the news every night. Because the other family members didn't relish this particular programming, he was glad to have her as company and explained everything following the broadcast. After hearing the current events, Mom excitedly raced home to notify her mother what was happening in the world. Polish cynic Bupchie grumbled that the information was a big lie. Before long, though, our grandmother was more receptive to the technology and bought a used radio for their living room.

Our mother's childhood family on McKinley Avenue adored Jack Benny. Because Bupchie didn't speak English or even understand much of it at the time, the kids had to explain why the radio audience and they were laughing. Even after they did, Bupchie still could not comprehend what was so hilarious. I guess something was lost in the translation.

Mommy and her brothers also tuned into baseball games. That's when she fell in love with the all-American sport and later read about her favorite players—Pie Traynor, Babe Ruth, Lou Gehrig, Hank Greenberg, and Roger Hornsby. To see them play was her biggest dream.

Because of Mom's passion for baseball, our family spent most summer evenings on the back porch listening to Pirates' games on the portable radio perched on the kitchen windowsill above the sink. Sipping lemonade and fanning ourselves with the eight-page *Vandergrift News*, we were joined by neighbors in cheering for the Pittsburgh boys of summer. Before the game, good ole Dad would always trek to the roadside fruit stand in Apollo, across the river. The crowd on the porch opened and closed the kitchen screen door throughout the nine innings and helped themselves to watermelon, peaches, and cherries. Swatting flies was Kenny's job, a very important function considering the many excursions to the kitchen table for fruity refreshments during the baseball game.

The Kitchen Table

At quarter past noon on school days, Barbara and Jimmy entered through the kitchen door for lunch. Taking our regular places, the four of us kids and Mom perched on plastic-covered chairs at the kitchen table. Barbara and I sat side by side across from the boys, who faced us and the wall with a framed picture of *The Last Supper*.

For some reason unbeknownst to me, Barbara refused to switch positions even though she was left-handed and sat at my right. When we bumped elbows while eating throughout the years, she insisted that I was at fault. The only way to have pleased her would have been to cut off my right arm. Okay, I may have professed many times in my life that it would be worth one prized possession or special moment; however, I was not going to sacrifice a limb for Barbara's stubbornness. As a result, I ate like a robot, moving only my wrist to avoid hitting her left elbow. No wonder I was so skinny.

When southpaw Kenny first came to the table from his high chair, he sat at Jimmy's right. They tapped elbows once or twice before Jimmy resolved the situation. Calmly pushing his chair back, our big brother rose, swooped up Kenny, and plopped him down in the other seat. Problem solved. No arguments. No more bangs and bruises. End of discussion. When I hinted to Barbara that maybe we could change locations, she adamantly refused to budge. Throughout childhood, high school, college, and many years later when I dared defy routine at that kitchen table, Barbara ordered me to "Move. You're in my spot."

More than any other food, Kenny hated mashed potatoes and adamantly refused to eat them. When Daddy tried stupidly to force them on him, his younger son snapped into an erect posture with arms folded and mouth zipped so tightly that his lips disappeared from his face.

One time at supper Mom responded to a phone call and left the table for almost 15 minutes, long enough for Kenny to start a fight with me. It could have been about any of a million matters. When he got cranky, I was the logical one to pick on. Until high school he was a foot shorter than I, but he always won our wrestling matches. I would have if he hadn't made me laugh. Once I started giggling, he had me pinned to the floor with his knees on my chest, forcing me to say "uncle." He knew better than to pull shenanigans with Jimmy or Barbara. Both could easily have swatted him as they could an ugly green fly zeroing in on unwrapped food on the counter.

As usual while Mom was out of sight, he kept bugging me until he finally got my goat. Out of frustration and the only way to shut him up, I grabbed my spoon, scooped up a chunk of mashed potatoes, and flipped it at him. The white gob splattered across his forehead and clung like homemade paste on construction paper. Just then, I heard our "I hate to talk on the phone" mother say good-bye and walk back to the kitchen. As her footsteps got louder, I begged Kenny to wipe the potatoes off his face, but he merely smiled devilishly. Jimmy and Barbara chortled as sweat streamed down my arms.

"What's going on in here?" were the first words out of Mommy's mouth when she saw Kenny sitting there with arms folded across his chest, looking like a jerk with those dumb mashed potatoes on his forehead. Gravy was dripping down his nose.

He blurted out the truth, "Diana threw them at me!"

What could I do? What any child in her right mind would do, I lied and vehemently responded, "I did not!"

At the same moment, Barbara and Jimmy, on my side when I needed them, also shouted, "She did not!" Three to one. Safety in numbers. The majority rules.

Thinking Kenny was fooling around as he always did, Mommy ordered him to wipe his face and behave himself. Unlike the baby of the family, I would have been punished. No wonder he was spoiled. If my mom had known the truth, I definitely would have been in big trouble for wasting food and then had been reminded of those starving children in China.

At that meal, as so many others, we heard anecdotes of Mom's childhood when there was nothing in the pantry to eat but stale bread. "And, furthermore, you kids should thank God for even one spoonful of mashed potatoes that children in the Depression would have considered a luxury like candy."

Talk of the hard times flowed on and on. A much-repeated vignette was about how her Uncle Andy had given our kid mom a dime that she lost in the outhouse when it fell down the stink hole. "There were no indoor bathrooms then; and you kids should feel fortunate to even have toilet paper, because as a child I had to use pages from the Sears and Roebuck catalog." Pumped-up Mom invariably continued to describe the index pages that were the softest. Once starting Depression-era stories, our maternal historian was on a roll. She recounted how teenage girls used red crepe paper left over from weddings to rub on their lips and cheeks in place of lipstick and rouge, which they couldn't possibly afford. More of the arduous days tumbled forth. When she and Daddy were children, they washed with lye soap; and mothers made bloomers from flour sacks and created knickers from bags of chicken feed.

"Most days we got down on our hands and knees to thank God for coffee with a drop of milk in it and a crumb of moldy bread." In the '30s, jelly was a luxury no one could afford, we kids heard quite often, especially after putting a heaping tablespoonful of jam on slices of fresh bread. "And now," she wistfully spanned the four of us around the table, "after all that suffering and starvation, I have a little boy who refuses to eat his mashed potatoes and even plays with them."

Even if she had uttered every hard-luck story in the world, Kenny was not going to eat those smashed spuds, no matter what he heard about the Depression or skinny kids in Peking. He would not even let them touch anything else on his plate for fear of contaminating other foods he liked or at least tolerated.

Jimmy hated eggs and anything with eggs in it. Daddy tried to sneak them in milkshakes; and just as soon as Jimmy finished one, he threw up on the kitchen table.

Our dad hardly ever ate weekday dinners with the family since they started at five. On the rare occasions that he did, though, he took his place at one end of the table, and Mommy sat at the other. Kenny's spot was next to the kitchen window, and Daddy faced it. Through the spotless glass panes, the two had a panoramic view of the cemetery uptown or "Boot Hill" as Kenny preferred to call it. There, on that sacred ground high above East Vandergrift, father and son would be buried side by side someday, both veterans of foreign wars.

At the daily meals, never dreaming what the future had in store, we discussed school happenings at midday then world events and history from 5:00 to 6:30. Daddy generally returned from work close to seven. A little later, Kenny and I listened to the radio while Jimmy and Barbara did their homework. By nine o'clock, we four kids were on our knees asking God to take our souls if we died in our sleep.

Life did seem simple back then.

Clean As a Whistle

Diligent Mommy had fixed household routines and never wavered from them. Monday was wash day. First, she soaked the clothes—colors and whites carefully separated—in aluminum tubs. Next was the cleaning process in the machine with its one setting, wash. Then, she maneuvered the clothes into the rolling rubber wringers at the top of the washer to squeeze out the excess water. Finally, she hung the garments on the back yard clothesline during warm weather and down the cellar in winter. When the clothes were dry, our efficient mother sprinkled them with cold water and rolled them up. Storing some in laundry baskets down the cold cellar, she put others into the refrigerator to await the hot iron.

Tuesday she ironed. The board was set up in the living room; the radio, Kenny, and I kept her company. We were extra careful near the cord, because as a crawling baby I pulled it and was badly burned on the cheek when the scorching iron dropped. "It's a miracle it didn't leave a scar," Mommy remarked every Tuesday.

On Wednesday and Thursday, she cleaned her mother's house from cellar to attic and washed clothes over there. While she scoured, Kenny and I fed the chickens in the back yard, raked and watered the garden, and passed the time with Bupchie. We had a ball with our grandmother, even though she didn't speak more than a few words of English and we couldn't understand much Polish.

Friday, Mommy cleaned windows inside and out, rearranged the attic, then pitched in with other women to spruce up the Polish Church.

Saturday was for heavy-duty housework: scrubbing the porches, cleansing cabinets and drawers, sweeping the cellar and coal bin, polishing furniture, and washing baseboards.

Barbara and I trained to be housewives by learning how to clean Mommy-style. Big sis was in charge of the upstairs—changing beds, dusting, vacuuming. Because my job was downstairs where I dusted, I never learned how to properly make a bed until college.

When I got older, another chore was swabbing the front porch, where I mopped to the music floating from the radio in the dining room. The instant I heard a big band song, I knew the door would soon swing open. Sure enough, my mom clad in peddlepushers would grab me and start jitterbugging. If someone walked by, we both waved enthusiastically while twirling around the wet floor. Her explanation for dancing on the slippery porch was that I had to practice in order to dance gracefully backwards in high heels like Astaire's partners. Not finding that justification plausible, Barbara was constantly worried that one of her friends would walk by and see her mother not acting her age.

"If the antics on the porch do not stop," Barbara warned me, "I shall die of embarrassment and never be able show my face in public again."

Our mother, too, didn't tolerate public displays of inappropriate behavior, but jitterbugging on the drenched porch was one of the rare times she didn't give a hoot what the neighbors said or thought. Mom loved to dance.

After the last mop and bucket were put away, she baked while Kenny and I ran to Hovanik's grocery store with a long, weekly food list that we dropped off for the Hovanik boys to fill and deliver.

When Daddy returned from the grind (as he put it), he found his best gal in the living room on the couch, waiting and puffing a cigarette, her trusty coffee nearby on the table. By the time her guy strolled in the front door, Mom had bathed for the second time and was wearing a stylish dress, full makeup, and Chanel No. 5, his favorite perfume. Every single evening she got gussied up for his arrival.

Appearing in the doorway when a slow song was playing on the radio or hi fi, Daddy reached out his arms, and she glided across the room to him. The very-much-in-love couple then waltzed cheek-to-cheek throughout the house. Starting at the front door, they continued through the hallway and living room, around the dining room table, and ended up in the kitchen kissing. I imagine they imagined that they resembled Ginger and Fred; and after seeing those remarkable movies, I do believe they were almost as smooth while cutting the rug, as you know who liked to say.

If they recently quarreled and were not speaking, silly Daddy picked up Kenny and me in his arms and shuffled through each room until his pouting partner gave in and tapped my shoulder to cut in. Beaming broadly, Daddy put us down, caressed his woman's face, and pulled her close to him. They swayed as one in rhythm with the music. Following closely behind the dancing fools, Kenny and I tried imitating the steps but mostly horsed around.

What Big Ears
You Have

On Sunday, after going to Mass and eating either a huge breakfast or a special dinner at noon in the dining room, the family went for a ride. Once a month the outing was to Grandma's house in Pittsburgh, where our dad grew up.

Going to Grandma Dell's was without fail a major production. The other Mrs. Dell made sure that we kids were squeaky clean and that our Sunday-best clothes were wrinkle-and dirt-free. Also, the maternal warning was to "be on your best behavior, or else!" The inflexible instructions were not to run through Grandma's house, not to fight with each other, not to interrupt grownups, not to talk back, not to get dirty, and not to leave anything on the plates set before us at dinner. Besides the six trillion rules and regulations, we were expected to smile, have fun, and be charming. It was as plain as the noses on our scrubbed faces that Grandma Dell and her daughter-in-law did not see eye to eye, and the Sunday afternoon visits to Pittsburgh were duty trips.

The stories of when Daddy and Mommy met, courted, and married drifted through my mind as we drove the 35 miles to the big city. (I'll jump ahead in the telling to show why the two Mrs. Dells didn't cotton to each other.)Our parents were secretly married by a justice of the peace in 1939, because Daddy was afraid to tell his mother about the marriage plans. It seemed every time he got serious with a young woman, Grandma Dell claimed she was too sick for him to leave home.

Following the simple wedding, Daddy remained at home, and Mommy continued living at Mel's boarding house, where she was a cleaning lady ever since leaving high school and East Vandergrift during the Depression. They didn't know how to break the news to his mother until nature helped solve the problem. Mom became pregnant with Jimmy.

When Daddy eventually told his mother, she ranted, raved, and disowned him, refusing to see or speak to him for three years. Grandma Dell finally came around and saw the light when Barbara was born. One look at her granddaughter and she was head over heels in love. There was something about our older sister that softened Grandma Dell's heart; and the affection she felt toward Barbara, her little fairy princess, was truly magical.

All car rides were adventures to Kenny and me. He counted cows on the left side of the road, and I kept score on the right. Any time a cemetery appeared, the cows on that side died, and the unlucky person had to start at zero again. Daddy changed the route each trip so that neither of us could possibly know which side had the fewest cemeteries or the most cows. I did mention how smart he was, didn't I?

Grandma Dell's little fairy princess frequently got car-sick and had to bring along an extra change of clothes in case her dresses became soiled with puke. When not throwing up in the back seat, Barbara had her nose buried in a book.

Jimmy, meanwhile, quietly stared out the window with a bored expression on his face, anxiously awaiting his 13th birthday, the milestone in his life when he could stay home alone while the rest of the Little Red Riding Hoods trooped off to Grandmother's house.

Grandma Dell may have been a witch (not her son's wife's choice word for her, but close enough) to our folks when they got married, but she sure was overly pleasant to the family during our sojourns. Slaving over a hot stove the day of our visit, she outdid herself with those extraordinary fried chicken legs and whipped-to-perfection mashed potatoes. Kenny devoured the mound of French fries cooked just for him. And from the moment we walked through the front door until the second we put on our coats to leave, the grandmotherly hugs and kisses were continuously passed around, most often to Barbara, the beloved grandchild.

Grandpa Steve—Grandma's second husband—was partial to Kenny and me, constantly propping us on his lap to help clean his pipes. Oh, that marvelous tobacco aroma smelled Heavenly and lingered everywhere in the house including upstairs, where Kenny and I hunched over the bedroom floor heating grate and eavesdropped on the adult conversation below in the living room.

While Jimmy plopped on the front porch steps, dreaming of his birthday and freedom from these obligatory social calls, Barbara curled up next to Grandma, clutching her hand. The grownups and the little princess, a straight-A student, discussed topics such as the Korean War, Senator Joseph McCarthy, the pros and cons of a back yard bomb shelter, as well as what Barbara wanted to be when she grew up.

Listening from above, Kenny and I started to doze off as Barbara droned on about the possibilities: a doctor, a lawyer, a mother, the first woman president. Everyone downstairs knew she was a brain and constantly compared her to Shirley Temple, from the time she started not just to talk but also recite nursery rhymes moments after her first words, "I smart," were spoken.

Whenever Grandma pleasantly purred, "Barbara, my gorgeous, exquisite angel, go find Kenny and Diana—I'm sure they're up to no good—and tell them it's time for some cake and ice cream," clearly the grownups were getting rid of her. Obviously, they wanted to dish the dirt concerning a subject not appropriate for "little pictures with big ears" to hear. Kenny and I held our breaths when Barbara called our names, not wanting to miss any juicy gossip about a relative or celebrity.

The for-adults-only information wafted up and entered our very big ears pressed to the grate. Kenny's eyes met mine, and smiles crossed our faces the instant Grandma (in almost a whisper) brought up the sordid episode of Ingrid Bergman and Roberto Rossellini's out-of-wedlock love child. Once television entered our lives and Kenny and I became hooked on old movies, Ingrid Bergman was on our A-list of choice actresses. Sinners and other baddies, of which Barbara was not one, intrigued Kenny and me.

After catching us spying, Barbara made us wash our hands and march behind her downstairs for the promised dessert. No dummy, she never squealed about our prying at Grandma Dell's, because we shared information with her that we gathered while snooping through the wall heating unit that separated the boys' room from Mommy and Daddy's. Eavesdropping plenty of times, we heard them murmur endearments, discuss money problems, and best of all, talk about what we were getting for Christmas and for birthdays. Kenny and I were like flies on the wall, always knowing what was going to happen before it did and warning Jimmy and Barbara about any doom coming their way.

I never exerted much effort, but Kenny tried plenty of times to get closer to Grandma Dell. The poor boy never seemed to ask the right questions or hit the suitable subjects to get the ball rolling. He chose instead to chatter about stuff like those famed robbers who got away with all that loot at the Brink's job in Boston. Stories pertaining to Lithuania, Grandma Dell's birthplace, was a topic he also loved hearing about, and she also hated discussing.

Going to Grandma Dell's house was a multifaceted experience. Barbara worshipped her as much as Kenny and I adored Bupchie, our East Vandergrift Polish grandmother. Daddy loved his mother. Mommy intensely disliked her. Delighted to see the family, Grandpa Steve was oblivious to any negative undercurrents. Jimmy was practically comatose from boredom. And Grandma Dell was a nervous wreck trying to please her extended family and to bury the past. Whatever the outcome or conversations, the trips to Grandma's house in Pittsburgh were adventures Kenny and I looked forward to, especially counting cows on the way there and snooping through the bedroom floor heating grate.

Once upon a Time

Wherever we were in the house or outside, any time Mommy shouted, "Kenny! Diana! Do you want to hear a story?" the two of us ran like Pavlov's dogs, claimed seats on either side of her, and silently waited for her to begin. Prefacing most of the narratives with, "This is a true story. Now listen carefully," she began recounting important history lessons of what the world was like before we were born.

Hearing about Daddy's branch of the family tree was fun, and we listened carefully. James Delcus and Susan Butkus, both born in Lithuania, met in Pittsburgh. Grandpa changed his name from Delcus to Dell, which sounded more American, in order to get a good job on the Pennsylvania Railroad as a railman. After he and Grandma were married in 1915, they had four children—Daddy (born in 1916), Johnny, Bobby, and a girl who died in the flu epidemic of 1918. Only a few months old when she passed away, her name was Clara, the same as Mommy's.

Grandpa Dell was a very handsome man, and people in the neighborhood said he looked and acted like a movie star. Sadly, though, he had a terrible temper, drank heavily, and gambled to boot. Grandma Dell and the children took many beatings from him, especially when he was sloshed or lost money gambling. It didn't matter, she was madly in love with him and overlooked his many faults and shortcomings. Extremely stern, he forbade Grandma to speak Lithuanian in the home. In spite of his desire and demands to raise an all-American family who spoke only English, Grandma secretly taught the kids her native language. Some of his commands, however, she could not repudiate.

Although Grandma was a devout Roman Catholic, he adamantly refused to let the children attend Mass or make their First Holy Communion because he had fought with the parish priest and was too stubborn to make up, as was the priest, an obstinate old coot.

As a boy while hawking newspapers on a street corner in Pittsburgh, our dad dreamed of becoming a reporter. "Extra! Extra! Read all about it! President Harding dies suddenly! Calvin Coolidge is the new President! Extra! Extra! Country has new President!" I imagine Daddy shouting headlines and looking jaunty in his knickers hitched up by striped suspenders.

Projecting an aura older than an eight-year-old, he was thrilled at the swarm of people thrusting two pennies at him for the paper that was most people's only source for news, other than the neighborhood grapevine. On eventful days the big-city tycoons sometimes tipped a penny! Newsboy Pop didn't interpret the news; he just sold the papers to a public clamoring to know more about sports heroes, scandalous movie stars, and daring gangsters made notorious by that noble experiment, Prohibition.

Daddy not only sold the newspapers, he also read them prodigiously hot off the presses. Later, he took copies to his teacher, Miss Paula Mahan, a beautiful, thoroughly Irish lass, every day until he outgrew short pants and headed for high school. "Extra! Extra! Read all about it! Lindberg does it! Flies to Paris in 33 1/2 hours! Extra! Extra! Read all about Lucky Lindy!"

An intelligent student, Daddy graduated valedictorian from high school. During his busy senior year, he had the lead role in the play, *Uncle Tom's Cabin*, and won an award for the part. For a brief time afterwards, with the applause still ringing in his ears, he dreamed of becoming an actor.

On graduation day, his father gave him a special present of a 30-day pass on the railroad, which enabled him to travel to Chicago to visit his godmother who was married to a judge. Upon returning to Pittsburgh, he found work at a steel mill but hated it so much that he started night school at Duquesne University for journalism and English. His fantasy by then was to be a newspaper writer.

Though very busy with homework and odd jobs, he kept in touch with his godmother; and following Daddy's second year of college, his godmother sent him another ticket to go to Chicago for the summer. With connections at the *Chicago Tribune*, her husband the judge helped Daddy land a job as a cub reporter. Loving the exciting world of deadlines and bylines and banner headlines, he decided to stay.

The best laid plans of mice and men. Daddy had to return home within the year when his father died. At that point, his hope of becoming a reporter was shattered. Instead of returning to college, he sold insurance to help support his mother and two younger brothers.

In his spare time for extra money, Daddy and his buddy Izzy organized and managed the championship Pitt football team during the off-season to play exhibition basketball games with Western Pennsylvania small-town fire departments and high school teams. It was a snap to recruit cash-strapped college players for $5 a game plus supper. The games drew large crowds, mainly because the collegiate champs clowned around on the gym floors, letting the beer-gutted fire fighters and hero-worshipping teen jocks win.

The Rose Bowl champions of 1937 (Pittsburgh 21, Washington 0) lived at Mel's boarding house near the University of Pittsburgh. My industrious future mother was a cleaning lady at Mel's since quitting high school at 15 during the Depression. A year earlier, the infamous flood of 1936 hit East Vandergrift. High school freshman Mommy and her family were trapped until firemen in boats arrived to rescue them. After being rescued from the top of their roof (Daddy told Kenny and me), they moved in with relatives uptown in Vandergrift for a few months, returning home after the river receded.

At the beginning of her sophomore year, Mom had to quit school and go to work. Although she was an all-A student, the administration gave permission for her to drop out. With too many mouths to feed at home and no opportunities for employment, her mother handed her $5 before putting her on a Pittsburgh-bound bus to find a job in the big city.

Daddy first spotted the woman of his dreams standing on a stepladder washing walls in Mel's boarding house kitchen. "I'm going to marry you someday," was the first sentence he spoke to her. Daddy, no moron, knew that women around the world were enchanted when the King of England, reputed playboy as the Prince of Wales, relinquished his throne for the woman he loved a year earlier. Those of the gentler sex, saps for romance, were still talking about how lucky Mrs. Simpson was to be adored so much and by royalty, no less.

Daddy was not a king, and petite workhorse Mommy was nobody's fool. With plenty of practice rebuffing propositions and proposals from her illustrious housemates, she took his opening salvo as merely another line from one more smooth-talking, tall, dark, and handsome Casanova.

When Jim Dell strolled into Mel's kitchen and proposed, Clara Maszgay thought he was crazy or, worse, making fun of her. Yet, her heart skipped a beat that moment when she first gazed into his exquisite green eyes. Unable to control her intense feelings, she fell in love with this good-looking guy at first sight but (clever her) played hard to get as Mel had advised.

Mom's boss and mentor was a 30-year-old college graduate who worked at the University of Pittsburgh's library. In the fall and winter Mel rented rooms to Pitt and Carnegie Tech students. Additionally, men who worked at J & L Steel lived there year round. In the summer, she let space to traveling performers who entertained at Duquesne Gardens and to a few baseball players with the Pirates.

Any time Daddy was present during a Mel's-boarding-house story, he'd always add his 2 cents. Feigning jealousy, he protested how difficult it was to win Mommy over because of the heavy competition, which included 10 circus clowns with red noses and floppy shoes, four muscular roller derby stars, six sequined ice skaters, and a carload of amorous midgets vying for her attention. Besides the show-biz suitors, he swore he had to stand in line behind medical students and future captains of industry just to say hello to her.

Poor Pop scrimped and saved for 5-cent hamburgers, 10-cent movie tickets, and 15-cent banana splits on dates. The gridiron heroes, on the other hand, could afford to show a girl a grand time because of the extra money and fancy cars handed to them by those earthly angels—executives in Pittsburgh—who sought out star football players as adolescent girls collect charms on bracelets. One fine place in the world to find bachelors was Mel's boarding house on Craig Street.

Mel, though, had no luck with men, who took advantage of her good nature. She paid the tuition for one student who promised marriage after graduation. When his classes were completed, before going home to Kansas, he pledged to return for the wedding, but she never heard from him again. The last young man she dated was studying to be an engineer. Mel picked out his clothes, paid his college bills, and even bought him a car. Following graduation, he said he was going home for a few days and would be back soon. Frantic with worry when she didn't hear from him for over six months, Mel decided to find him. Shortly after arriving at his hometown outside New York, she discovered he had married his high school sweetheart. Poor Mel.

Mommy loved the excitement of living at Mel's boarding house with college kids, engineers, teachers, football and baseball athletes, mill workers, circus performers, boxers, and various entertainers. Every week there was a big party; someone was always celebrating a birthday, graduation, or special occasion. Best of all, Mel treated our teenage mother like a daughter. She liked Daddy but always warned him to treat Mommy well, or else.

I can see him now (as he described it) trembling in his shoes because he's brought his date home one minute past curfew and finds Mel waiting up in the kitchen with a rolling pin in her hand. The family historian completed the scene:"There Mel would be, in the kitchen, just waiting to joke around with your father. I'd go to bed, and they'd stay up for hours gabbing, drinking coffee, and laughing. Daddy adored Mel. Everybody loved Mel." Everyone, that is, except her Mr. Right.

Daddy's opening comment about wanting to marry Mommy was no line. The man was head over heels in love and set out to woo her; she finally consented 12 months later at the end of 1939. They were young, madly in love, and optimistically facing the future for the rest of their lives together; but storm clouds were on the horizon. The Japanese bombed America into World War II a year after Jimmy was born, and another baby was on the way. Nothing would ever be the same again.

The trio left Pittsburgh in 1942 when Daddy got a new job servicing candy machines in Vandergrift and surrounding towns. They moved to East Vandergrift and stayed with Bupchie because they couldn't find a place to rent, and Mommy was expecting Barbara in a couple of months. (My sister was the only one of us kids to be born at home.)Following Barbara's birth, the young Dell family found a place in Apollo with two acres of land, a big chicken coop, and a large house.

Because every able-bodied man had either to enlist in the military or to work at a defense job, Daddy gave up servicing candy machines and reluctantly went to work at the Avonmore Foundry. He hated working in a steel mill, but the dirty job sure as heck beat subjecting his 27-year-old body to rigorous training geared to gung ho 18-year-olds.

Mommy loved that farm. Besides raising chickens, she sold 500 fryers every three months along with eggs. She also prepared jelly and canned vegetables and fruit. But best of all, they had a calf, two dogs, 12 baby ducks, 16 rabbits, and a big scarecrow that Mommy constructed herself. Daddy liked the farm but didn't enjoy the work that accompanied it. In sharp contrast, Mommy thrived throughout every backbreaking minute.

Gregarious Daddy spoke fondly of the neighbors during the times he reminisced of those early war years on the farm. Let's see, three daughters were part of the Barringer clan, a 15-minute walk away. The girls baby-sat Jimmy and Barbara after school and on weekends. Riding by on his way into town, Mr. Kepler always turned into the driveway to find out if his neighbor needed anything while Daddy was at work contributing his part on the homefront.

Similar to Will Rogers, Daddy said, "I never met a farmer I didn't like, except one." Mr. Dingle, who lived down the road apiece, thought that a sign of a good neighbor was one who didn't know his neighbors. Apparently this cantankerous man wanted others to mind their own darn business as well. The dairy farm kept him, his wife, and their five sons busy from sunup to sundown, with no time left over for socializing. The little leisure time he allowed himself was spent with his family.

The cranky farmer kept to himself, but the long arm of the draft did not. The Dingle dairy farm was one cow short for all five sons' exemptions; and for that reason, the youngest of the brood traded his overalls for a pair of fatigues and marched off to defend his country. "How you gonna keep 'em down on the farm after they've seen Paree?" never was a consideration for the boy, who upon boarding the train had all intentions of returning to Apollo. But for one cow he might never have left the farm. If Mr. Dingle had purchased just one more cow, the boy would not have died on a beach during the Normandy landing on D-Day, June 6, 1944.

Daddy, too, was called up on a technicality. When the war broke out, he registered with the draft board in Pittsburgh, which could never fill its quota. Our father wasn't overjoyed when his draft notice arrived from the city, but like the other draftees he followed orders. He regarded his Army experience as a temporary inconvenience, but a duty he could not shirk.

Mommy had to move after Daddy was drafted because she couldn't drive and had to find other work to support herself, Jimmy, and Barbara. They returned to Bupchie's house.

The day after her man went into the Army, our mom got a job waiting tables at The Liberty Restaurant. She was part of the evening shift so that she could be home during the days with Jimmy and Barbara. Aunt Veronica played with them from 4:00 p.m. to 8:00 p.m. and told them a terrifying story before putting them to bed.

Mom did very well waitressing because money flowed like water during the war. Employed around-the-clock in the steel mills, men made money hand over fist, while the soldiers fighting the war couldn't even sustain their families back home. It really wasn't fair, but at least those who stayed in the States felt guilty when they saw a soldier's wife working as a waitress and left generous tips.

At the train station, Daddy expressed how scared he was going off to the battlefront. Yet, these civilians, safe and sound in their hometowns, used to brag about how many Germans or Japanese they would kill if they were "over there." Our normally cheerful mother once became enraged when she overheard some big, strong draft-dodger tell his other burly draft-dodger buddies what he would do to the enemy. She defiantly asked him why he didn't prove it by enlisting.

"Do you know what he told me?" Mom asked Kenny and me for the hundredth time. "That he was essential at the steel mill. 'Huh!' I huffed, then added that plenty of men in the service gladly would trade places with him. Guys like that, who talk patriotically but don't put their money where their mouths are, make me sick," she declared repeatedly throughout the decades.

Mom had two wonderful Greek bosses with the last name of Agnos, a shortened version of a family name nobody but a Greek could pronounce. Socrates and his brother Aristotle arrived in Vandergrift from Athens in 1913. After laboring in the steel mill for five years, they had enough money saved to open a restaurant, which soon became the largest and busiest in town. Initially, the two brothers intended to make their fortunes and return home; but after many years had passed, Socrates and Aristotle Agnos, as most of the immigrants, decided to stay.

When the brothers Agnos arrived in Vandergrift before World War I, they spoke no English, knew not a soul, and had nothing but ambition, drive, and $20 between them. This country for them was the land of opportunity and freedom. Sadly, though, much the same as so many other immigrants who after time forgot the hate and resentment they first encountered, the Agnos boys also became prejudiced toward Negroes.

Mom only spoke of the good Socrates and Aristotle Agnos did, but Daddy remembered a specific time after World War II when he dropped by The Liberty Restaurant across the street from his candy business. A black American soldier with a chest full of medals, among them the Purple Heart, approached the counter, ordered a beer, and drank it without saying a word to people sitting beside him. Socrates, who was talking to Daddy and other businessmen, marched over to the black hero, picked up the empty beer glass, and smashed it against the wall. As the humiliated veteran stood speechless, Socrates turned to the other customers and announced that he didn't have enough soap in the restaurant to clean the glass thoroughly so breaking it was cheaper.

Trying to control his temper, Daddy tossed 50 cents on the counter for his yet-to-arrive 35-cent lunch and escorted his brother veteran out the door. Standing on the sidewalk while searching for the right words, Daddy apologized to the man, who thanked him then left with his head downcast. Enraged at the embarrassment felt by the combat veteran, Daddy swore he would never eat at The Liberty Restaurant as long as he lived. He abided by that decision but felt somewhat guilty for not giving his business to Socrates who was great to Mom while she waitressed during the war. Guilt or no guilt, he could not in good conscience remain friendly with a bigot, especially one who treated a returning soldier with such disrespect and disdain.

Per Private Dell's strange request from the front, waitress Dell started collecting sugar coupons with some of the money she earned. What she could not buy with cash, she bartered for with meat and gasoline rations left as tips. Just as soon as he returned home to his young family in 1945, our father took his sweet savings plus the $1000 of sugar that the Army gave to soldiers who wanted to start a candy business and struck a deal with the Mello Company to set him up in the wholesale-candy business in exchange for the valuable sugar they desperately needed to keep up production.

The postwar period was frenzied. Personal savings were amassed during the austerity of wartime. Afterwards people wanted to spend, spend, spend. The pursuit of personal happiness and consumption quickly replaced the four years of sacrifice and deprivation the country had endured. Consumer goods were in short supply with the nation switching rapidly from war to peace. Thousands of soldiers were discharged a day. They, as well as homefront Americans, craved items limited or unavailable during the war: beef, ice cream, toys, alcohol, cars, and candy.

Possessing a sweet tooth himself, Daddy understood the pent-up desire for candy and seized the moment. Candy was his future. Private First Class James Albert Dell of Company F, 318th Infantry put away his military uniform and stored his Good Conduct, European African Middle Eastern Theater, and Purple Heart medals in a trunk. Donning a gray flannel suit with a matching fedora, he set out to do battle in the world of business. After renting a store in Vandergrift, he bought a truck and named his new venture "The PX."

Nine months to the day after Daddy set foot back in East Vandergrift, I was born along with millions of other babies who officially kicked off the baby boom of 1946.

Uncle Bobby

Daddy's younger brother Bobby lived with our family when we rented from Mrs. Berostek across the street from our home. I don't remember much about him; he only stayed for two years then entered a hospital in Arizona a few months before Kenny was born. Jimmy, though, later talked fondly of the constant piggyback rides, and Barbara remembered strolling happily to church and to the playground with Uncle Bobby. I'm really not sure what I recall and what stories from others were planted in my brain. In my memory he is merely a tall, shadowy figure.

The neighbors remembered his peculiar condition called Tourette's Syndrome, involuntary twitching, speaking, and swearing at inappropriate times. When Mrs. Berostek admired his tie as she passed him on the way to church, he thanked her then called her vile names. Simply put, he could not control his behavior, which was the reason Grandma Dell took him out of the seventh grade and never sent him back to school. Teachers staunchly affirmed that he had a disruptive mental illness, but Grandma Dell refused to have him committed to an institution and instead kept him at home tied to her apron strings.

After his older brother returned from overseas, Uncle Bobby begged to come and live with us. Grandma Dell never allowed him outside, virtually imprisoning him without friends or a social life. He was 18 when he moved from Pittsburgh to East Vandergrift and enjoyed the most gratifying two years of his life—working hard with Daddy at the candy business, baby-sitting Jimmy, Barbara, and me, and befriending those neighbors who genuinely liked him and nonchalantly accepted his condition.

Besides Tourette's, he also had a dreadful case of asthma that became so severe he had to check into a sanitarium out West for treatment when Mommy was pregnant with Kenny. Uncle Bobby died of a heart attack not long after he left. That I remember. It was Kenny's first Christmas and the first time I saw my dad cry when Grandma phoned two days before the holiday with the terrible news. Death had no meaning to me. I simply could not understand why sad Mommy and tearful Daddy were silently taking down the tree and putting away decorations before Santa delivered our presents.

Kidz N the Hood

The summer before I started the first grade two new events occurred. Kenny was not yet four and said he was three-and-a-half when asked. I was five-and-a-half. Well, almost. This was the memorable season of our first television set and first paying job—running numbers for Mrs. Pinchek.

Initially, the pay was a dime to deliver the secret bets a few blocks to the housewife-bookie; then a quarter, when Kenny and I found out what we were doing and forbidden to do it. Dodging the chance of a licking was well worth a quarter; back then in 1951 a nickel bought a six-ounce bottled Coke. While the Korean War raged and the Rosenbergs awaited execution, Kenny and I sang "Getting To Know You" from the hit musical *The King and I* in between sipping the rewards of our 10 minutes of easy, albeit illegal, work.

The bookie lived a few houses down from Bupchie on McKinley Avenue. We were later informed that the state police kept surveillance on the bookie's house. Although barely out of the toddler stage, we were smart enough to know that the cops would never suspect a five-year-old and her younger brother who still had to hold her hand to cross the street.

At first, Mrs. Pinchek said we were delivering recipes to the lady who lived down the street from our grandmother. The alleged recipes were wrapped in white Kleenex and bound tightly with a rubber band. Mrs. Pinchek gave strict instructions not to tell anyone about the rendezvous, including Mommy, her law-abiding, next-door neighbor.

Every morning at 11:30, Kenny and I sat on the back porch steps that faced the Pinchek yard and stared at the tulips until we heard our neighbor give the agreed-upon signal, "Psst." Then, she waved for us to approach the fence that separated the two properties. The barrier also kept her vicious cocker spaniel, Fifi, safe from people in the neighborhood who wanted to poison it. Even gigantic male dogs strolling down Quay Street crossed over to the other side when they passed the Pinchek yard. Fifi truly was a bitch.

"Where's your mama?" our neighbor whispered through pinched lips. (Daddy called her "Prune Face" when he thought kids weren't listening.)Assured that our energetic, workaholic mother was cleaning somewhere in the house and out of ear shot, she handed us the tissue and a dime. Not two nickels. A dime. Stuffing the Kleenex into my overall pocket, I let Kenny take the dime for our later use. Like clockwork, I then found Mommy in the house and told her we were taking a walk before lunch.

It was clear that the secrecy somehow covered up wrongdoing, but the dimes were too good to be true. As self-appointed leader by height and advanced age, I clutched the so-called recipes and Kenny's hand as we walked down the dirt alley and over to McKinley Avenue. But first we checked out the chickens in their coop behind Mrs. Bielak's house, sniffed Mr. Kocur's roses on his vine-covered gate, kicked rocks, and stopped to pet dogs and cats along the two blocks to our town's version of Al Capone. I wonder if other crime figures baked apricot squares and chocolate chip cookies.

Kenny was cranky one hot day and refused to budge an inch until I got him something to drink. He had such a bad temper that arguing with him about making the delivery before he wet his whistle, as Daddy loved to say, was useless.

Before starting the daily delivery for Mrs. Pinchek, I led him into the kitchen, placed the Kleenex atop the Formica table, and poured some lemonade that Barbara had made early in the morning. As we slurped loud enough to wake the dead (Pater's words), Mommy breezed in and spotted the tissue.

Asked what it was, I informed her, "It's nothing important."

She immediately reached to toss it away. The woman was a fanatic about anything, except food, on the kitchen table. A comb placed on the table was an unspeakable act in her crazy-clean mind-set; a dirty Kleenex was worse.

Methinks I doth protested too much. Hurriedly peeling apart the little white parcel, she knew in a flash its purpose the instant the five-dollar bill fluttered to the floor, exposing a list of numbers on a crumpled piece of paper. I knew it couldn't be a peach pie recipe, and for a moment fear gripped me. Could these be atomic-bomb secrets intended for a Soviet agent in a housedress? Spies were in the news and on everyone's lips; and I had visions of being hauled off to jail by the FBI and executed for treason.

"Truman says Russia seeks world conquest."

"J. Edgar Hoover warns that Communists are going underground."

"Movie canceled about Henry Wadsworth Longfellow, since Hiawatha, an Indian peacemaker, is seen as a Communist sympathizer."

"Spy ring busted. Diana and Kenny Dell arrested for espionage."

Radio announcers and newspaper editors warned daily about reds, pinkos, and commies on every corner, under every rock, who were disguised as ordinary, everyday people like Mrs. Pinchek and the bookie on Bupchie's street. This situation looked like explosive trouble. Not only would the G-men be called in, but Kenny and I could also get the licking of a lifetime.

After an eternity of terrifying thoughts, I saw Mommy smile. The five-and-a-half years of life stopped passing before my eyes, and I sighed with relief as she explained the numbers racket. Saying we were being played for suckers with the recipe story, she neglected to ask how long the trips had been going on or if we were being paid. Without pausing for a breath, she put a stop to the daily mission then and there

(she thought) by ordering "never, ever deliver the numbers again."
Regaining her composure, she softened a bit. "Just tell Mrs. Pinchek I
don't allow you two to cross McKinley Avenue by yourselves."

What that meant, I guess, was she didn't want to make a big deal out
of it. It was useless confronting Mrs. Pinchek. Ours was but a tiny
neighborhood in such a small town, and each person tried to get along
as best he or she could without bothering anyone else. That was true, of
course, until Mr. Pinchek got loaded, chased Fifi with an ax, and tried
to beat up his wife. At those frightful times, Daddy stepped in to protect scrawny Mrs. Pinchek. Meek when he wasn't drinking, her husband
thanked his neighbor the next morning and all was forgotten until the
next time Mr. Pinchek closed the Slovak Club and attempted to substitute his wife for a punching bag. Mildred Pinchek played the numbers;
John Pinchek got ugly drunk.

When I explained to Mrs. Pinchek why Kenny and I could not
deliver her (snicker, snicker) recipes, she increased the commission
from a dime to a quarter, and our first business—the illegal courier
service—resumed.

Too young to know about bank-savings' accounts (piggy banks were
for hoarding money usually given as gifts), we spent the easily earned
dough as fast as it came in. A quarter bought a slew of soda pop, cho
chos, and other sugary treats at Joe Stemplensky's candy store that summer. Kenny and I gorged sweets like piglets and later picked at our supper. As a Great Depression survivor, our mom's biggest worry was our
never eating. Yet, she never had a problem with Jimmy and Barbara.
They cleaned their plates at mealtime while Kenny and I, with candy-
filled bellies, practically threw up at the sight of food. Instead of feeling
sorry for those starving children in China mentioned three times a day,
we desperately wanted to ship them the chow on our plates. Just as soon
as the cops raided the bookie, remarkably our appetites returned.

Bupchie

Kenny and I earned legitimate wages by carrying odds and ends from our house to Bupchie's. Before we made a delivery, however, Mommy warned us not to take any money. After we informed our wonderful, white-haired grandmother what her daughter had said, Bupchie replied right on cue, "Take it and don't tell mama." The comeback was in Polish, but the gestures and inflection were universal. Slyly, we pocketed the change Bupchie thrust at us without a peep to anyone. Like clever children, we rationalized that since Bupchie was older and our mother's mother, we had to obey her. Bupchie always won as far as cash was concerned. Even when no dough was involved, going to her house still was fun. We loved her for caring so much about us, two scruffy little moppets.

Bupchie kept a wad of bills in a handkerchief tucked in the pocket of her extra-large housedress. Short and round with long white hair tied in a bun, Bupchie was the embodiment of central casting's ideal grandmother. Everyone loved Bupchie, especially her grandkids. She could be gruff and tough, but never to children.

By the time Kenny and I were old enough to conduct messenger service to her house, Bupchie had already been in America for over 50 years, given birth to eight children, grieved when one of them tragically died, lost her first husband to cancer, fled her home because of floods, survived the Depression, remarried a man with four children she gladly raised as her own, and watched her sons go off to war to defend her adopted country. Yet, during those five decades, she never learned English and faithfully dreamed of moving back to Poland, her beloved homeland.

Bupchie's second husband was our only Ju Ju—grandfather in Polish. Our real Ju Ju meant nothing to us, except when he came alive during our mother's childhood stories. As Kenny and I got older and Bupchie's presents got larger, she whispered after handing us some cash, "Don't tell Ju Ju." When I think back to those times, I never remember him ever giving us anything, so why would we ever go against her advice or in any way confide in him?

Since our mother was first-generation American, she and her siblings spoke two languages: Polish at home and English elsewhere. In contrast, Bupchie figured she didn't have to learn the new language. Most of her life she planned on returning home to Poland.

Our grandmother, however, did know a few important English phrases: "Don't tell your mother," or "Don't tell Ju Ju," and especially "I love you!" which she proclaimed often to our delight. We could strike out at bat or get bad grades, but the world was safe and secure because Bupchie loved us unconditionally and enthusiastically.

Being typical second-generation Americans, we kids never learned any language other than English. No matter; we communicated with silver-haired Bupchie just fine. She spoke in Polish, and we responded in English. If not able to fully comprehend what she was saying, we simply nodded affirmatively and hustled out the kitchen door. Our antics continuously made her laugh. Entertainment evidently was the purpose of our existence; we knew this and played it to the hilt. It did not take a genius to realize that two little rascals were not required to carry one bowl of Jell-O two blocks to their grandmother. Kenny and I loved the attention and the moolah.

Bupchie's house smelled of cooking cabbage and moth balls. The kitchen table was covered with one of those 1940s, gaudy, stiff, wipeable, kidproof, stainproof, wild-flowered, plastic tablecloths. In one corner was Ju Ju's silver-plated spittoon, which we used as a potty when we were toddlers. The only wall decoration was Da Vinci's *The Last Supper*, one of our first introductions to fine art. She also had a formal dining room that was rarely used. In it was a long oak table Bupchie's first spouse built; it was covered with a beautiful lace tablecloth Bupchie bought during one of her trips back to Europe. A religious painting of Christ with an exposed heart decorated one wall. After Barbara received her First Holy Communion and formulated plans to enter a convent as her life's vocation, she genuflected each time she passed the picture on her way through the dining room toward the bathroom upstairs. Never would she have considered using the spittoon.

Sometimes Kenny and I visited Bupchie without a purpose and beat a hasty retreat the instant she started pulling out the magical and mystical, money-bulging handkerchief. I suppose this was an innocent way of showing that we cared for her and not only for the monetary gifts. Then, at other times, we gleefully skipped over to Bupchie's house without a delivery and stopped dead in our tracks with disappointment upon seeing Ju Ju in the kitchen, which meant no surprises from Bupchie. I think he liked us, maybe even loved us, but he certainly didn't know what made kids happy. Money and a big lap to sit on were on the top of our wish lists. After becoming movie addicts, Kenny and I compared Bupchie with Ethel Waters. Attitude, not color, counted. Ju Ju was Walter Brennan in his grumpiest role.

Bupchie had a gigantic yard with a vegetable garden and a chicken coop in it. Raising chickens became illegal during the mid-1950s when a newly passed town ordinance forbade farm animals in town. The result of the regulation was similar to Prohibition. Most people broke it. Bupchie reluctantly gave in a few years after the decree was enacted when the town council threatened to raise the taxes of scofflaws. Plainly she understood the language of money.

Those darn chickens scared the stuffing out of Kenny and me; viciously they pecked at us when Bupchie wasn't watching. When she did look, they then turned into gentle pets. All of them had special names and responded to her commands like obedience school gradu-ates. There was a major problem with those ornery poultry: they did not understand English. And the only Polish Kenny and I knew included (this is how we said them, not how they're spelled) "Yitch da duomo sputch," which loosely translated means "go home and go to bed," and "sha looney goovno" for "green shit."

Obviously, her feathered friends, who demanded all her attention, were jealous of Kenny and me; but if a choice had to be made, even those chickens knew that we kids would win. Kenny and I were cocky regarding that unspoken truth. In our hearts, we were sure of one thing: In a lifeboat situation, Bupchie would save us before them. I kid you not, they taunted us with a vengeance while her back was turned; but we showed them who had the upper hand by gluttonously devouring our favorite meal, fried chicken.

Once those miserable cluckers were removed from the premises and eaten, Bupchie created a beautiful flower garden to complement her bountiful vegetable patch. Gorgeous red roses and luscious tomatoes were ours for the picking.

The Chicken Business

About three days after our family—minus Kenny and me—moved to the farm in Apollo during the war, Daddy brought home 600 baby chicks. His ordinarily unflappable wife was in total shock, because she didn't have a clue how to raise chickens. Frantic, Mom turned to one of the neighbors for help.

In Mom's own words: "With baby chicks it can be a disaster. They need special care or else they die. Mr. Barringer brought his incubator over, and we set up a warm place for the wee chicks inside the coop for three weeks so they could get enough strength to survive the cold. I followed Mr. Barringer's instructions and all but 40 survived.

"Before going off to war, Uncle Caz helped care for them during those first three, critical weeks, and in three months they were full-grown chickens. Salesman that he was, your father found a restaurant owner who purchased them for a dollar apiece. Daddy then bought 600 more baby chicks; and when this batch grew to fryer-hood, he sold them as well. This time, though, we kept out 50 that I raised for eggs and eating. Our family had chicken every Sunday, as did Bupchie and her friends.

"Your grandmother also sold the eggs to people in East Vandergrift for 50 cents a dozen and had 30 customers who claimed hers were the best eggs they had ever tasted. If Daddy hadn't been drafted, we planned to continue and expand the chicken business. When Jimmy, Barbara, and I moved back to East Vandergrift during the war, I taught my mother all about raising chickens."

When Mom left her memories and returned to the present, she began laughing at how the mere mention of those fowls made Kenny and me scrunch up our faces in total disgust.

Our First Boob Tube

Daddy's candy business boomed, and he happily bought new appliances for our home. The iceman cameth no more when the Kelvinator refrigerator with the bottom drawer for storing potatoes arrived, and the radio was relegated to an obscure corner in the dining room as soon as our first television appeared on the scene. The 12-inch, black-and-white Philco, with dark mahogany finish and a jewel light at the base to indicate when it was turned on, sat center stage in the living room. Thrilled about the new toy, Kenny and I were also ecstatic with the big cardboard box it came in.

Daddy and Jimmy spent the whole morning on the roof setting up the antenna. Kenny and I had the time of our lives making a fort with the container and running in and out of the house to tell the guys on the top of the house when the reception was getting better so that they could make adjustments every which way. Daddy spent most of the time on the roof swearing, sweating, and waving to the neighbors. Jimmy worked.

The entire neighborhood was buzzing with excitement about the first TV in East Vandergrift. Thrilled too, our family had a party that Tuesday evening to stare at the case with doors that opened to a small, snowy screen. Mr. and Mrs. Welkon, who lived two blocks up Quay Street, came over with their kids, Sylvia and Joannie, to join in the celebration.

Huddled in the darkened room, the gang viewed Mr. Television (Milton Berle) on the Texaco Star Theater. Truly, there was magic in the air that night, but no one had the faintest idea that what we were looking at would have significant impact on American life. Television was simply a novelty.

Mrs. Welkon and her brood visited often and in awe watched Lucy and Ethel get themselves into some awfully big pickles, Arthur Godfrey strum on his ukulele, Groucho Marx crack jokes and chomp on a cigar, Arlene Francis and pals in formal evening wear and fancy masks try to guess who the mystery guest was, and Ed Sullivan's fabulous variety "shoe" wow America.

There was one rather frightening afternoon when Kenny and I decided to sit with Mommy and Mrs. Welkon while they observed a bunch of men talk or not talk and "take the fifth" instead. During a station break, Mom explained the workings of the Senate Crime Committee hearings chaired by Senator Estes Kefauver. Underworld figures appeared as what Kenny and I imagined gangsters looked like. One guy allowed only his hands to be photographed; and before our television arrived, Bugsy Siegal's girlfriend, Virginia Hill Hauser, roared at the Committee, "You goddamn bastards. I hope an atom bomb falls on every one of you." Oh, how Kenny wished he could have seen her with his own eyes.

The crime hearings hit too close to home for the wide-eyed numbers runners squirming on the floor, facing the black-and-white screen. Kenny and I may have been alarmed at the thought of having to testify on television some day, but not enough to give up the quarters Mrs. Pinchek was paying. We just went outside to play until something better came on. Out of sight, out of mind.

Before the newness wore off, Kenny and I were glued to the set keeping an eye on the Cisco Kid and his sidekick Pancho, Wild Bill Hickok and his pal Andy Devine, and Roy Rogers with cowgal Dale Evans. Loving those cowboys with a passion, Kenny ran around the house calling me "kema sabe" while the masked man and his faithful companion rode off in a cloud of dust after another day's program. Later, hearing

Buffalo Bob ask Kenny and me, "What time is it, boys and girls?" we screamed at the set, "It's Howdy Doody time!"

Kenny loved to drink from shot glasses the same way as cowboys, claiming pop tasted better in the little tumblers. He even practiced getting drunk. Most of the time, I had to be the dance hall girl and bar maid to his cowboy in the saloon. Kenny owned a Hopalong Cassidy suit and changed the saintly character into a drunken one, although everyone knew full well that Hoppy did not cuss, smoke, mess with dance hall girls, and he certainly did not drink booze.

I was forced to be Dale Evans as a dance hall girl, even though Dale was as pure as the Blessed Virgin Mary and only had eyes for Roy. Sometimes Kenny made me mimic Gabby or, worse yet, Tonto. My speaking parts consisted of repeating "ugh" and, of course, "kema sabe." My Lone Ranger also insisted that his Tonto get rip-roaring drunk on fire water. Mommy did not approve of these games and sat us down numerous times to describe how alcohol and moonshine had ruined many people's lives. We heard a great deal about heavy-drinker Grandpa Dell, and how our father had suffered because of the booze.

There was never any liquor in our house, except for a few bottles of Iron City beer in the fridge for Mommy's younger brother Caz, our bachelor uncle who lived at home with Bupchie and Ju Ju. I never saw my dad take a drink, and Mom held a highball glass at weddings but never drank from it. Neither, though, minded other people's drinking in moderation. Their only addictions were Mommy's cleaning and the old man's eating.

Daddy loved food, even Army chow and meals from hospital cafeterias. In fact, he couldn't resist the chocolates in 5-pound boxes that Kenny had bitten into and decided weren't to his liking. Daddy always saved his son from those God-awful creams and mints, which he hated as much as mashed potatoes. Since these were the pieces no kids favored, we asked Daddy what idiot at the candy factory insisted on including them in the assortments. With a straight face, Daddy explained, "This is the only way for fathers to get any of the goodies." At the time that sure made sense; and come to think about it, it now certainly sounds logical.

Nobody in those early years bragged about not tuning in to zany Amos n' Andy or the endearing Swedish Mama or loquacious Molly Goldberg hanging out a tenement window; and thousands of kids all over America knew it was time to wash for dinner the instant they heard rotund Kate Smith melodiously warble "When the Moon Comes Over the Mountain" at the end of her late-afternoon show. Pops was right when he declared, "It's not over till the fat lady sings."

Box Seats

Mommy remembered once, when she was nine years old, listening to a Pirates' game with her brothers: "Every time someone hit a home run, we got excited and jumped up and down clapping. During a commercial, I remarked that it would be wonderful to be able to see teams play in the radio. My brothers laughed and said I was nuts. When the broadcast was over, the boys ran outside and told their friends about my 'crazy comment,' as they called it. Those boys teased me relentlessly for weeks. Huh! Look who has the last laugh now. Who would have ever guessed?" she remarked while watching a baseball game in the living room.

Uncle Caz

At this early point in television history, Uncle Caz started spending more time with Kenny and me. The three of us became TV buddies. After he got off the graveyard shift in the steel mill, downed a shot and a beer at the Polish club, then went home for a nap, he caught up with Kenny and me in the early afternoon for "Mr. Wizard," "Ding Dong School," and the cowboys we enjoyed so much.

Uncle Caz was such a kind and gentle soul with us kids, but he hollered at Aunt Veronica whenever she told scary stories that made us cry. Fairy tales to him were too frightening for children; he chose non-fiction sagas instead: fights he got into as a kid, pranks he and his school chums pulled on teachers. Even better yet, he told World War II stories. I remember how he predicted when it would rain, because, he said, the shrapnel in his body caused him severe back pain any time a storm was on the way. He might have fibbed and knew the weather forecast from the radio, but who cared? The shrapnel in the back sounded mysterious and heroic.

During the war, he became disabled when the jeep he was riding in hit a land mine. The five other soldiers with him were instantly killed, but Uncle Caz was blown out of the doorless vehicle before it became engulfed in flames. Unconscious for a very long time (he wasn't sure just how long), he came to as German soldiers were turning his pals' bodies over to make sure they were dead. With half-opened eyelids, Uncle Caz watched in horror as they bayoneted the dead Americans, most with missing limbs. Holding his breath as a German swinging a bloodstained weapon approached, he silently prayed, certain he was soon to follow his friends to the afterlife. Suddenly, however, when the squad's sergeant barked an order, the soldier ready to stab Uncle Caz quickly turned and ran toward his leader. The group then marched away down the road. Uncle Caz passed out and was found two days later by a platoon of GI's. At first they thought he too was dead, but a medic among them detected a faint heartbeat and shouted with joy, "This man's alive!" Our uncle convalesced in an English hospital for a year before coming home to East Vandergrift at war's end.

Following the jeep incident, he never drove a car. Extremely superstitious, he was afraid that if he got behind the wheel he might cause a horrible accident. Because of all the walking, he was in great shape, considering he smoked two packs of cigarettes a day and downed a six-pack with them.

Swearing like a sailor, although he was in the infantry, Uncle Caz was always straightforward and honest with Kenny and me, never glossing over any of our questions regarding the war, including the ones concerning comely nurses and fetching farm girls he met overseas. What a lady's man he was! From his stories at least. The only subject about that time he would not discuss with us was Uncle Stanley, his stepbrother who died in the war.

Mom explained: "Caz and Stanley were very close, and Stanley's death devastated Caz. Your Uncle Caz can't even mention our brother Stanley's name without getting terribly sad.

"During a leave in Paris, Caz glanced across the Champs Elysees and spotted Stanley. Figuring that no Parisian would ever have a nickname like our brother's, he yelled, 'Hey, Stush!'

"Stanley responded with Caz's boyhood name, 'Hey, Cutsca!'

"They raced across the wide boulevard and hugged until soldiers passing by started to whistle. Partying all night, my brothers hit Pigalle (where the prostitutes plied their trade), took in the show at the Follies Bergere, and climbed the Eiffel Tower. Culminating their celebration at the famous Pont Neuf bridge over the Seine River, they watched dawn appear. How lovely that must have been! Before parting, they made plans to meet in London in a few months if they could swing it with their CO's. The hug good-bye at the mobbed French train station was the last time Caz ever saw Stanley."

At the end of the Paris anecdote, Mom remarked, "Try to understand why he will not talk about Stanley. It's only because he does not want you children to see him cry." Kenny and I did understand that about Uncle Caz, our mutual godfather, who always tossed a smile and a nickel each time he saw us.

Soldiers

Kenny and I played cowboys and Indians and GI Joe fighting Nazis. Sgt. Rock, however, was our all-time beloved hero. Superman was cool, but he wasn't real like Sgt. Rock. Even before we could read about the tough soldier's brave exploits, Jimmy sank into the couch—with Kenny and me glued to each side of him—and read aloud his comic books. Afterwards, our older brother let us play with them, giving the oldies to Kenny when he bought new ones.

In those early '50s, World War II was still fresh in everyone's mind, and the Korean War kept getting hotter. Because of hearing war stories from our mother, male relatives, and neighbors, Kenny and I knew which men in East Vandergrift had stayed out of harm's way by being 4-F. We also were aware of who remained at home making bunches of money in the steel mills, while brave men left their wives and children to go fight the Krauts and the Japs. Those were terms Mommy forbade us to use, but we said them anyway. Sgt. Rock and Uncle Caz did.

Man Mountain, the guy who ran the post office and rarely had a kind word for kids, was a genuine hero. He received the Silver Star after he single-handedly fought and defeated 10 Jap soldiers. There were bayonet scars on his stomach to prove it. We never saw the marks, but everyone said they were right there on his gut.

Kenny and I quietly opened the post office door, darted past his cage to our box, turned the dial with the correct combination (left-5, right-2, left-4), reached in to get the mail, and raced out, terrified he would be offended and pounce. It's surprising that those 10 Japs didn't immediately surrender when they first laid eyes on Man Mountain. His giant build alone could make anyone tremble with fear.

Whenever we found a pink slip indicating a package too large to fit in the box, we had to go to his cage. Oh, Kenny and I hated pink paper in our post office box, just as people dread them in their pay envelopes. We were filled with relief when we approached the window and saw his wife, a large courteous woman who always knew our names. She could afford to be gentle, not having to kill her enemies then pull four bayonets out of her belly as her husband did. Not a war hero, she at least had the good sense to marry one. Kenny referred to her as "Woman Mountain" a few times, but the tag never caught on.

The post office was in a red-bricked building next door to Blue Heaven, a bar. On warm days the stench of cigarettes and beer wafted through the screen door; and the tavern's regular customer, Danny Boshkus, could be seen perched on his bar stool, right next to the door.

Danny fought his way up Heartbreak Hill and had been in the Inchon Landing in Korea but was court-martialed shortly after General MacArthur—that old soldier who never seemed to fade away like the one in the ballad—destroyed the port-town in order to retake Seoul and save Korea's capital from Communism. Kenny and I could almost feel Danny's shame. Nobody would say what he did to deserve that horrendous reprimand from the Marines, but we knew the pain would follow him forever.

People whispered that not only would he never be forgiven, but also that he lost his right to vote and would never to be allowed into federal buildings. Someone must have forgotten to notify Mr. and Mrs. Man Mountain about Danny's ban from government property, because we spotted him in the post office often and could not help staring at his bulging muscles covered with tattoos. My kid brother and I loved our mother, too, but neither of us would prove it by letting somebody stick a needle in our arms.

Danny was always friendly to kids, although he was known around town as a thug. Responding to his hello, we could not look him the eyes. It was hard to bear the dishonor they held, or at least the humiliation Kenny and I thought we saw. With a pack of Camels protruding from his rolled-up T-shirt sleeve, he resembled a war hero like Sgt. Rock, but we knew he was just the opposite, almost a coward. Kenny and I had no room in our lives or hearts for anyone as lowly as a court-martialed soldier; we didn't want to be seen in his company. In retrospect, whatever he did during the Korean War, he certainly did not deserve our childish scorn. I see that now, but was blind to it then.

When Man Mountain, in contrast, occasionally flashed a smile or laughed at something we said, our hearts swelled with pride. Pleasing a war hero, we felt blessed.

Hovanik's
Grocery Store

Darting home with the mail (we never walked anywhere), Kenny and I then got the next assignment. Frequently, it was a jaunt to the grocery store with a list and the orange credit book that everyone termed "the store book." Comparable to other families who shopped at Hovanik's corner grocery market, we charged our food orders and paid once a week on Friday.

Mr. and Mrs. Hovanik, the classic old man and woman who lived with their sons above in the second-floor apartment, owned the store. Both short, round, and jolly, they looked sort of like the Clauses. Unlike Santa, though, Mr. Hovanik spoke with a thick Polish accent. Mrs. Hovanik displayed an amiable disposition. He grinned incessantly, while she stood behind the front and only check-out counter, tallying up the purchases and recording them neatly in the orange credit book. Her penmanship was as grade-A as his meats were.

Mr. Hovanik ran the butcher shop section in the back of the small store. When anyone ordered hamburger, he ground it fresh from pieces of "this" and pieces of "that." With steak requests, he stepped into the walk-in refrigerator and brought out what appeared to be half the cow, sliced off a slab within the customer's eyesight, then trimmed off the fat which became part of the "that" for the next person's ground-beef purchase.

Once a month was kishka day. You could smell the stuff for blocks, and its unique aroma made mouths water. To kids, kishka was a mysterious kind of sausage. When Barbara asked Daddy what was in it, he answered, "Don't ask. You'll enjoy it more if you never know." He said the same thing about hot dogs. In fact, kishka was created from a month's worth of scraps from the butcher department then stuffed into an animal's intestines. Selling for 10 cents a pound, it tasted best freshly made and served piping hot.

Throughout the kishka day, Mr. Hovanik emerged from the trap door leading from the cellar with platters of this yummy specialty. Women stood in a line that stretched beyond Butch's family's combination candy store-pool hall next door, waving their orange store books, screaming out quantities they wanted.

"Four pounds!"

"Six pounds!"

"Ten pounds!"

Because everyone had big families, no one shopping at Hovanik's grocery store ever ordered anything less than a pound. I'm not even sure Mr. Hovanik's butcher scale could dip below 16 ounces.

Before recycling became au courant, each person and all businesses in our hometown recycled everything. Nothing was wasted. People either returned pop bottles or gave them to Mutsy Futsy for the deposits, the milk man picked up empties from porches each morning, and the rag man on Saturday—with his tired old horse and beat-up wagon—bought scrap metal for 15 cents a pound. Mothers reused the plastic and brown paper from clothes the cleaner uptown delivered to the homes. The traveling egg man refilled cartons from original purchases. Paper bags were cut up to line kitchen shelves and drawers, cover school books, and make Halloween masks. Those left over were returned to the grocery store when one of the high school Hovanik boys dropped off the Saturday order. He got back the bags and a dime tip.

Down the Field

Kenny and I hunched on the wooden bleachers down the field with pride and joy in our hearts when Jimmy, the star pitcher for the Polish National Alliance (PNA) team, hurled a no-hitter against the Slovak Club players, the rival team. They were the bad guys who deserved no mercy. I didn't have a clue then, nor do I know now, why the Polish and Lithuanian people despised the Slovaks, but they did. Rightly or wrongly, the Slovak kids (Mutsy Futsy was one) had reputations as bullies, mischief-makers, and meanies to animals and old ladies.

All the boys in their snazzy uniforms on the field were Catholics, and each guy up at bat made the sign of the cross. It sure must have been difficult for God to choose the winner, since every one of the youngsters—most altar boys—was praying for His help.

Kenny and I were regulars at games down the field, a baseball diamond directly below the dump owned by the steel mill. The refuse heap was filled with dirt mounds, trash, and discarded metal. Uncle Caz, Kenny, and I spent many Saturday mornings there, collecting scrap iron to sell to the rag man the next week, keeping the dump from encroaching on the ball field and also making money.

It was sad whenever Uncle Caz stared up and recalled as a child picking junk and dodging rocks thrown by the boys uptown at the top of the heap. Those bad guys, who obviously did not live in glass houses, not only threw objects, but they also slung epithets.

"Hey, Hunky, what's you doin'?"

"Hey, Polak, lookin' for somethin' to eat?"

Uncle Caz still felt the stings; yet, he could not understand the connection between the names those troublemakers hooted and the derogatory terms he used when speaking of war enemies, the "Japs" or the "Krauts." His sister did though.

Our mother refused to listen to ethnic jokes and abruptly left the room if words such as "dago," "wop," "chink," or "nigger" were uttered. The only exception to her iron-clad rule was the phrase describing white Protestants of Anglo-Saxon descent. God only knows where the nickname "pie-eater" came from, but that was the expression I heard sporadically to describe most of the people living in Vandergrift, who voted as solidly Republican as East Vandergrifters voted Democrat.

Over the years the field gave way to the dump, eventually becoming too small for regulation matches but just right for unorganized, non-Little League pickup games. Once, however, it was an honest-to-God baseball field, and the three clubs in East Vandergrift and the one Catholic Church in Vandergrift used it for games.

The players from the Milan Stefanik Slovak Society, or Slovak Club, were members of Holy Trinity Slovak Roman Catholic Church. Adolescents from St. Casmir's Lithuanian Roman Catholic Church belonged to the Beneficial and Brotherly Society of the Grand Duke of Lithuania, the Lithuanian Club. Jimmy, a parishioner and altar boy of All Saints Polish Roman Catholic Church, pitched for the Stephen Czarnecki Society No. 791 Polish National Alliance, the Polish Club, generally termed the "PNA." Few of the jocks could pronounce the complete names of the clubs, so they called them the Polish, Lithuanian, and Slovak clubs and left it at that.

The PNA Janitor

There was a studio picture of a blond young man in a military uniform in the PNA bar above the cigarette machine. A portrait of the old janitor who lived and worked in the club, the black-and-white photograph depicted him as a youthful, decorated officer in Poland's army.

For many years after that freeze-frame moment (when his glory days were gone), he drank unceasingly and repeated stories to anyone who would politely listen of his younger days when he fought alongside the great Polish general, Jozef Pilsudski, against the Russians in World War I. Later, in 1939, he led an escape into Romania after Germany attacked; and when hearing that Russia had also attacked his homeland 14 days later, he then made his way to Paris to fight in the Resistance. When the pro-Nazi Vichy Government of France took control, he fled to England, signed on for the duration, and fought the Germans under Britain's flag.

Over 50 years old during World War II, the future PNA janitor courageously battled against Nazi tyranny and fought for other people's freedom in North Africa, Norway, Italy, Normandy, and the Netherlands. When the war ended and the Communists seized Poland, he found exile in America. A broken man without a free country, without a future, there was nothing he could do but get soused and tell stories of his younger days, fighting for his country's independence. What little passion he had left was expended hating the Reds.

"So," our mother would sternly advise, "if you see kids making fun of him, I want you to stop them and repeat what I'm telling you. Remember, the Polish Club janitor may appear to be an old drunk, but in reality he's a great hero with lots of medals to prove it. And don't you ever forget it."

The PNA, where the Polish patriot swept, slept, and swigged the sauce in exile, was diagonally across the street from the post office. Several blocks up McKinley Avenue, near the school, the Lithuanians built their club, named for a powerful ruler of Lithuania who helped defeat the Teutonic Knights in 1410. Finally, the Slovaks constructed their center, recalling one of the founders of the modern state of Czechoslovakia. Each club had a private bar, large areas for weddings and wakes, and a meeting place for baseball teams.

The rivalry was fierce. When Jimmy pitched, Kenny and I in turn ran home between innings to give our family up-to-the-minute reports on the game.

Jimmy was quite the sportsman, competing in football and basketball as well as baseball. Consequently, he filled the cellar with hoops, helmets, balls, bats, gloves, padding, shin guards, and those necessary cups every baseball player hates to wear but appreciates when they stop wild pitches. Generous to a fault, Jimmy let Kenny and me borrow the equipment without asking his permission.

We practiced hitting, throwing, and catching baseballs in the alley, until Kenny became so good that Mrs. Pinchek, spying on her numbers-running employees from a second-floor window, convinced Mommy that the Pinchek windows were in jeopardy. Drunk Mr. Pinchek smashed plenty of glass and Kenny never damaged any; yet, off we were shoved down the field to practice when the big boys were not using it.

Frankie Poleski

On the way down the field one day, we bumped into a new friend, Frankie Poleski, who lived at the end of Quay Street. I thought he was my age that first time we three said, "Hi!" in the alley, although he was as tall as Barbara. When Kenny asked how old he was, Frankie raised three fingers. That simple gesture was the beginning of a friendship between the two boys that lasted until the day Kenny died 18 years later. After asking his mother's permission on that first morning, he joined us and instantly became a constant playmate.

A burly, clumsy tyke, Frankie wore a black patch over his right eye to correct its laziness. In contrast, Kenny was small and agile with perfect vision, which remained so throughout the years of his sitting inches away from the television screen.

Kenny figured out early in their friendship which buttons to push to get Frankie so angry that in frustration he scampered home crying. I liked Frankie a lot; and compared to Kenny, he seemed even sweeter than he actually was. Having no sisters, only a younger brother, he was very shy around girls.

Kenny and Frankie collected baseball cards and haggled for hours over their trades. Neither of them could read, but Jimmy revealed to his baby brother who the players were, and Kenny memorized the faces on the cards then cheated Frankie in the swaps.

Following hours of negotiations, Frankie glowed with delight when he got a Stan Musial or a Ralph Kiner. Heroes in hand, he gleefully ran home to share his good fortune with his father. When his dad remarked that the baseball cards featured, say, Willie Mays and Mickey Mantle (two rookies), Frankie tore them up and cried until his mother called ours and announced what Kenny had done. Immediately, Mommy made Kenny go to the Poleski's and give Frankie the valuable cards. Happy again, Frankie shook his pal's hand and forgave him; but the next day Kenny pulled the same or another trick on Frankie.

I felt slightly jealous of Frankie and Kenny's friendship. The two of them started to exclude me from games when they finally realized that I was a girl. When I strolled onto the front porch during a card-toss game and asked to be included, they got snooty and retorted, "No girls allowed."

No girls allowed! The nerve! I could not believe my ears after all I had done for them. Who taught them how to slide into a base? Who taught them how to throw a football? Who taught them how to whistle? Who taught them how to blow bubbles with the chewing gum they shoved into their mouths after excursions to Joe Stemplensky's candy store for even more baseball cards? The ingrates!

My best friend now had two best friends, and Frankie and I had to share him. If he got angry at Frankie, which happened at least 57 times a day, Kenny played with me. When he got mad at me (I could not even venture a guess as to how many times that was), he played with Frankie. Mr. Popularity lorded it over both of us.

Resembling fools, Frankie and I caved in to his every whim so as not to get on his wrong side, the Mr. Hyde one. This preschool acquiescence created a spoiled brat who made both our lives miserable unless he got his way. If the blond-haired, blue-eyed shrimp of a monster did not outrun, outthrow, or outcatch either of his two best friends, Kenny simply outcried us and won by default.

We Are Not Amused

There must have been an accidental switch at the hospital when Barbara was born, because she did not seem to fit into our boisterous family with its Eastern European roots. If there were only one word to describe her, it would be "proper." I wonder who carted home our baby girl.

Barbara and her friend Sylvia played together; and one of their special games was serving tea. The two little girls got decked out in Mommy's and Mrs. Welkon's old clothes: hats with veils and feathers, old coats with fake-fur collars, open-toed, spiked high heels, and housedresses. They acted like fine ladies sipping tea from China cups, when in fact, they looked more like chubby midget hobos.

Snootily, they pretended not to notice Kenny, Frankie, and me as we hovered near the wash-tub-turned-upside-down table making fun of them. Maintaining the aura of a dowager queen and her lady-in-waiting in the castle-cellar laundry room, they thought they appeared regal next to the wringer washing machine with its one setting, wash.

Dragging baseball bats and tossing balls in the air, Kenny, Frankie, and I stuck out our tongues and ridiculed their baby dolls sitting in opposite chairs. It really didn't matter how obnoxious we were; they were in their own correct realm and kept up their mannered conversation, "More tea, Lady Barbara?" "Yes, thank you, Dame Sylvia," as though we loutish interlopers did not exist.

Leaving Home

For years I daydreamed of going to school with Jimmy and Barbara, but when the time came I didn't want to go. Kindergarten, recently introduced to the East Vandergrift grade school, was where I was headed.

My reluctance began when spunky Stella Ruzbacki, convinced that her son Timmy was a genius who should skip the kiddy class, interceded. A mover and a shaker determined to beat the system or at least bend it to her wishes, she forced the school officials to do a study of five-year-old first-graders. The guinea pigs were to be tracked through high school to see how well they did scholastically. The first step was putting the children through a battery of tests to make sure they were mature enough to handle the early placement in first grade. A dour college psychologist conducted the oral testing.

I remember being afraid of making a fool of myself and flunking; and the only question during the hour-interview I recall is, "What is the difference between mother and money?" Now, really! Did that neurotic, anal-retentive Ph.Der not realize he was testing a businesswoman who ran numbers? Or was he preparing me for a lifetime of blaming problems on my mother? Taken aback with the stupidity of the question, my suspicious mind at this early point in my educational training formed the unspoken notion, "Is this a trick question?" Nevertheless, I somehow passed (with flying colors) and with trepidation entered the first grade.

I did not want to leave home, even though East Vandergrift's elementary school was only four blocks away on McKinley Avenue. It had taken me five long years to discover everything there was to know regarding my secure neighborhood world. School represented uncharted territory, and I started to have conflicting emotions about it.

Jimmy hated school. Barbara loved it. There seemed to be way too many rules and regulations. The only person I knew who would be in my class was Timmy, but we weren't that familiar with each other. I wasn't sure I was cut out for school as was Barbara, who took to it like a fish to water. Worst of all, I would be leaving Kenny behind for the first time in our lives.

As Barbara and Jimmy clasped my hands and led me down the back porch steps, Kenny, his arms wrapped around Mommy's leg, began to cry. At the sight of his first tear, I also started to wail. Scared before, I now was terrified of the new terrain that lay four blocks away. Was it fear of growing up?

"You have nothing to fear, but fear itself!" Mommy called out as Jimmy and Barbara practically dragged me past the desert sage, still in bloom, decorating our side of Mrs. Pinchek's fence. Since she was going to quote something from the Roosevelt era, I wish it had been the lyrics from "Happy Days Are Here Again" to bolster my confidence instead of the inauguration quote which reminded me of my cowardice.

I do not exactly remember the basis on my dread, but after those first few tearful mornings, I fell madly in love with school. Every summer for the next 12 years, I counted the days, wishing they would speed by so that school could begin again.

I do remember that dress the folks bought me at Geraci's Children's Clothing Store (for the discriminating child). Yet, they always said it was a sin to discriminate against anyone on the basis of race, color, religion, or creed, whatever that meant.

Oh, that dress! Yuk! Brown and white plaid, it had a peculiar feel next to my skin. I think it was velour, but to a girl who lived in overalls, it was unbelievably uncomfortable. I couldn't chase chickens or little brothers in a dress. I couldn't slide safely into home plate or replay World War II battles with Kenny and Frankie. I wasn't allowed to get dirty in a dress.

How in the world could I lie on my back and stare at the floating clouds or count the stars? How could I dig for earthworms after a rain without getting a dress soiled with mud or worm slime? Dresses were absolutely impractical, although some people thought they looked pretty.

Off to the first grade I went, dressed to the nines and minus two front teeth, for which the tooth fairy had given me a quarter. Barbara, my first mentor, divulged the truth concerning the dental legend, but I never let on that I knew that fact of life. I wanted to get the cash for each and every baby tooth in my mouth.

Run, Spot, Run. Dick and Jane. First grade was a snap after years of Sgt. Rock comic books. The drill was easy: listen to and obey Miss Claypool's strict rules of behavior, and I was a shoo-in for success. There was, however, one initial drawback. Painfully shy at first, I hid behind Barbara's skirt all the way to school, and once there, without her big sisterly support, I was afraid to raise my hand, even to ask to be excused to go to the lavatory. My nickname was "Puddles" for the first few embarrassing days. Still, even those wet moments didn't dampen my growing affection for school.

After I learned how to get permission for the girls' room, first grade was the greatest. The class was made up of 14 kids, seven boys and seven girls. Except for four kids born in 1946, the beginning of the baby-boom generation, the students were from the 1945 births. The first grades that followed for years to come were much larger. Because of our smallness, we became a very tight group and received plenty of individual attention from teachers.

By the end of the year, six boys and six girls remained, traveling together like a pack of wolves. The blond little girl who lived on Vandergrift Lane moved away in the middle of the school year; and the redheaded boy, whose family rented in the same apartment building—the only one in East Vandergrift—as the Welkons, left also.

Carrot-top considered me his girlfriend and was forever to my annoyance trailing me home from school, trying to kiss me. Just before going away, he was chasing me as usual to make his daily pass. In my consternation, I picked up a clump of snow from the street and crashed it down on his head. To both our surprises, the clump of snow was really a chunk of ice. He darted away bleeding, and I wet my pants, feet frozen in my tracks with fear he would die.

The next day, the last time I ever saw him, he arrived totally bandaged above his ears. Miss Claypool took one look at him and in a concerned voice asked what had happened. Staring straight in her eyes, Red said he had bumped into a tree. Then he turned to me and winked. Shocked that he had lied to a teacher for me, I nervously smiled but really wanted to kiss him right there in front of the whole class. After all these years, I still remember how gallant he was his final day and wish I had followed him home for a good-bye peck.

Mitzy's Candy Store

Across McKinley Avenue to the right of the school was a candy store owned by an old lady who resembled a witch, or what kids imagined a witch would look like. Her name was Mitzy. The only reason kids ever shopped there was when Cokes went up to 6 cents, she continued selling them for a nickel. I guess she must have made a truckload order at one point and was still trying to put a dent in the overstock.

The candy was stale, the store stunk, and there was a layer of dust over everything, including the unwrapped chocolate pieces in the glassed-display case, which was so filthy that a kid could barely see through it to consider a choice.

Mitzy lived in the rear of the store and owned the building, a big brown triple-decker that had not been painted since before the St. Patrick's Day flood of 1936. There were two other mice-infested apartments in it that never had renters. Big surprise.

The wooden floors creaked; and when kids walked in, they made sure they did not enter alone. There were too many stories circulating about children disappearing mysteriously. Rumor had it that Mitzy concocted soup from the bones of the missing children. Kids constantly warned each other to make sure to watch her open the pop in case she slipped in poison while getting it from the back room.

Mitzy wore ratty old housedresses and had her cruddy, stringy hair wrapped tightly in a bun, just like most of the grandmothers in town, except they smelled pleasant of talcum powder, perpetually smiled, and had clean tresses. She, on the other hand, reeked of BO and growled as though we, the customers, were intruding on her space when we came in to buy a bargain Coke. Kids shivered in her presence but were dying to find out what was behind the curtain separating the shop from her living quarters. Shrunken heads? Skeletons? Nobody knew for sure. Or they weren't telling.

While we sat on the front porch sipping the just-bought pop, she charged out with a dirt-encrusted broom and swept us off like some fallen leaves from the neighbor's tree that had the audacity to land on her property. Mitzy could have successfully worked as a sales clerk at Saks Fifth Avenue or Lord and Taylor; she had the utmost contempt for paying customers.

The nasty old woman once had a husband and offspring of her own, who moved away as soon as they turned 18. They never returned to visit their mother, and she never acknowledged her children's existence.

Poison. Dead bodies in the back room. Cannibalism. There were many tall tales and rumors relating to Mitzy, but the truth probably was simple. A bitter grouch who hated the world, she only perceived the bad in it and herself.

Our parents remembered her beating her kids with a belt buckle until there were welts and calling her daughter a whore as she ran crying across the street to enter the first grade. People Mitzy's age, or those who went to school with her kids, claimed she was always mean and hateful, never having friends, nor wanting any.

Never having done a kind deed in her life, the one redeeming quality of her being was that kids wanted to be good and avoid ending up down below some day, because sure as shootin' Mitzy would be there, ready to torment them for eternity. All Catholic kids knew from their Catechism how very long that was. Passing her beat-up establishment on the way to the Polish Church was an added incentive for kids to really pray the rosary before Mass, not just pretend. They needed all the extra indulgences they could muster to avoid the fires of Hades and pitchfork-wielding Mitzy.

Cindy

Cindy Petrouski, the tallest and most outgoing girl in first grade, became my best friend. It seemed only logical since I was the shortest and shyest. As I helped her with homework, she kept me in stitches. Cindy found humor in everything.

Even though we played with everyone at school, our two closest companions were Timmy Ruzbacki and Francis Pluciennik. Cindy and Francis were neighbors and sort of boyfriend and girlfriend; and somehow everyone assumed that Timmy, the shortest boy in school, was my fella. Not so. I was sick of being small, and being Timmy's sweetheart made me feel tinier yet. I also had a major crush on Francis, but never revealed it to anyone, not even Cindy.

The niece of our gossipy neighbor Cazzy and his brother Lefty, Cindy was the class ringleader and self-appointed social director. With an imagination that was boundless, she opened new worlds to me. Besides teaching me how to play Monopoly, Red Rover, and other extraordinary games, she let me help tend her roses and allowed me to hang her family's laundry on the back yard clothes line. On lazy afternoons, I loved sprawling on her front porch glider and waving to the man in the train caboose chugging by across Railroad Street. The guy in the cute gray hat bringing up the rear always waved back.

Taking me over the tracks and down to the Kiskiminetas River, Cindy showed me how to skip rocks on its surface. Contaminated by the town's sewage and the steel mills' waste, it flowed through the eastern part of East Vandergrift. She reminded me, though, that a long time before it was polluted, the Indians fished in it and set up their teepees on the banks.

With long, thick, dark brown hair cascading down her shoulders when not in pigtails, Cindy pretended she was an Indian maiden and dressed the part that first Halloween we became chums. Into Indian legends big time, she considered the Kiskiminetas her river.

According to John McCullough, a guy captured by the red men, Kee-ak-kshee-man-ni-toos meant "cut spirit," she excitedly told me. Later, we both learned from Miss Claypool that there was another explanation. Our first grade teacher explained to the class of Native American folklore lovers about how a man by the name of John Heckewelder, a Moravian (this was written in big block letters on the board) missionary and authority on the Indian language, hypothesized (on the black board, too) that it came from the word "Gieschgumanito" and meant "make daylight," which was the impatient cry of a warrior in haste to take the warpath.

Imagine, if you will, 12 first-graders at recess running around the cowering kindergartners and screaming, "Gieschgumanito!" "Gieschgumanito!" Puddles, I assure you, was one nickname shared by a lot more kids that year.

As Cindy, Francis, Timmy, and I threw rocks at rats on the banks of the river, out of the blue Cindy began history lessons. Dramatically pointing to Apollo, the town across the river, she firmly stated that it was once called "Warren" in honor of her great-, great-, great-, great-, great-grandfather, Chief Warren. Trying to convince the three biggest skeptics in first grade that she was a direct descendant of Indian royalty, Cindy swore on a coloring book that she had been adopted by the people who claimed to be her parents, Sophie and Stap Petrouski. When she cut through the Indian princess crap, her pals ended up learning something new concerning our town.

Cindy's Aunt Laura was a prodigious reader, whose favorite topics were American history and anything in *True Confessions*, which she hid on the top shelf of her beauty shop (located in Cindy's back yard) where Cindy could not reach them. However, Aunt Laura sat often on the salon porch with her niece, telling her about East Vandergrift's earliest inhabitants.

Aunt Laura informed her, then, of course, Cindy shared the new knowledge with Timmy, Francis, and me.

Apollo, across the river, and East Vandergrift, which was once labeled "Morning Sun," were parts of territory known as Three Bottoms. The four of us got a nervous chuckle out of that; the word "bottom" sounded like a swearword. Anyway, Three Bottoms (tee hee) was owned by Chief Warren, and the land was at one time or another known as Warren's Sleeping Place, Warren's Sleeping Ground, and Warren's Sleeping Grove.

"He was one very powerful and important man, my great-, great-, great-, great-, great-grandfather," Cindy breathlessly concluded.

Everyone in our class knew, even before starting school, that Chief Warren's grave was discovered during the excavation of the Stepkevich cellar in 1910. Thereafter, no one dared dig up a basement for fear of finding a dead body in it. Cindy, natch, was positive there were lots more sacred sites nearby.

She remarked often, "You are living on my tribe's burial grounds and will be cursed for upsetting the dead spirits."

We laughed uproariously at her macabre prediction, and yet, every time we dug in the dirt, we crossed ourselves first, just to be on the safe side.

Miss Claypool

Cindy loved the mystical and spiritual, but sensible and no-nonsense Miss Claypool, whose father was one of the 42 property owners who petitioned for the incorporation of the Borough of East Vandergrift, preferred fact to fiction.

Miss Ruth Claypool was born in Morning Sun when most of its landed gentry were of Anglo-Saxon descent. After selling the homestead, her father moved the family uptown to Vandergrift shortly after Morning Sun officially became East Vandergrift. She never voiced it, but I guess he wanted to live with his own kind of people uptown once the immigrants started flocking to East Vandergrift. If her family had stayed, they would have been the only Protestant one in town. The move didn't change much; her roots were in East Vandergrift, and what history she did not actually live through, she learned as a child while sitting on her father's knee.

Miss Claypool's ties to our small borough in the valley were very strong, and it seemed as though she had been teaching the first grade there since time immemorial. When most of our parents entered her class to begin their short-lived education, Miss Claypool greeted them wearing her hair in a bun and sensible black high-buttoned shoes, just as she did when we started school.

After zipping through the alphabet, cursive writing, adding and subtracting, first-graders then got to the good stuff—history. Dick, Jane, Sally, Spot, and the whole gang were ho-hum, but we loved hearing about real people doing daring and exciting deeds, especially in East Vandergrift. Our first teacher loved telling stories of what it was like before we were born and even before she was born, which was anyone's guess as to when that was. Miss Claypool brought history alive, and the 12 of us hung on to her every word, even if we did not always understand its meaning.

Sitting at little desks with inkwells (the same ones sat in by most of our parents while they dipped their pens and scratched letters and words on paper), we listened attentively to Miss Claypool. Without making excuses or glossing over the facts, she vividly exposed the white man's cruelty toward the Delaware Indians who once lived in our nook of the planet. After enduring years of maltreatment and degradation, the destitute Indians finally gave up, left their ancient homeland along the Kiskiminetas River, and headed West.

Circa 1896, the year Bupchie arrived in America, the portion of Three Bottoms that later became East Vandergrift was cut into lots and sold piecemeal. The cheapest deals were in our town made by the poor newcomers, who wanted a home but couldn't afford the more expensive property uptown in Vandergrift.

"There is nothing wrong with being poor," Miss Claypool remarked often. "Some of the greatest people in the world came from poverty. If you work hard, study diligently, and be a good person, you can be anything in this world you want to be. One of you boys could even become President of the United States."

Remembering her father's stories, she informed the class of how hard the newly arrived immigrants from Eastern Europe worked. Although having the worst paying jobs in the steel mills, they still saved their money, bought homes, and raised children to be good American citizens.

Hey! Miss Claypool was bragging about our grandparents and parents. As proud of them as she was, we became upset when she told us about the owners of the mill company constructing a high board fence along the boundary line of Morning Sun. Those big wigs (all Republicans, I might add) put up that stupid barrier to discourage (this also was put in large block letters on the blackboard) the laborers, who lived in the lowlands and worked in the mill farther away on the other side, from purchasing these cheaper sites. The bully, rich mill owners tried to force the lowly paid immigrants into buying the more expensive tracts in Vandergrift.

There was another reason for the construction of the fence. George McMurtry, the mill president, intended to purchase the land in Morning Sun and resell it at a higher price; but, a man named W.S. Bean heard about the plan and beat him to the punch. When McMurtry tried to buy the land from Bean, the price had tripled. Furious at being whipped at his own game, pious-Episcopalian McMurtry considered the barbed-wire fence his retaliation.

Mr. Family Man-Regular Devout Churchgoer didn't give a hoot that going around the barrier meant many extra miles to and from work in the mill for the underprivileged and weary refugees. Tired but clever, the workers defiantly cut holes in it and bravely climbed through, not sure if doing so meant the loss of their jobs. Finally, fearing that the workers might move on to better jobs in Pittsburgh and he wouldn't be able to replace them (who else would work for slave wages?), McMurtry gave up and eventually tore the fence down.

Because Miss Claypool's father was a leader in Morning Sun when it became incorporated in 1901, he had been in the thick of the battle with McMurtry. In Miss Claypool's description of our town's early history, her sympathies were with the immigrants, who had to put up with a lot of baloney from George McMurtry, a hero to the first-graders uptown in Vandergrift.

Miss Claypool did not loosely use the word "hero." George Washington was a hero whose portrait graced a classroom wall. Her father and the humble immigrants who started new lives in Morning Sun and helped make America great were heroes. With his eyes only on the almighty buck, George McMurtry was certainly not among that

select group. In our judgment, Miss Claypool was also a hero for showing us how our grandparents were important people in history who
developed our special community, adding one more piece to the puzzle
that made up a strong and viable America.

Chief Warren's Bones

East Vandergrift, our small town 30 miles from Pittsburgh, was a Delaware Indian village in the mid-1700s. The grave of Chief Warren, owner of the bottomlands of the Kiskiminetas River that flowed through town, was discovered in 1910 during the excavation of the Stepkevich cellar, a few blocks from our house.

Mr. Stepkevich almost had a heart attack when he found parts of a skeleton while digging near the coal furnace. Upon closer inspection by Mrs. Stepkevich, who raced down the basement the instant she heard her husband's death-rattling shriek, a feathered headdress and other Indian artifacts were unearthed near the bones. After putting her husband who was as white as her sheets to bed for the day, she scuttled down McKinley Avenue to the school house blaring, "Indians! Indians!" akin to a pioneer woman in the Old West alerting the other white settlers to an impending massacre.

Hearing the bizarre warning, a school marm stuck her head out a window and admonished Mrs. Stepkevich to go home and sober up. Not understanding much English, Mrs. Stepkevich screeched up at her in a mile-a-minute Polish. Immediately, children in the grades one through eight dashed to the windows, pushed their perplexed teachers out of the way, and in Polish heard the report of the mysterious skeletal unearthing. Quickly translating, they explained the situation to a bright young teacher, who instantly realized what had happened. Excitedly, she gestured for Mrs. Stepkevich to come inside the building; together they went to the principal's office and telephoned the superintendent of schools, who notified the University of Pittsburgh's anthropology department. The very next day a professor from Pitt arrived in East Vandergrift. The expert examined the bones and artifacts—a bayonet, arrow heads, musket ball, and stone beads—then pronounced "his" treasure a once-in-a-lifetime discovery. From that historic moment on, Indian folklore acquired a new significance in the East Vandergrift school house; and Mrs. Stepkevich, with her recently gained renown, began studying English by devouring Zane Grey novels.

Huddled Masses

There wasn't a kid in town for decades later who couldn't recount the victory over the Indians in 1764 at the Battle of Bushy Run, not far away. Driven from their homes, the Ancient tribes at that point started their migration West. Coincidentally (yeah, right), Western Pennsylvania was opened to further settlement by white pioneers from the British Isles.

The Indian hunting and fishing grounds along the Kiskiminetas River became known as the village of Morning Sun when a white settler perceived the beauty of the rays at dawn spreading through his vineyard. Schoolchildren learned that his name was Dentist Cochran but were not sure if he pulled teeth or just had a strange Protestant name.

During the booming 1890s, long after the natives left, Morning Sun's destiny meshed with the likes of the local steel tycoon, George McMurtry, owner of the flourishing Apollo Iron and Steel Company across the Kiskiminetas River. At the same time, the new wave of immigrants arrived from Southern and Eastern Europe. These newcomers had peculiar customs and spoke little or no English; most were Roman Catholics. They came in droves to work in mills and mines as cheap laborers. Making the factories prosper, the foreigners provided the human resource that transformed America into a major industrial power.

The American-born were the owners and operators of the plants. Immigrants who had been here from the beginning of the 19th Century were the managers and foremen. However, the muscle that stoked the blast furnaces, laid the railroad tracks, dug deep in the earth for coal, and supplied the brawn and sweat that built the nation in the late 1800s and early 1900s were the just-off-the-boat immigrants. Newcomers, including both sets of our grandparents—Bupchie, Ju Ju, Grandma and Grandpa Dell—flocked to Pennsylvania, the Keystone state, the nation's top steel producer, and started fresh lives.

There was a popular song that people in Europe sang and evidently believed. Passed along from village to village in the 1800s, it was presumably straight from the hearts of the American people, eager to welcome the new arrivals.

"We have room for all creation, and our banner is unfurled, here's a general invitation to the people of the world: Come along, come along, make no delay! Come from every nation, come from every way! Our lands are broad enough, don't be alarmed, and Uncle Sam is rich enough to give us all a farm."

A peasant boy squatting in a hovel in Krakow, Prague, or Naples must have imagined a brass band meeting him when he got off the ship. And God only knows where those fables pertaining to streets paved with gold got started; tall tales abounded of gilded opportunities and bountiful riches to be made. All that aside, it was better to take the leap of faith and make the journey to America than to stay at home and face poverty, war, oppression, ignorance, and abuse, with no hope in sight.

People who have nothing to lose are usually the most courageous. And so it was for the brave and hardy immigrants who left their wretched peasant lives and found an asylum in the New World. Many of them, like Bupchie, wanted to make their fortunes in America and then return home, but few did go back. They uprooted and transplanted themselves in America, and the few possessions they still cherished from their homelands in the years that followed were their memories. Although the misery was erased from their minds, the longing for what was left behind remained. The immigrants came to America and settled wherever the jobs were, and Pennsylvania had plenty due to the iron and steel mills that prospered after the Civil War.

George McMurtry, Captain Jacob Vandergrift, and a group of businessmen purchased the Apollo Iron and Steel Company in 1886. Their timing was brilliant and expansion immediately followed. While the Industrial Revolution was in full swing in the country, and the demand for iron and steel was monumental, they set up a second plant on farmland they had earlier acquired. Then they put into motion plans to build a town to house the workers needed to work at the two sites. Buying other farms encircling the new plant, they advertised the formation of a model town named for Captain Vandergrift. His namesake officially became a town of Pennsylvania in 1887.

As workers and their families poured in and bought lots in the new town, Mr. Bean, that shrewd investor, bought the farm in the lowlands and offered lots at a much-reduced rate. McMurtry was fit to be tied, but there wasn't much he could do with regard to where these people wanted to live. The SOB's main concern was getting workers, and the immigrants obliged him. The Apollo and Vandergrift steel mills hired many of these foreigners, who then made their home in the village of Morning Sun. A handful of the immigrants worked in coal mines. One was located below the entrance to Morning Sun and was owned by the Pennsylvania Railroad. A smaller one, farther down the lane, belonged to an early resident.

Incorporated as a borough of the Commonwealth of Pennsylvania in 1901, the town was henceforth known as East Vandergrift, though old-timers still called it Morning Sun for years later. Shortly after Chief Warren's bones were discovered, there was a movement to change the name back to Morning Sun, but nobody seemed to know how to file the appropriate petition, and the idea was dropped.

The Poles, Slovaks, and Lithuanians were the three main groups of Europeans who arrived in East Vandergrift in the early 1900s. Of peasant stock, they had left extremely poor conditions in their homelands, most under foreign domination. The transformation from the rural peasant existence in Europe to a new life in the bustling industrial communities of Western Pennsylvania was, to put it mildly, not an easy one. These non-English-speaking outsiders encountered monumental prejudice from the American-born inhabitants who regarded them as odd, untrustworthy, and economically dangerous.

As if it were not bad enough to be maligned, reviled, and treated with open contempt by the local citizens, the Ku Klux Klan (violently anti-Catholic and anti-immigrant) increased its influence in Pennsylvania during those early years with its cross-burning intimidation toward the new arrivals. For protection against the hooded hate-mongers, these bewildered poor people sought out their own when they arrived in the land of the free and the home of the brave. The immigrants in Morning Sun, all Eastern Europeans, felt a sense of security in living side by side with people who shared a common heritage.

Bupchie and her husband, along with the other residents of Morning Sun, gazed out their windows many nights and observed crosses burning on the cemetery hill. Trembling with fear, they watched as dark figures shook their burning torches in the direction of the town in the valley, home of immigrants.

Many prominent, sophisticated, and intelligent Americans, including that great Democrat, Woodrow Wilson, felt threatened by the foreign flood they believed would destroy America. Oh, Lord, the blame attributed to the immigrants! Increases in the rate of illiteracy, unemployment, indigence, disease, immorality, and crime were just a few problems the refugees were said to have caused. Well, at least they escaped starving in Lithuania or being killed by sword-swinging Cossacks in Poland.

America, the promised land, was (the foreigners believed) the nation of opportunity for those who worked hard, saved money, and sent their children to school, where they would learn to be good citizens. Be a good citizen—that was the immigrants' mantra that was drilled into their American-born children's minds.

Between 1901 and 1914, approximately one million foreigners a year came to the United States; more began arriving following World War I. In 1921, the year our mother was born, the surge of immigration stopped when Congress passed a new law, which explained in concise language just how many immigrants from each country were allowed in. Aimed at those from Southern and Eastern Europe, this new edict was devised to cut down on the number of Greeks, Italians, Poles, and Slavs coming to America. Immigration from China had stopped in 1882, and the numbers allowed from Japan had been cut to practically nothing. People from Northern and Western Europe were considered, well, to put it bluntly, better than those others.

The major enticement for the Eastern European immigrants who settled in Morning Sun was the steel mills. Such great numbers of foreign workers were employed there that safety signs in the plants were written in six languages—English, Polish, Lithuanian, Slovak, Italian, and Greek.

Who could have imagined then that one day, decades into the future, the immigrants' grandchildren, entirely American, would be annoyed whenever they spotted signs in Spanish or Vietnamese in public places, the whole time blaming the ills of America on the newcomers, some from places their grandparents had never heard of when they first disembarked as wretched refuse at the beginning of the 20th Century?

When young women from the old country found their way to Morning Sun, the steel workers boarding in private homes married them and then procured homes of their own. Many immigrants had relatives or friends here who had blazed the trail from the homeland. Once established with a job, room and board, they in turn sent for the others. Running a boarding house became one of many lucrative enterprises for those hustling immigrants.

The Important
Three R's

Education was a fundamental concern of the foreigners who settled East Vandergrift. Having little or no formal schooling themselves, they wanted their children to be model students. No monkey business, or they got the strap as punishment. The immigrants expected their offspring to study hard to help with medical and legal matters. Other practical concerns, such as reading the American newspapers and conveying basic information relating to life in America, also became the responsibility of the school children. Learning to read and write was the immigrants' dream for their children; going to college became the hope for their grandchildren.

East Vandergrift's first school was a two-room, two-story structure built in 1898, after much pressure from Miss Claypool's father. Expansion over the years resulted in an eight-room building; adjoining the main site was a portable one-room house for the first grade, which our mom attended in 1926. Miss Claypool was her teacher, and the only difference about her back then was that the first grade schoolmistress's hair was not gray.

In the spring of 1933, the school burned to the ground; and the East Vandergrift children hiked uptown and attended classes at various facilities, wherever there was room. With the help of Roosevelt's Works Progress Administration, better known as the WPA, a new building arose and was ready for use in 1939. Still looking brand new, it was shiny clean when I first entered it to begin the first grade in 1951.

East Vandergrift's last school had 14 classrooms and an auditorium-gymnasium put to use for every town function, from Halloween dances to Christmas parties to church events.

Mr. Mathews, the principal ("Principal ends in p-a-l, because that is what he is to boys and girls," explained Miss Claypool) was ardently involved in everything the town's citizens arranged. He also raised money for extracurricular activities when the budget was strained. If any kid ("A kid is a baby goat," Miss Claypool explained) became ill, Mr. Mathews drove him home. Whenever there was a wedding, Christening, funeral, or church picnic in the community, he attended. An amateur historian and genealogist, he had an open ear as well as an open door policy at school. Parents were always welcome to visit the classroom unannounced and drop by to see him without an appointment. Focusing on educating children, he believed being naughty was self-defeating. When he picked up the phone to call a parent, there was never any argument at the other end of the line. Because Mr. Mathews was always right, parents took his word as the Gospel truth. He knew many parents on a first-name basis, since he had been a teacher in East Vandergrift when they were children themselves.

The soft-spoken Mr. Mathews lived in Vandergrift with his wife and children, but his heart remained in East Vandergrift with its students. Very kind, he believed that school should be a pleasant place to spend the day and learning should be loads of fun. Rarely did a teacher threaten a child with a trip to the principal's office. Everyone knew that he just did not have it in him to punish a student, although he had per-mission from parents to use the ruler on bad bottoms (tee hee) any time he saw fit. Teachers handed out the verbal and corporal punishments, and he tossed smiles whenever he passed any of us in the hallway.

The guy was great to the teachers, whom he admired as much as the parents respected him. Holding students in high regard as well, he reg-ularly commented that the East Vandergrift school children (he never called us kids) were the smartest and the most polite in the whole district, probably the entire state, maybe the whole world. Trying to live up to his constant praise, we studied extra hard to keep him proud of us.

And what a heart he had! It was limitless. Before schools had ramps for disabled students, he carried the children stricken with polio from room to room and up and down the stairs before the change of classes. I distinctly remember his big, strong, yet gentle arms wrapped around small steel braces while tiny fragile arms encircled his neck. Together, principal and handicapped student, climbed the stairs cheek-to-cheek several times a day. I recall seeing him cry when a little girl with polio died. Lovely in appearance and manner, she was in the kindergarten class, the one I was almost in before entering the first grade. From the smile on Mr. Mathews's face as he carried her up those stairs, I could tell he loved her very much.

Polio seemed to strike children more often than adults, and the hot summer months were the most feared by parents. Frighteningly, the beginning symptoms were common ailments. Whenever a child complained of an upset stomach, a headache, and a stiff neck in July, mothers panicked and prayed that fever, convulsion, and paralysis would not follow.

It seemed as though everyone knew somebody who had been disabled by the horrible affliction, but children usually thought they were invincible. During polio season and afterwards, however, staring at other children wearing heavy steel braces on their legs or sitting in wheelchairs, many older kids thanked God for sparing them a lifetime of misery. Our folks also prayed extra hard that none of us four would be polio's next victim.

Visiting a woman her age confined forever to an iron lung, my mother used a phrase I heard for the first time: "There, but for the grace of God, go I."

Not only did school children have to worry about becoming crippled, but we also dreaded having an atomic bomb dropped on us by Russia. Because of this very real threat (or so most Americans truly believed), we drilled often. Led by the teachers, the classes met in the hallway, then in single file we followed Mr. Mathews to the bomb shelter in the cellar during frequent air raid drills. Sometimes we just had to crouch under the desks and wait for the all-clear signal that wailed from the fire station.

Daddy thought the precaution was stupid, since, he reasoned, if a bomb fell anywhere near East Vandergrift, nobody would survive. If by some miracle a few did, he added, the radiation fallout would kill them after emerging from the shelter. He believed, and voiced this opinion quite often, that the exercise in school was just government propaganda to make everyone aware of the dangers of the atom bomb. If we feared Russia's nuclear capability, we would not complain when the American Defense Department demanded more money to build more bombs to counter the Communist threat. Air raid drills created a climate of fear.

"What did you do in school today, Dear?"

"Well, we had show and tell, I learned the capital of Arizona, and we went to the bomb shelter."

Americans, our father explained regularly, were kept apprehensive through their children; and their fears kept the defense industry well oiled; and the smooth-talking, God-fearing anti-Communists (of both political parties) created the most devastating arms' arsenal in the history of humankind.

But, at the time, mostly we had fun getting out of class and checking out the janitor's small rest area he decorated for himself in the cellar. The cozy space had a couch, lamp, magazines, and radio. While hunkered down and snooping into the janitor's belongings, we talked about where we wanted to be when the bomb landed; all the kids supposed it would be at home with their families. Yet, I don't think we really thought about dying. When you're young, you know you can't die; though other kids did.

(But I digress. Back to that peach of a principal.)Mr. Mathews had a soft spot for talented people who were having a rough time of it. During the Depression, students were treated to marvelous musical assemblies he arranged. Then a history teacher, Mr. Mathews found the money to hire out-of-work musicians, singers, and actors to entertain students. One such down-on-his-luck troubadour who traveled from school to school was Burl Ives. While not on the road, he boarded with Mr. Mathews and his family free of charge. Remaining friends over the years, they exchanged phone calls and letters; and later, when the entertainer became famous, Mr. Mathews kept everyone in town informed as to the status of his friend's career—movie parts he was offered, new albums being released, other notable people he had met.

If Norman Rockwell had ever painted a picture of a grade school principal, it would have been a portrait of Mr. Mathews behind the big, walnut, cluttered desk in his office, waving enthusiastically to his precious children during the change of classes.

George's Town, Uptown

And now a brief background on that pompous, cruel tough guy. George McMurtry traveled widely during the prosperous days of his steel mill, returning frequently to his homeland Belfast, Ireland, since his birth there in 1838. More important, he visited Essen, Germany, where the Krupps—Hitler's pals during World War II—had established a model village for their employees. The cooperatives of Belgium and various English experiments came under McMurtry's scrutiny as well; and in America he witnessed the Frick Coal and Coke Company making efforts to beautify mining towns. Paternalism, with its control of the worker's private and community life, was featured in the new towns.

Paternalism may have been the way the executives described this way of life, but Tennessee Ernie Ford's hit song, "Sixteen Tons," in the mid-1950s depicted it in a far different way: "Sixteen tons and what do you get? Another day older and deeper in debt. St. Peter, don't you call me 'cause I can't go. I owe my soul to the company store."

In 1892, the Apollo Iron and Steel Company acquired the 640 acres that later comprised his dream town. With high hopes of establishing a working-man's paradise, with him at the helm in total control, McMurtry published a brochure announcing the creation of a community he labeled "Vandergrift," named for one of his business partners. Going all out, he even commissioned the well-known landscape architect, Frederick Olmstead, for design work. Olmstead was famous as the designer of the World's Fair in Chicago and of New York's Central Park. The company broke ground for the new town in 1895, and Vandergrift was born.

Captain Vandergrift

East Vandergrift was a completely separate town from Vandergrift; the only thing the two places shared was a name. The towns' namesake, Captain Jacob J. Vandergrift, George McMurtry's good friend and business associate, was born in Pittsburgh in 1823. On his own at the tender age of 15, he turned to the river, since at the time steamboat travel was the principal means of transportation between Pittsburgh and the West. Starting as a cabin boy, he labored vigorously, and his energy attracted the attention of his employers. Becoming captain of the boat in less than 10 years, he was the first commander to use the space in front for cargo. Vandergrift also introduced the method of towing barges, which gave rise to mining in the Pittsburgh Coal Field.

J. J. Vandergrift later owned a craft named the "Grey Fox." After turning it over to his brother, he set out to try his luck with oil in what later became West Virginia. When the Civil War began, the United States government chartered the Grey Fox to carry war supplies until it sunk somewhere in Ohio. Being a war-profiteer did have some risk.

Vandergrift suffered heavy losses in the oil fields as well and went to Oil City to start over. As oil shipper, he was the first entrepreneur to make a pipe line profitable. With all this dough, he founded an oil company, sold it, then became a major stockholder in the Standard Oil Company. Any time someone threw the guy lemons, he quickly built lemonade stands.

Later, moving his family to Pittsburgh, he began investing heavily in real estate. Soon, though, becoming bored with being a landlord, he searched for fresh horizons. Interested next in the manufacture of sheet iron, Vandergrift became associated with George McMurtry and his ideas for a steel mill combined with a working man's paradise, as they preferred to dub it, as though the reasons for the town were strictly benevolent. Captain Vandergrift expired in Pittsburgh before his namesake was completed and before Morning Sun adopted his name as well.

Fred and Fran's
Bar and Grille

Fridays were meatless as dictated by the Roman Catholic Church. The dinner tradition in our house was for each kid to take turns and plan supper that day. Items on the menus included macaroni and cheese, potato pancakes, tomato soup with grilled cheese sandwiches, and fish sandwiches from the Blue Heaven bar. Later that evening at 11:45, a mere 15 minutes away from Saturday, a phone call was made to Fred & Fran's Bar and Grille on McKinley Avenue, across the street from the Polish Barber's shop and home.

"Fred and Fran's. Fran speaking."

"Fran, it's Clara. I'd like to order 10 hamburgers. Jim will pick them up in 15 minutes or as soon as the next commercial's on."

"What are you watching?"

"*Of Human Bondage.*"

"With Bette Davis?"

"Uh Huh."

"She's my favorite actress. You know, Clara, you remind me of her. Who plays the male lead?"

"Leslie Howard. Oops, it just started. Sorry, Fran, I gotta go."

"Tell Jim the hamburgers'll be ready in 15 minutes, and I'll keep them warm until the next commercial. Bye."

Fred and Fran's hamburgers were the finest in the world. Fran's secret was that she never cleaned the grill; she just scraped the grease into the side pans and threw on another patty.

The family, glued to the television screen, not missing a single Bette Davis-exaggerated and familiar gesture, munched away on Fred and Fran's best, washed down with cold bottled Pepsis. Friday night late movies at our home were as much a staple as those burgers. The whole family viewed vintage films from the '30s and '40s. Flicks with Bette Davis, Joan Crawford, Mae West, and Rosalind Russell were Kenny's favorites. The feistier the woman, the better.

Getting Scalped

The barber shop, with a red and white-striped pole outside, was on McKinley Avenue, as were all businesses in town. I never heard anyone ever refer to the white-haired owner by any name other than "The Polish Barber." At reunions throughout the years, he's come up in nostalgic conversations; at those times, he's always called The Polish Barber. In his shop there was only one chair for customers, and he gave all the boys the same haircut—as short as possible.

There were three reasons why Kenny liked to go for a trim: (1) The old man gave lollipops after he was through tickling little necks with a shaving cream brush and applying grownup cologne. (2) His wife was very friendly and gave the prettiest-wrapped and most-delicious treats at Halloween to her husband's regular clients. (3) The Polish Barber had piles of dirty adventure magazines—scantily dressed women being rescued in jungles by men with bulging muscles—that Kenny enthusiastically perused while waiting his turn to get scalped.

The Polish Church

The Catholic Church was an important part of our lives when Pope Pius XII ran the show in Rome. While Peter's successor and his legions of cardinals and scholars directed affairs at the top, the local scenes—the parish churches—were managed quite efficiently thanks to the housewives of America, whose careers were at home with husbands and children.

Mom was one of these active women who selflessly gave their time and boundless energy to the Church by belonging to such organizations as the Ladies Auxiliary. Regularly raising money, they held raffles every time you turned around; and the children of the members of the Ladies Auxiliary were sent from house to house selling tickets. Big prizes were ten-inch, black-and-white television sets donated by local merchants. If a businessman could not afford to donate a large item for a raffle, he could, and really felt obliged to, take out an ad in the brochure for the next church event. There were so many.

For whatever occasion (Easter show, Christmas pageant, church feast), the booklet contained less than six pages of program information and at least 25 pages of ads. Those Ladies Auxiliary women sure could sell space. Nothing fancy mind you; because a generous printer donated the typesetting and printing service, the women, to show their gratitude, didn't want to burden him with extra work or any needless fuss. He, of course, got a free half-page ad.

Advertisers had three choices of copy, no matter what size. The ladies pushed full-page ads with the sure-fire sales pitch, "It's for a good cause." The ads started with "Best Wishes," "Good Luck," or "With

Regards." Simple headlines were followed with names of the businesses and their addresses. Every announcement had the same type-style, and the lucky businessman paid twice as much for the space in the booklet with a circulation of 250 as the only newspaper uptown charged with a readership of nearly 5000.

The Ladies Auxiliary put on extravaganzas that would have made Otto Preminger green with envy. Covering every national—Polish and American—and religious holiday, they brought in tons of money for the Polish Church. Steady cash unceasingly flowed in weekly with the raffles at bingos. The winning stubs were drawn from a big barrel at the Friday bingo, a must-event for everyone in our family. The school week ended with a bang: kids planning supper, racing to bingo, then returning to a classic Hollywood movie with Fred and Fran's hamburgers. Who could have asked for anything more?

Not only were there bingo games and prizes, but there were also hot dogs, popcorn, and fabulous homemade baked goods for sale. The women of the Auxiliary worked at the bingo; old ladies of the town, wearing babushkas and carrying wads of bills in their change purses, gambled.

Kenny loved greeting the old ladies with the Polish phrase older women gave each other, "dzien dobry pani." It means "hello, Mrs." Oh, my, did they eat it up and marvel at his fluency in their native tongue. After enjoying their hearty laughs and oohs and ahhs, he didn't mind at all putting up with the hugs and kisses, because the grandmotherly affection was usually then followed with dimes. Kenny had a way with women at an early age, no doubt about that.

One week the cash prize of the raffle was $200, donated by a businessman wanting to remain nameless. If his name had been made public, he would have been deluged with requests from every other women's church and temple group in the surrounding towns. How could he have said "no" to the thousands of women who never took "no" for an answer. They would have driven him out of business by boycotting his company. It was safer to stay anonymous and seem humbly generous. The $200 winning voucher was drawn by Barbara, and she handed it to Mommy at the microphone. Flustered, Mom announced Kenny as the winner. He and I cheered the loudest upon hearing his name.

After the applause died down, our decorous parent pledged, "The money, all of it, will be donated to the Church." There were 154 witnesses to the obviously fair drawing; however, Mom remarked later, "It did not look right for Kenny to win Barbara's draw from the barrel." Constantly concerned with appearance, her remark, "What would the neighbors say?" was heard in our home regularly.

Hearing his mom donate the $200 prize to the church, Kenny, I thought, was having a heart attack right there in the church basement. Turning white as a ghost, he stood perfectly motionless, his mouth hanging open as though he were silently exploding. He was really close to releasing the primal scream at that moment, let me assure you.

By and by, he knew the futility of complaining. He also surmised that although he had won, he would never see the money. What was his mom going to do, let him buy $200 worth of chocolate in one candy-store trip? My calculating brother pouted just long enough to get all the hot dogs and sauerkraut he could possibly eat and enough bottles of Coca Cola to satisfy 10 thirsty men crawling on their bellies after a month in a desert searching for water.

Since Fridays were meatless, the women of the Auxiliary saw an opportunity to make even more money by selling pierogis filled with cheese, potatoes, or lekvar (delicious crushed prunes) every Friday from noon till five. The Polish Church basement had an industrial-sized kitchen, and the women cooked in it for most church events. The members of the Auxiliary running the bingos were the biggest pierogi customers of the ones creating and selling the filled fried dough. When Kenny heard that Protestants served only cake and coffee at their affairs, including weddings, he could not believe that anyone wanted to remain in that denomination.

These industrious Ladies Auxiliary women also conducted bake sales, church bazaars, picnics, and dances to complement the yearly calendar of programs, raffles, and bingos. They did just about anything and everything to raise dough for the Polish Church. All this, and God bless them, they acted as the church's cleaning service.

Women on their hands and knees scrubbed the floors. Women crawled over the altar dusting, polishing, waxing. Women on ladders washed the stained-glass windows depicting various saints and religious scenes in beautiful rich vibrant colors; when sunlight streamed through, the church was flooded with a warm and comforting glow. Women vacuumed the long red strip of rug leading from the huge solid oak front door to the walnut altar railing. Women above the confessional in the choir loft in the rear of the church dusted the organ and polished the pipes. After everything was spic and span for another week, the ladies arranged dozens of flowers on the center altar and the two side ones. There were gladioli at Eastertime and roses and poinsettias during the Christmas season, starting right after Thanksgiving—what was good enough for Macy's was good enough for the Polish Church. Flowers decorated the church every week for Sunday masses; some arrangements came from popular funerals, others were donated, but most of the floral displays were a common expense of the Ladies Auxiliary budget.

The women of the Ladies Auxiliary were comrades in arms. They raised money, cleaned and decorated the church, and had great fun doing anything that Father Shezocki wanted done with and at All Saints Polish Roman Catholic Church.

Father Shezocki (Ed to Daddy, who was never Christened) was their confessor, marriage counselor, religious leader, and good friend. Since the Depression, he had ministered to the 901—give or take—souls of his congregation. He brought with him when he came to East Vandergrift a wonderful, whimsical sense of humor; compassion; generosity; kindness; and his own housekeeper, Mrs. Jarenski, who also wore the hats of organist, Ladies Auxiliary adviser, Sunday school (held on Saturday) teacher, pageant organizer, and choir leader. In other words, she was Father's right-hand woman.

They were as comfortable together as a pair of old slippers. Nobody found it the least bit strange to ring the rectory bell and have Mrs. Jarenski answer the door in her black slip then direct visitors, including the Bishop, to Father in his musty, book-filled study. After making the guests comfortable, she would excuse herself without a blush to finish dressing, then moments later appear in the den with refreshments, coffee for the adults and pop for the kids, along with cookies and cakes baked by the women of the Ladies Auxiliary.

Father loved company and often shouted out the window of his study when he saw some kid on a bike ride by. Those tykes, no matter what church or religion they belonged to, were then summoned to come into the house for a huge piece of cake and some lemonade. By the time the youngster rested his bike on the kickstand, Mrs. Jarenski was opening the door with one hand while holding a plate of chocolate cake with the other. Father, meanwhile, was rushing down the hall (often in his pajamas) holding three glasses and a pitcher of lemonade.

After Mass and 18-holes of golf with the Protestant ministers and the Jewish rabbi uptown, the good Father took pastry and baked goods with him on daily rounds to shut-ins and poor families he knew could not afford any extras or luxuries like sweets. There was a large strawberry patch in the front yard of the rectory house, and during the harvest season, quart baskets filled with the luscious fruit lined his porch banister, waiting for any strawberry-lovers to help themselves without asking.

The under-50 parishioners cherished him, but the old ladies who went to Mass every morning to repent for their sinful youths thought he was a young whippersnapper, even though he was middle-aged in the early 1950s. Petty *puni* detractors said he laughed too much and had too much fun at church picnics, wearing scandalous Bermuda shorts and quaffing beer. They thought his sermons were too short, none in the summer months, and not serious enough.

"Why did he always tell a joke from the pulpit, and then explain that the reason he told jokes was to make sure nobody was sleeping in the audience. Hrrumph. That man had a lot to learn about being a priest," vocalized the old biddies. Instead of him, they wanted someone like the Slovak Church priest, always with his hands in prayer and never a smile on his face. "Now he was a priest." Never allowing kids on the church playground wearing shorts, he would rather die before he let beer touch his sacred lips. Oh, Lord, those old bats could not stand the sight of Father Shezocki.

When a family was in financial difficulty, Father Shezocki came to the rescue immediately after the Sunday Masses were over and the collections were counted. The loans to the needy parishioners came under the miscellaneous column in the church books, without mention of any names. The debts were expected to be repaid in one of two ways. Once the families were on their feet, they could either anonymously help other families in need or drop more money in the collection basket. No proof of repayment was required. Father Shezocki was a tad loose with the church's bookkeeping; yet, the Polish Church continued to thrive, his Masses were practically SRO, and he was the first person parishioners turned to with good news or bad.

There was a slight problem with this close arrangement. Knowing the parish kids very, very well, he easily recognized our voices with his eyes closed or in the darkness of the Confessional.

"Bless me, Father, for I have sinned. I made my last Confession last Saturday. These are the sins I have committed since then. I disobeyed my mother twice. I disobeyed my father once. I had dirty thoughts after reading Cindy Petrouski's Aunt Laura's *True Confessions* magazines. I used God's name in vain once, but it was because my brother made me so mad that the swearword just slipped out. I accidentally ate meat on Friday. It was two minutes past midnight, but our clocks were fast, and

I didn't find out until after I already ate the burger. I told two lies, but they weren't big ones. Just little white ones. That's all, Father. For these, and all the sins of my past life, I am truly sorry."

"For your Penance, Sweetheart, I want you to say three Hail Marys, three Our Fathers, and make sure your clock's on time before you take a bite of Fred and Fran's hamburger. Auctoritate a Summis."

"Thank you, Father. (big breath)Oh my God, I am heartily sorry for having offended Thee,(big breath)and I detest all my sins, because I dread the loss of Heaven and the pain of Hell,(big breath)but most of all because they offend Thee, my God, Who art all good and deserving of all my love. (big breath)I firmly resolve, with the help of Thy grace, to confess my sins, to do penance, and to amend my life. (big breath)Amen."

"Patris et Filii et Spiritus Sancti. Amen. Oh, by the way, Diana, tell your mom and daddy to call me after five. Mrs. Jarenski and I want to show them the new carpet we bought for our living room."

Did God break the mold after He created Father Shezocki? I suspect He did.

The Hunchback of All Saints Polish Roman Catholic Church

Little kids could not help gawking at the serene midget lady with the massive mound on her back, sitting in the back pew beside her beautiful sisters. Older brothers claimed that when the hump was touched while making a wish, after asking her permission, whatever you hoped for would be granted. Older sisters revealed that if you were kind to the deformed young woman, good luck would always be yours. The poor soul of Notre Dame was shunned, but the Polish Church hunchback was the most popular parishioner, beaming broadly as she bent down to let awed, yet polite, youngsters make a wish.

Rain or Shine

The smartest person in town (or so everyone claimed) had a Ph.D. in physics from Carnegie Tech, wore a derby and black raincoat, carried an umbrella with a knife at the tip, and refused to speak to anyone except his mother.

Not heeding the constant warning to stay clear of him, a group of ruffians taunted him one day; and he stabbed two of them with his umbrella. A judge sent him to Torrence State Hospital for the insane for five years. Upon being released, he returned to East Vandergrift. Refusing to speak to anyone but his mother, he sauntered around town all day, wearing his derby and black raincoat and carrying his umbrella with the knife at the tip. Nobody bothered him after his return.

The Steel Workers

Except for Daddy, Mr. Hovanik, Joe Stemplensky, Father Shezocki and the other two priests, gossipy Cazzy, The Polish Barber, the school janitor, and a handful of others, most of the men of East Vandergrift worked in the steel mills. Staunch union men and loyal Democrats, they carried lunchbuckets as they walked along the railroad tracks on their way to and from work. Afterwards, still dressed in dirty clothes, they headed to the clubs for a shot and a beer chaser, even if they had just gotten off the graveyard shift as the sun was rising over the Kiskiminetas River.

Most of these hard-drinking, church-going, family men had toiled in the mills since boyhood. They believed education was the only way out of the dirty mills and were unusually harsh to the college boys who worked beside them in the summer months. They did not want the smart-aleck kids trading studies for a weekly paycheck and a bleak future. Before gaining as much wisdom as the undereducated, older steel workers, the college-trained men needed many years to realize that the summer cruelty was really kindness in disguise.

A History Lesson

"Kenny! Diana! Would you like to hear a story?" Mommy shouted so frequently that neither of us thought for a second what our response would be. In the cellar or on the porch, upstairs or downstairs, we dropped whatever we were doing or into and ran to our history-loving mom sitting on the couch, getting ready to continue the oral tradition of storytelling that undoubtedly had been going on since prehistoric times. It's not difficult to imagine two cave-dweller children, barefoot and animal-skin clad, running to their mother, claiming seats on the rock on either side of her, and silently waiting for her to begin a B.C. history lesson.

More than any other story, we loved hearing Mom's tales of Tekla Mocadlo, the Polish girl who became our grandmother, our Bupchie.

"Your grandmother was born in a small village in a part of Poland called Galicia, a province then controlled by Austria-Hungary. Most of the people in the hamlet were peasants and worked for rich Polish farmers or Austrian or German businessmen. Poland at that time was divided into three parts and was ruled by Russia, Germany, and Austria-Hungary.

"Bupchie had two brothers and four sisters; six others died at birth. Life was difficult and my mother became a farmhand when she was 10 years old, working in the fields every day except Sunday, walking five miles to and from home, even in the snow and rain.

"The family home in Poland had only three rooms, and the six children slept on the floor on mats. They ate mostly potatoes, cabbage, and, once a week, meat. Well, it was really bones with some clinging meat.

Still merely a child, yet worried about her family's health and well-being, your grandmother brought home a gallon of milk each day because she didn't take off for lunch and instead took on additional work for the farmer's wife. The milk was an indulgence for the family.

"Her older brother Steve left for America first, followed by sister Sophie. Shortly after his arrival, Steve wrote that jobs were easy to find. Not much later, when Sophie sent word that she had married, Bupchie expressed that she, too, wanted to go to America and promised to send back money. Determined to go to the Promised Land, she went to work for a German construction company carrying cement, a man's job, but she persevered. By saving half of each paycheck, after a year there was enough money for the boat trip.

"My Aunt Sophie wrote that my mother could stay with her and her husband Chester in Lilly, Pennsylvania, a coal-mining town. In this little borough, Chester labored in the pits, while Sophie boarded 12 lodgers and worked as a seamstress for the well-to-do ladies of Lilly.

"Bupchie set sail for America in 1896, when she was 16. Traveling third-class, she and the other passengers slept on the floor and ate one meal a day, barley soup and water. The voyage was so bad that most of the people were seasick and had lice.

"Your grandmother didn't talk to anyone on board, fearing someone would steal her belongings—a steamer trunk and two pillows her mother made for her as a wedding present. Also, she kept $6 wrapped in a rag tied to her slip.

"It took 14 days to get to the Philadelphia dock. After she and the other immigrants got off the ship, they boarded trains and rode to Ellis Island in New York. While there, everyone had to have a doctor's examination, and anyone with a contagious condition was turned away, sent back home to Europe.

"At Ellis Island, the U.S. Public Health Service doctors screened Bupchie for tuberculosis, scalp and nail fungus, and measles. Another unacceptable condition was trachoma, a highly contagious eye infection that causes blindness. Physicians used a buttonhook to turn my mother's eyelids over and inspect inside. Individuals with a blotch or patch were restricted. Those detained due to medical problems had chalk initials marked on their clothing to indicate the doctor's findings or suspicions: "L" for lameness, "X" for mental disability, and "E" for eye trouble.

"Ellis Island was a no-man's land, the barrier between the country left behind and the terrifying, although thrilling, new home ahead in what the immigrants—including my mother—believed to be the greatest nation in the world. Reaching Ellis Island, after a tumultuous trip by crude steerage class, Bupchie's and the other immigrants' journey was not over; it was only the beginning for millions of brave and adventuresome individuals like your grandmother.

"Following the medical examination, the Red Cross gave her a hearty meal, a little American flag, then helped her get to the final destination. One volunteer was a Jewish woman able to speak Polish; she took Bupchie to the train station and helped her buy a ticket to Lilly, Pennsylvania, and a new life."

Only 10 years before Bupchie was helped on the train to her new home in America, another Jewish woman, well aware of the suffering of her people in Russia and Poland, wrote a simple poem, which was engraved on the pedestal of the Statue of Liberty, a gift from the French people commemorating the 100th anniversary of the Declaration of Independence. Poet Emma Lazarus, who worked with the refugees flocking ashore, just might have been the woman who helped Bupchie buy her first American train ticket. Mommy doubted she was the woman Bupchie remembered, but Kenny and I insisted that maybe, just maybe, she was the same one who urged the tired and the poor to come to America.

"My mother stayed with her sister Sophie for six months then moved to Pittsburgh, where she worked in a big hotel as a dishwasher and later found a better job as a cook's helper.

"On Sundays the Polish people had dances and parties; and at one of those functions, she met my father, Frank Maszgay, who lived in North Vandergrift and worked in the Vandergrift Sheet and Tin Plate Company. On his days off, he visited his friends in Pittsburgh, because it was the only way to meet women. At that time, there were 15 men to every woman, and it was not easy for men to find wives.

"Twenty years older than my mother, Papa proposed the first time he saw her. After dating for a year, my parents finally had a big wedding in Pittsburgh, then moved to East Vandergrift, or Morning Sun, as it was called then. A beautiful picture of them on their wedding day was lost in the flood of 1936.

"The grandpa you kids never knew was a 6-foot tall, thin man with a curled mustache. I remember how he loved to read and sing. Oh, I miss him so much.

"By the turn of the century, your Bupchie had given birth to two children; and when Walter was three and Eleanor one, she decided to make a trip back to Poland. She and Papa had a few thousand dollars saved, and her dream was to buy her mother a farm. With my father's blessing, Mama left from New York with Walter and Eleanor, traveling third-class back home to Poland. Six years had passed since her maiden voyage to America; she was a little braver this time, not afraid to ask for anything on the ship and knew that with a dollar she could bribe workers for better food.

"After reaching Poland, your grandma took her parents shopping for a farm, a 20-acre tract with a barn and a four-room hut for $1700. My generous mother also purchased two cows, four pigs, chickens, and a horse for plowing. This loving gesture was the most significant event in my mother's life.

"Bupchie and my brother and sister remained in Poland for a year, regularly receiving letters from Papa. Each message conveyed how lonesome he was, begging her to return home to East Vandergrift. My mother later remarked that she was very confused then, because she loved her husband but also missed her mother and homeland.

"Desperate, Papa went to see Uncle Steve, Bupchie's brother with whom she did not get along at all. Steve was upset about her excursion to Poland and the new farm she bought. Never helping anybody, he was jealous of his sister.

"My father pleaded with Uncle Steve to write a letter to Mama, because none of his seemed to do any good. He was frightened she would stay in Poland for good.

"It was a big mistake going to Steve, who not only contacted Bupchie, but also conveyed a message to their mother, telling her how my mother had no love or compassion for her husband. He sang the praises of his brother-in-law, the one who allowed his wife to spend their hard-earned savings to buy her parents a farm; and to show her gratitude for having such a wonderful man, she decided to stay away from him for over a year. Besides making Bupchie appear to be the world's worst wife, he castigated her as a mother who tore the children away from their grieving father. Papa did not know what had been written. As a result, though, my mother returned home to my dad; and from then on, she had very little to do with Uncle Steve.

"Immediately upon her arrival, she took a night-job cleaning offices for a steel executive to save money for the next trip to Poland. It was no secret she wanted to move back to the Old Country, but my father often said he never had the desire to return. He loved this country and never wished to step outside its boundaries. As far as Papa was concerned, America was home.

"Sure enough, two years later my mother was ready to travel again. For the second time, my father let her take the money they had saved; and off she went across the Atlantic with three children. My brother Johnny was born a year after her return from the first trip. This time, however, to calm her frantic husband, she swore on a Bible that she would return home in half a year.

"When Bupchie arrived in Poland, her mother had bad news. Uncle Andy, who still lived at home with his parents in the village, had been drafted into the German Army. He was so upset that my mother bribed an Army official to take Andy with her to America. Paying 400 American dollars, she obtained a passport and snuck him on the next ship to America. Because of Uncle Andy, Bupchie had to depart two months earlier than planned.

"Upon landing in East Vandergrift, she mentioned to no one except Papa about her brother Andy. In an attempt to surprise her brother Steve, she had my dad pick him up and bring him over to the house. Uncle Andy hid in a cupboard, and when a very worried Uncle Steve wanted to know why his sister had come home sooner than planned, out popped Andy to surprise him.

"Predictably, Steve yelled, 'Why in the hell did you bring him here. I hope you don't think I'm going to keep him, because if so, you're dead wrong.'

"Instead of being pleased at Bupchie's surprise, he was rotten. At that point, Andy began to cry, and my father blurted out that the kid brother could stay with his family as long as he wanted. When my mother, trying to calm down Andy, offered to find him a job herself the next day, Uncle Steve laughed at her, snarling that she was too stupid to know how.

"Sure enough, the next morning your gutsy grandmother marched her brother Andy to the Vandergrift Mill. When she asked to speak to the big boss, the personnel director came out, and she tried to explain to him in Polish the nature of her visit. The accommodating man found someone to translate and heard how Andy had arrived in America the day before and now needed work. Smiling at Bupchie, the company executive cheerfully announced that this was her lucky day. Just that morning, the mill owners decided to open another department called the "rolling mill" and needed six men to run it. Now that her brother Andy was here, he needed only five more men. Then and there, thanks to Bupchie's gumption, Uncle Andy was the first person hired for the new section.

"The very next day Andy was in training. And after that, life was smooth sailing. Regularly promoted at work, he learned English within a year and became an American citizen 10 years before his older brother Steve, who was insanely jealous of his kid brother's good fortune. The one sad note was that my mother never returned to Poland and never saw her mother again."

Offspring of the immigrants in East Vandergrift went away to fight in World War I while Bupchie was giving birth to her fourth child. Shortly before Helen's birth, Eleanor, the second-born, died after a group of boys who were playing with torches accidentally started her clothes on fire. She passed away in Bupchie's arms on the milk-run train to the hospital. Uncle Walter and Uncle Johnny, who both moved away and rarely visited, remarked how I resembled Eleanor. Sometimes, when I saw the way Bupchie stared at me, maybe she thought so too. Often I wondered if the ache at the horrible loss ever dulled, or if Aunt Helen's birth helped ease the pain.

Prohibition ushered in the '20s, and during that prosperous decade, Clara (our mother) and three more siblings, Joe, Caz, and Veronica, were born. Shortly after Mommy was born in 1921, Walter, the oldest child, ran away from home when he was 15. Following a terrible fight with his father, he left when Grandpa threatened to send him to a reform school unless he stopped getting in trouble for stealing. Mom never even knew she had a brother Walter until she was eight years old and he returned as surprisingly as he had departed.

Life was good in early 1927 when the baby of the family, Aunt Veronica, was born. Bupchie had a loving and fine husband, seven healthy children, and a house of her own, bought two years earlier for $5700 in cash.

Sadly, however, Grandpa Maszgay became ill in the winter of 1927. At the hospital he was treated for an ulcer and given morphine for the pain, but he suffered terribly. A week before he died, Bupchie called in a new physician, fresh out of medical school, who diagnosed the cancer, which she nor any of the neighbors or relatives had ever heard of before.

Bupchie's husband died in 1928. Mommy loved him very much and said she would always miss him, that wonderful man, who loved to sing and tell stories. Besides having a great disposition, he was quite handy— repairing shoes, cutting hair, painting, wallpapering, making furniture.

Before he died, Christmas with him was the best time of the year, with a big tree decorated with bright candles, lots of lovely homemade presents and delicious baked goods, along with loud and happy singing. He was very funny when he had a few drinks, though he never got drunk. From the time he died until World War II, when Jimmy, Barbara, and Mommy stayed with Bupchie, the house on McKinley Avenue never had a Christmas tree.

Grandfather Frank had lived a full 67 years. After leaving Poland and before coming to America, he and a friend from home traveled around South America, where they went to work on a construction project for three years. They signed a contract stating that their pay would be deposited in a New York bank for them and they could get it after the agreement was fulfilled. When they went to New York after the three years, they discovered there was no money waiting for them. They were swindled. The bank book they carried with them at all times in South America was a fake. Never regretting the South American stay, Grandpa told the kids it taught him a hard lesson to always check everything carefully before signing on the dotted line.

In the United States he was by trade a blacksmith and always had work and made a good living. Happy-go-lucky and carefree most of the time, Grandpa, however, often spoke with sadness of his parents and one younger sister in Poland. After leaving his homeland, he never saw his family again but missed them terribly and thought about them all the time. He was constantly torn between love for America and the longing for clan in the Old Country, a place he never wanted to return to, even for a short visit.

After Grandpa's death, Bupchie took a job at the Schenley Whiskey factory to support her seven children. One year later, the Depression hit the country, not with a whimper but a bang.

The times Kenny and I begged our mother to tell stories, most of them were regarding the 1920s, the Depression, or World War II. The one anecdote that impressed us the most is still distinct now as I close my eyes and let my memory of childhood take over. I imagine my mother going down the cellar steps, where she catches Bupchie leaning over a wash tub, scrubbing clothes, and crying.

"What's wrong, Mama?" 12-year-old Mommy asks.

Heaving from sobs, Bupchie tells her the banks have closed, their savings are gone, and the only money she has left in the house is a quarter. From that day on, Bupchie kept her nest egg under a mattress.

Bupchie married her second husband, our Ju Ju, in 1935. He had four children he had been raising since his wife's death a few years earlier. She needed a husband; he needed a wife; the kids needed both mother and father. Things were certainly clear-cut back then.

Into my mother's world entered a new father, another sister, and three more brothers. The economic bad times dragged on and on with no end in sight; and just when things could not possibly get any worse, the flood of 1936 wreaked devastation on East Vandergrift and the lives of its citizens. Shortly afterwards, Mommy left home to find her way in the world and met Daddy. After his return from the war, East Vandergrift became our family's permanent home; and from that moment on, Bupchie became an important part of our daily lives, a fact we cherished then as well as now.

Morning Sun

Morning Sun was a three-year-old village when Bupchie and her first husband arrived to begin married life. The first map drawn for the new town was mislabeled and referred to Morning Sun as "The Borough of Sunshine." This by college-trained engineers whose first (and probably only) language was English. The initial building erected was a general store, followed by hastily built dwellings for the European-born residents coming by the hundreds.

In 1901, the Court of Quarter Sessions of Westmoreland County decreed "That the village of Morning Sun in Allegheny Township, Westmoreland County, Pennsylvania, be and the same is hereby incorporated into a borough under the name, style and title of 'THE BOROUGH OF EAST VANDERGRIFT' with all the rights, privileges and powers conferred by law upon boroughs within this Commonwealth." Four of the 42 property owners who signed the petition for the incorporation could not read or write. An "X" marked their historic deed.

Bupchie and her husband lived happily in the new town of 700 inhabitants in that turn-of-the-century year. At that time, the streets and alleys of the town were unpaved and extremely muddy during rainy weather. This sloppy predicament was remedied by the construction of a 4-foot plank walk on either side of the main street, McKinley Avenue. The town, from one end to the other, measured 4000 feet, with three streets running parallel to the Kiskiminetas River and seven small-town roads intersecting them.

McKinley Avenue, the street of our grandparents' future home-of-their-own, ran from the ball field and steel mill dump at one end to Sheridan Road and The Cut at the other.

Sheridan Road, hardly a road while we were children, let alone when Bupchie was a young wife, was more like a footpath, unpassable by car. The Cut was the shortened version of the West Penn Cut that appeared on old maps drawn following the Civil War. Around that time, the railroad replaced the canal as standard means of transportation for people and goods, and The Cut, used by children as a playground and lovers for necking, was the approximate grade of the first railroad in the area.

During the early part of the 20th Century, McKinley Avenue became the setting of the three churches (Polish, Lithuanian, and Slovak), three ethnic (Polish, Lithuanian, and Slovak) social clubs, the school, and all the businesses (what there were of them) built to accommodate the residents.

McKinley Avenue was in the middle of town and the longest street. The other two major streets were Quay and Railroad Streets. The later was nearest the river, where the Pennsylvania Railroad kept a busy schedule before highways carted away their freight and passengers, just as the rails had replaced the canal. In the other direction, toward Vandergrift Lane, the hill into the town of Vandergrift, was Quay Street.

During the early life of the town, a ferry operated to Apollo, across the Kiskiminetas, but it went out of use before World War II. After its demise, there was only one way in and out of East Vandergrift. Men used the railroad tracks to and from work, but that was the only exception. When the Lane was closed during snowstorms, the town was cut off from the rest of civilization.

Quay Street, a few hundred feet long, was the shortest of the three major streets. All of the short streets that ran perpendicular to the three long ones were named for Republican bigwigs, ardent Republican property owners with Anglo-Saxon names. The immigrant tide eventually flooded them out of town. As the Eastern Europeans moved in, the

American-born residents moved uptown to Vandergrift, although the property there was higher priced. At least up there they could speak with their neighbors in English. Once the predominantly Protestant and rabid-Republican group left, East Vandergrift became inhabited by immigrant Catholics, parents of future dyed-in-the-wool liberal (a revered word back then) Democrats.

Fashion Store

Size-5 Mom was a snazzy dresser and bought clothing at Fashion Store, owned by Mrs. Shepler and her daughters, commonly referred to by practically everyone as "the Shepler girls." Married women with children, the Shepler girls lived in Pittsburgh with doctor husbands. After Mr. Shepler passed away, his wife brought the young women into the business, but Mrs. S, as some customers named her, was the CEO and a genuine balabusta, a very, very bossy lady.

Bupchie and the Shepler family went way back to the time Mr. Shepler sold garments from a pushcart, not long after arriving in America from Poland with his young wife. Venturing into East Vandergrift for the first time, he encountered ugly prejudice from the Catholic immigrants who hated Jews, blaming them, I suppose, for killing Christ, who they forgot was himself a Jew.

Bupchie met Mr. Shepler when she chased away (with a broom) hooligans who were harassing the young peddler. While sweeping the sidewalk immediately afterwards, pretending nothing happened, she offered him a cup of coffee and a piece of babka. After he thanked her and accepted the invitation, they sat at the kitchen table and savored warm coffee, delicious cake, and congenial moments talking about their mutual homeland. Instantly liking the clothes' peddler and judging him to be a fair businessman, Bupchie began buying his merchandise.

Our granny was his original customer in East Vandergrift. In return for her kindness, beginning with the mitzvah performed with the whacks on the rowdy shlemiels' tokhises, he extended her credit during the Depression. During those tough times, her growing children needed duds, but there wasn't much money to buy them with. Without the installment plan, she would have had to forgo milk and bread to buy new shoes for kids whose feet mysteriously grew by inches overnight.

Customer and vendor formed a loyal bond, and Bupchie continued doing business with Mr. Shepler when he opened a storefront uptown on Grant Street. Referring friends and neighbors to his showroom, she advised him as to which clientele paid their bills and who were deadbeats.

Over the years, the clothing racks in Fashion Store were jammed with the prevailing styles; however, a section to the side was reserved for housedresses that the Sheplers' old and loyal patrons, like Bupchie, preferred.

Twice a year Bupchie went to Fashion Store to buy housedresses. And as soon as our grandma opened the front door, Mrs. Shepler enthusiastically yelled from the rear of the store, "Tekla! Dzien dobry pani. Shalom! Shalom!" and trotted to Bupchie with arms outstretched. Then, abruptly turning to her daughters, no matter what they were doing, she commanded them to go and get two cups of coffee from Isaly's across the street, "plenty cream mit three sugahs" and pastry from the bakery down the street. "Mach shnel!"

Daddy said that whenever Mrs. S ordered her girls to jump, they asked, "How high, Mama?" And, boy, was he right. The younger soared out that front door, pencil still firmly attached to her ear. Mrs. Shepler then pulled up two chairs that the other daughter had raced to the back room and schlepped out with. Mrs. S and Bupchie plopped in them in the middle of the store, drank coffee, and noshed on pastry, while smartly attired shicksas negotiated around them, heading toward the curtained dressing rooms.

Bupchie, wearing her customary housedress, and Mrs. Shepler, dressed to beat the band in a chicly tailored suit, shmoozed in Polish about the good old days, their dead ("Oh Vay, God rest their souls") husbands, and Poland. Without pausing for a breath, Mrs. Shepler called Kenny and me over, "Kennala! Dianala!" and placed me on her lap and motioned Kenny to climb onto Bupchie's.

It was obvious to everyone in the store how much respect these two women had for each other; and glancing at Bupchie, I felt incredible love.

CEO Shepler remarked in broken English, with a little Yiddish thrown in, how wonderful Bupchie was, "Your bouba's a mensch," and how much she assisted her late husband during the hard times, "many, many mitzvahs. Tekla is very good voman."

Mom and the Shepler girls smiled expansively as their mothers carried on in Polish in the center of the shop, oblivious to the teenagers gaping at them as though they were from another planet. Some of them even kvetched about the inconvenience the two old ladies were causing by blocking the path to the changing quarters.

Into this scene entered Daddy, hauling loads of boxes from Geraci's Children Store (for the discriminating child) and gripping Barbara's hand. Big sister dashed over to Bupchie for a kiss, and Daddy quickly marched to the back room for another seat.

Dragging the chair, the whole time dramatically pretending his eyes were closed as he passed the dressing room cubicles, Daddy maneuvered a place between Mrs. Shepler and Bupchie at center stage. Fedora resting on his lap, he soon had both arms encircling the shoulders of the two old friends. Having learned enough Polish over the years, as well as a smattering of seven languages as a paperboy, he entertained the two punis with jokes in pidgin Polish and Yiddish.

Time flew by during these twice-yearly visits; and after embraces and kisses were exchanged, Bupchie sadly opened the door. As the tiny bell at the top of the door ting-a-linged that our grandmother was leaving and wouldn't be returning for another six months, Mrs. Shepler clutched her dear friend's housedress and implored, "Don't be stranger, Tekla. Shalom! Shalom!"

Pokey

"How much is that doggie in the window?"

"Arf! Arf!"

"The one with the waggily tail. How much is that doggie in the window?"

"Arf! Arf!"

"I do hope that doggie's for sale," sang Patti Page on the radio as Kenny and I sat on the couch, putting on socks and shoes and getting ready to go uptown by ourselves for the first time.

The occasion was for Kenny to buy himself a birthday present with the $5 Grandma Dell had sent him. He didn't have an inkling what to get. I knew what I wanted him to buy—a puppy—but wanted him to come up with the idea himself.

Looking over at him while Patti Page chirped the familiar lyrics, I noticed there was no reaction from him, so I joined in, "I must take a trip to California, and leave my poor sweetheart alone. If he has a dog he won't be lonely, and the doggie will have a good home." Still no response from Kenny as he finished tying his laces.

Mommy buttoned our coats and waved good-bye from the door as we started uptown. There were 85 steps, three houses down and across Quay Street, which led to Vandergrift Lane, but kids used the shortcut down near the field. To reach the time saver, we had to cut through Mrs. Laski's yard, pass under her grape vine, and wind up the dirt path to the top of Vandergrift Lane, which ran into Franklin Avenue. On the corner of Franklin and Grant was Dr. Benjamin Franklin Lear's house-office; his home address was Grant Avenue, and the door to the reception room was on Franklin. (Contrary to what Jimmy had stated as he crossed his heart and hoped to die, the doctor's youngest child was not named Shanda.)

Barbara and Jimmy took Kenny and me uptown plenty of times; we both knew to look each way while crossing the streets and to hold hands. Walking down Grant, we passed Fashion Store, waved to the Shepler girls, then went on to the five-and-ten. For a change, we entered our favorite store through the door that led into the record department. I knew that the Patti Page hit would be played if we lingered in that section long enough.

No loitering was necessary. The instant we opened the door we heard, "How much is that doggie in the window?"

"Arf! Arf!"

"The one with the waggily tail. How much is that doggie in the window?"

"Arf! Arf!"

"I do hope that doggie's for sale."

Kenny advanced toward the candy counter with such speed that I had to practically run just to catch up with him. Like a magnet to iron, the smell of chocolate beckoned, and he tracked the scent. Mommy had given him a quarter for candy so he wouldn't have to use any of the $5 on anything but a present. After buying me a nickel's worth of chocolate stars, he got the same amount of malted balls.

Munching the candy, we strolled up and down the aisles looking at everything, and doing so, he saw way too many items he wanted. We would have needed at least $500 to buy them all, instead of the $5 in his jacket pocket. Besides, he was searching for something unique, something that nobody else would think of buying him. Since his party was in two days, he knew he was going to rack in the presents, stuff we were examining at the five-and-ten. No, he wanted to buy something original for himself with the $5 from Grandma Dell.

I wanted to scream, "Buy a puppy, dummy!" but held my tongue, knowing it had to be his idea, or he would tell Daddy he wanted a puppy. Mommy would say "no," and that would be the end of that.

Once she put her foot down, there was no arguing with her. But, and this was a big "but," she didn't suggest what not to buy as we left the house; and once it was bought, she wouldn't want to upset Kenny by returning it, or so I was counting on.

As Kenny inspected the puzzles, I started singing. "I read in the papers there are robbers, with flashlights that shine in the dark. My love needs a doggie to protect him and scare them away with one bark."

Putting the puzzle down, he picked up a toy flashlight. "Just like the robbers use," he remarked. I wanted to shake him until his teeth rattled but smiled instead.

"Let's go visit Mr. and Mrs. Geraci," I said, taking his hand. "Maybe they have an idea what you can buy." Exiting near the fish tanks, we stopped to count the dead fish, which became so dull we stopped at 25.

It was a short walk to the children's store and our parents' good friends since the farm days. At that time, the Geracis owned a fruit stand on River Road in Apollo. Urging them on to bigger and better things than bananas, my wise dad talked them into starting a children's clothing store for all the babies who would be born right after the war. He was right on target about the baby boom, and the Geracis' business expanded along with the population.

The second Kenny opened the door to Geraci's Children Store, I thought Mrs. Geraci had seen a long-lost relative or something the way she squealed with delight and clapped her hands together. Rushing toward us, she stooped down for hugs and kisses. Kenny's head nestled in her thick black hair, and mine was against her perfumed neck, which smelled pleasant. When I gave her a big squeeze, I realized what record was playing on the hi fi in the back room: "I don't want a bunny or a kitty. I don't want a parrot that talks. I don't want a bowl of little fishes. You can't take a goldfish for walks."

Mrs. Geraci twisted around and screamed, "Larry! Turn that damn thing off and get out here! Look who came to say hello!"

The music stopped abruptly, and Mr. Geraci came into view, his long nose leading the way. More hugs and kisses and a piggy back ride for Kenny, then lollipops for both of us.

A while later, with instructions from his wife, Mr. Geraci clutched our hands, and we three sauntered next door to Ross's pharmacy. He lifted us up, put us down on two counter stools, and waved to the teenage soda jerk.

"Two cherry cokes for my friends here," he said with a wink. "And anything else they want, just come next door and I'll pay for it." With that, he kissed us and went to the store to do whatever it was he did. Mrs. Geraci did the buying, advertising copy, and floor sales. Maybe he counted the money.

There we sat, gulping large cherry cokes, while the big girl behind the counter leaned on it staring at us.

"Want anything else, kids?"

When we shook our heads "no," she whirled around to turn on the radio, flipping the dial for a good tune. Her choice was too good to be true. For the millionth time in a week we heard, "How much is that doggie in the window?"

"Arf! Arf!"

"The one with the waggily tail. How much is that doggie in the window?"

"Arf! Arf!"

"I do hope that doggie's for sale."

The three of us sang along until a teenage boy walked in and sat at the counter. Kenny and I were history as far as she was concerned. Practically purring, she wiggled like Marilyn Monroe over to get his order, the whole time batting her eyelashes. This young woman saw too many films and read far too many movie magazines.

It seemed as if there was no way Kenny would think of a puppy as the present to buy with Grandma Dell's $5. After slurping the drop at the bottom of his glass, he wanted another, but my signal to the clerk didn't make her come running as Mr. Geraci's had.

I got up, walked over to where the big boy was sitting, and waited for her to notice me. She didn't, but he did. As luck would have it, he was a ballplayer for the St. Gertrude's Church team and knew Jimmy. He said he had seen Kenny and me at the games on the bleachers, cheering the loudest any time Jimmy pitched. Yep, that was us.

The big boy slid down the counter stools to sit next to Kenny and me and even bought the next round. Kenny mentioned what we were doing uptown, and as he did, Patti Page finished singing.

"Why don't you get a puppy?" he asked. I wanted to kiss him, and probably would have, but the soda jerk was cutting some bread with a knife and did not appear too happy that he fancied our company to hers.

Kenny thought a pooch was a great idea and asked me why I hadn't thought of it. What is it about little boys and the way they look up to big boys? Everything they do is astonishing to the shorter of the two. This tall one was rather nice; and as we said "thanks" and "good-bye" to George Esposito ("Call me Spider"), we skipped blissfully down the street. "See you two at the next game."

The pet store was next to the bakery that smelled wonderful, though the stuff they sold was never as good as homemade desserts or the pastries the traveling, opera-singing baker sold in the summer; but it all appeared good.

After checking out the cupcakes and cookies, we concentrated on the puppies and kittens in the pet store window. Daisy the kitten could never be replaced; our attention was focused on the puppies, who were awfully cute and responded enthusiastically to the taps on the glass. The smallest one leaped at Kenny and put his paws on the window glass exactly where Kenny's hands were. That was it. Shopping was done. My baby brother had chosen his present.

The stench as we entered the store was really bad, mostly from the birds in the dirty cages. P U! It stunk to high Heaven, and it took awhile for us to get used to the odor.

Obviously used to the rankness, the grinning clerk informed us that "dogs cost $6 and the leashes are $1."

"Oh," I responded and must have looked disappointed. I said we only had $5.15. With that, we wanted to buy a puppy and two chocolate-marshmallow ice cream cones at Isaly's, which we had just passed on the way to the pet store.

"Double scoop or single?" he asked.

"Double," Kenny answered, without pausing to ponder the question. If Isaly's had sold triples, that would have been his response.

The pet store man hit his head with his palm. "I forgot. There's a special today on puppies. The cost for one is $4.85, and a leash is thrown in free for good measure."

I started counting, and before I reached the thumb on the first hand, Kenny blurted out, "I'll take it!" Amazing what a head he had for figures, just like Bupchie.

The nice fellow told Kenny that his pick was the runt of the litter and very, very slow. After he put the leash and collar ("no charge since it's your birthday present") around the tan puppy's neck, we strolled over to Isaly's to get the cones. Kenny waited outside with the puppy, because no pets were allowed inside.

What a glorious place Isaly's was! The young guys behind the counter, wearing white peaked hats, were always friendly, even when a kid accidentally rolled a coin into the ice cream drums beneath the narrow glass counter.

Chocolate-marshmallow ice cream cones in hand, we began to think up names. Rover? Spot? Blackie? Fido? Pokey finally came to mind because that's just what he was—we had to stop the whole time going home to let him catch up.

"What a slow-poke my mutt is!" Kenny said 50 times on the way back to East Vandergrift.

The expression of utter horror on Mommy's face when she saw Pokey at the front door was priceless. We were afraid she would make us take him back, but she didn't.

Throughout the day, everybody in the family welcomed the new pet to the household. Barbara fixed a bedroom for Pokey in the cellar near the coal furnace, and he had the whole huge cement room to romp in.

Pokey cried a lot the first few days. Annoyed, Jimmy suggested additions to the sleeping space of old rags in a cardboard box. Daddy included a hot water bottle and a wind-up alarm clock to fool him into thinking it was the sound of his mother's heart. Not only was Pokey slow, but also he was stupid. Snuggling next to the clock, he fell asleep to the loud ticking.

Kenny got a ton of presents for his birthday, but none as wonderful as Pokey. Not realizing it was my idea in the first place, he gave the credit to Spider Esposito for suggesting a puppy. Oh, well, at least I was in good company. Patti Page got no acknowledgment either.

The Battling Felines

No ifs, ands, or buts about it, Kenny was the tattletale of the family. If Jimmy, Barbara, or I did something bad at school (pass a note to a friend in class or talk in line at the water fountain and get yelled at by a teacher), the three of us promised to stick together to make sure our strict mom didn't find out and punish us. Grabbing Kenny eavesdropping at the door, we threatened to kill him if he squealed. Convincingly, he promised; but the minute we let him go, he ran with the bad news, and we three were punished. Never able to keep a secret, he was not be trusted.

On the other hand, if he did something wrong, Jimmy, Barbara, and I stuck by his side, and a team of wild horses couldn't drag the secret out of us. Kenny, the baby of the family, never seemed to learn by sibling good deeds.

That boy got away with murder. Take for instance the time that the Polish Church had an extravaganza for Father Shezocki on the Jubilee of his ordination to the Holy Priesthood.

The 25-year celebration had been in the planning stages for months. Church Committeemen, All Saints Church Choir, Holy Name Society, Rosary Mothers, Young Ladies Sodality of the Children of Mary, and the Ladies Auxiliary, all groups under the superb direction of Mrs. Jarenski (the Church organist, Catechism teacher, Father's housekeeper, and, rumor had it, secret wife) worked with feverish love to put on the biggest program the Polish Church had ever witnessed.

This gala event consisted of folk dances, an accordion duet by Jerry Ruzbacki and Modesta Falenski, tap dance numbers, Polish songs by the choirs (junior and senior), and speeches by dignitaries. Mom was an organizer and choir member. Altar boy Jimmy was an usher. Barbara, one of the Children of Mary, popped out of a gift box and read a speech she wrote. Daddy took out a full-page ad in the program booklet. Kenny and I were in the Our Little Darlings' chorus line. We Little Darlings came right after John Majeran's trumpet solo, just before dinner, immediately after a nap.

Wearing kitten costumes designed by the Ladies Auxiliary, the little girls danced around the little boys, who were dressed in the same attire, kneeling on the floor. Thefinale was the girls kissing the boys on the cheek. At that crucial moment, Kenny at center stage decided that there was no way Joannie Welkon was going to kiss him in front of those people in the audience, all 302. He threw a tantrum and wailed at the top of his lungs. Upon doing so, he threw all the kittens, boys and girls, into a panic. The stage was chaotic with frantic Little Darlings running here and there and everywhere, crying for their mothers.

Kenny had his arms folded and didn't move a muscle but kept screaming as Joannie, also possessing a stubborn baby-of-the-family streak, tried desperately to finish the number. She tried kissing him; and each time she did, he swatted her with his paws. Grabbing his tail, she spun him around, pounced on him, and pounded him with her mitts to break his resolve. The more she tried to peck him, the louder he cried, while kitties, with whiskers askew and tails swinging from side to side, ran into each other, trying to get away from the unrehearsed scene. These kids would never have survived on live television with its unplanned moments.

The curtain came down; and mothers dragged children off the stage, trying to calm them down, long enough to wipe their noses. While this bedlam was happening, I calmly exited stage left, smug with the knowledge that Kenny was really going to get it this time, no matter what.

Just that morning, he had snitched to Mommy after he caught Jimmy and Eddie Lazinski sneaking a butt in the garage. She was furious when she walked in on them, Kenny in hand. When she learned that they were smoking one of her Lucky Strikes stolen from her purse, she became enraged. Smart Eddie scurried home as fast as his 12-year-old legs could carry him, and Jimmy got 10 lashes with the strap. Barbara and I cried just watching him get hit. Not realizing the punishment when he tattled, Kenny rushed to Daddy to say it was not his fault.

Anyway, back to the Jubilee when the curtain was raised a jiffy later by Eddie Lazinski and Jimmy, who did not want anybody to miss Kenny's naughty conduct.

There Kenny and Joannie were, still frozen in their spots, still brawling. To my complete surprise, the audience went wild with applause and gave the two sparring felines a standing ovation. Two bratty stars were born at that moment. Somehow I knew that my spoiled Little Darling brother would come out of it without a scratch.

And, to make matters worse, it just so happened that the bishop and his priestly entourage fell head over heels in love with the battling cats. The clerics lavished them with praise, quarters, and hugs when the curtain finally came down, along with Jimmy's and Eddie's smiles.

Our busy mother and Mrs. Welkon saw none of this part of the program; they were in the school kitchen putting the finishing touches onto the meal, which was to be served immediately following the kitten chorus-line kiss.

The bishop had Kenny on his shoulders, and a superior court judge was giving a grinning Joannie a piggyback ride through the audience to more cheers. I could not believe my eyes. There was no way Mommy could scold him now, not in front of the VIP-adoring fans. Kenny and Joannie were hits with the brass from the archdiocese and state government, no doubt about it.

I had observed Daddy's reaction in the first row as he viewed the whole fiasco on stage. He was laughing so hard that his face was red, and tears were running down his cheeks. Father Shezocki sat next to him, slapping his own and Daddy's knees. They thought it was a hoot. There really was not much Mom could do about punishing Kenny, without looking like a spoilsport.

Kenny and Joannie, the headliners of the Jubilee, were treated to dessert before dinner. They were conspiratorially licking the icing off cupcakes when I walked into the kitchen to find my mother and get the praise I felt I rightfully deserved for doing my kitten part, precisely as written, rehearsed, and performed.

Shooed away, I had my hand slapped as I grabbed for a cupcake myself. With bruised feelings, I turned to my brother for moral support. Wrong. Kenny stuck out his tongue, licked a big gob of icing, and pointed tongue and chocolate in my direction. He then slid his four-year-old arm around Joannie's shoulder and whispered in her ear. Listening intently, she slowly turned her smiling face to his, and they kissed. ON THE LIPS! I could have killed both of them at that amorous moment.

I found out later that the reason he was crying was because he emphatically avowed he would not do his part on stage unless he had a cupcake first. Mommy firmly stated that he could not have a treat until after dinner and then shoved him in the direction of the stage. Not shrieking because Joannie was trying to kiss him, he threw a public hissy fit because of that dumb cupcake that he was now feasting on before dinner.

Kenny Starts School

Kenny entered kindergarten when Jimmy was going to the seventh grade; Barbara, the fifth; and I was beginning second grade at the East Vandergrift elementary school.

Feeling like such a big shot, I gripped Kenny's and Frankie's hands all the way down McKinley Avenue to school. Stopping first at Hovanik's grocery store, we lingered for Cindy, predictably late, and her little brother Lenny, who was also starting preschool.

After the Petrouskis arrived, we five—hands held—rendezvoused with Bonny Zalenski and her youngest brother Benny, another kindergartner, at the intersection of Vandergrift Lane and McKinley Avenue. They were leaning against the Blessed Virgin Mary statue in front of the Slovak Church. The seven of us, linked together, then made our way the remaining one block to the nursery school classroom.

That first day Kenny's teacher sent for me close to a hundred times because he wouldn't stop crying over something or other, mostly about sharing toys. Even though Barbara and Jimmy were in the same building, because I was the Dell who brought him to school, he became my responsibility. Moreover, Judy Petrouski, Chrissy Zalenski, and Barbara notified Cindy, Bonny, and me in no uncertain terms that Lenny, Benny, and Kenny were not their problems and wanted absolutely nothing to do with them or us.

"Do I make myself clear?" Barbara added.

Frankie Poleski was odd man out and on his own, as far as the older sisters were concerned.

Seventh-graders Freddie Petrouski, Danny Zalenski, and Jimmy Dell were oblivious to everyone's existence, except the young women in their class who were starting to wear lipstick and training bras.

Kindergarten lasted until lunchtime, when Lenny, Benny, Frankie, and Kenny hustled to my classroom. We second-graders and our kindergarten brothers, plus Frankie, walked home together. Just as soon as the little lads spotted Barbara, Chrissy, Judy, and their other girl-friends, they ran with heads down straight toward the girls. The fifth-graders scattered like bowling pins.

Then, the more mature sisters yelled, "It's not funny!" at their chortling younger sisters, strolling ten paces behind as ordered.

Kenny loved Mother Goose nursery rhymes, especially "Georgie Porgie." For a week after first hearing about the mischievous little boy who kissed the girls and made them cry, Kenny followed suit and wrecked havoc every morning. Joannie Welkon protested the loudest when he kissed her and wailed the hardest when he did not. His teacher even sent a note home with me describing the disruption he was caus-ing. I wanted to, but knew I could never, not give the message to Mom. Disobeying parents was a venial sin; disobeying a teacher was equiva-lent to a mortal sin.

After reading the kindergarten teacher's note, Mommy hollered at Kenny and advised him to "behave yourself."

Daddy shook his head from side to side, muttering, "That's my boy."

Our mom did not think it was comical and told Daddy to "stop encouraging him. He's been a bad, bad boy. And he better stop it or he'll be sorry." Daddy kept smiling.

Certainly getting mixed messages, Kenny went a bit too far by trying to kiss the first-graders, who towered over him, at the water fountain. No-nonsense Miss Claypool put a stop to his antics and made him sit in a corner of her classroom until he promised to behave. She did not have to send notes home to get the proper behavior she expected.

The kindergarten room was near the boys' bathroom at the end of the first-floor hallway. I loved to stroll down there, peek in, and wave to Kenny, who had such an excited look on his face when he spotted me, as if he hadn't seen me for years. The absence between seeing each other at the water fountain an hour before and the peek in the doorway definitely made our hearts grow fonder. Kenny's affection for me quickly evaporated, though, if I beat him in a race home for lunch.

The Grolski Family

In the middle of the school year, two new girls entered Kenny's kindergarten class. Newly arrived immigrants, Jesse, age eight, and her five-year-old sister Tina spoke no English. Their parents had been concentration camp prisoners at Dachau during the war.

Shortly after Germany invaded Poland in 1939, the young women in Mrs. Grolski's village were rounded up and taken away to Germany, where the blue-eyed Polish girls went to a special camp and were impregnated by German soldiers. Their babies were given to childless German couples to be raised as their own. The brown-eyed girls, like Mrs. Grolski, were railroaded to forced-labor camps.

While at Dachau, Mrs. Grolski met her future husband, who smuggled extra food and a blanket to her. He had been a Polish resistance fighter, turned in by a Nazi sympathizer from his village. The Grolskis were secretly married in the camp by another prisoner, a Catholic priest; and Jesse, their first child, was born at Dachau a week before it was liberated.

Mr. and Mrs. Grolski and Jesse were then transported to a displaced-person's camp in Germany, where Tina was born, for another two years. Subsequently, they found work and lived in Munich while anxiously waiting to get the paper work necessary to go to the United States.

Father Shezocki, our parish priest, through an international organization that helped Polish Catholics imprisoned during the war, sponsored them to come to East Vandergrift. After the family arrived, the Ladies Auxiliary of the Polish Church (our popular mother was the president) pitched in and helped the family get settled. The members of the church group rented a house, bought clothes and food, secured the husband a job, and offered endless moral support.

Kenny and I, as well as other kids the girls' ages in school, were summoned to help the girls learn English. I don't remember how the other children reacted to this chore, but Kenny and I were excited to go to the Grolski house. For one thing, we were impressed that Tina and Jesse, almost our ages, could speak two languages and assumed they were awfully smart to be able to do that.

Mrs. Grolski was very sweet, even when Mr. Grolski, old enough to be our grandfather, rolled up his shirt sleeve and showed us the tattoo of numbers on his arm. His wife grimaced while Kenny gently touched each digit, knowing there were going to be many stories once the family mastered the English language.

The former Polish resistance fighter and concentration camp survivor, after returning home from his job at the steel mill and finding Jesse, Tina, Kenny, and me at the dining room table, would sit down with us. Yet, instead of horror stories of war, he recounted tales of his childhood, before his world turned upside down and inside out. The only reminder of the most terrible time in his life was that tattoo on his arm. And the only time we ever heard him raise his voice in anger was when Mrs. Grolski, who always wore long sleeves, suggested that they see a doctor about having their brands removed.

"Never!" he screamed, then quietly continued telling a cheerful childhood story in his normal, gentle way.

Tea and Crumpets

One of Aunt Veronica's childhood friends had enlisted with the WAC's during World War II and had been sent to London, where she worked in a motor pool helping Princess Elizabeth, doing her royal bit for the war effort, fix carburetors.

During her London tour of duty, Sgt. Marie Pojenski of East Vandergrift acquired a British accent and a Polish pilot husband, whom she enchanted at an RAF dance. Both thought they got quite a prize in the other; but she fancied remaining in England after the war, and he yearned to go to America.

With very few jobs in Europe after the war, they headed to America. Her hero-husband was a little disappointed, to put it mildly, when they settled in East Vandergrift. It was then he discovered that his new wife was not a member of a rich family as he was led to believe during their courtship.

After mastering his job in the steel mill, he spent more time at the Polish Club than at home and cursed himself for ever going to that RAF dance.

Subscribing to British magazines, she had tea time—the whole she-bang—every day, named their twins Philip and Elizabeth, and would not let anyone in town ever forget that she had once rubbed elbows, literally, with the future queen of England.

Another War Story

Our family historian told the following tale many, many times over the years. In the spring of 1933, Mommy met her Aunt Sophie and Uncle Chester for the first time when they came to East Vandergrift to say good-bye to Bupchie. They were on their way back to Poland for good after making America their home since 1894.

For nearly 40 years of marriage, the couple had existed on a small portion of their earnings and saved the remainder. The nest egg was just for this moment in the autumn of life when they could return to their homeland rich. Compared to most people in America and starving folks in Poland, they were very wealthy indeed. Their one daughter was married with children of her own, and they had nothing holding them back from their dream of four decades.

Following a big family reunion, the pair made their way to New York by train and then traveled first class across the Atlantic to buy a farm next to the one Bupchie had bought her mother almost 30 years before.

Consummate letter-writer Uncle Steve kept in touch and remarked how Aunt Sophie and Uncle Chester were the richest people in their parents' village. While Poland, like the rest of the world, suffered during the Depression, Aunt Sophie and Uncle Chester's American dollars went further than they ever could have dreamed. Besides 10 cows, they had a stable of horses and five farm hands who worked for pennies a day.

Uncle Steve was tempted many times, after reading the letters from Poland, to do the same and move back to the old country. The life there sounded marvelous; and he had quite a tidy savings he knew would be a fortune in Poland, but he had become more American than he liked to admit. Here in America he felt like a big man with his tin Lizzy, his large house in Vandergrift, and his steady job in the steel mill. And Steve was tight with a buck, so tight that George Washington screamed with pain, as he liked to brag. Also, he wasn't too sure he'd be happy on a farm, even though Aunt Sophie's letters made it sound as though they were living high off the hog and in grand style, lording it over everyone else in the village.

After the Germans attacked Poland in 1939, the letters stopped reaching Uncle Steve and his to Poland were returned unopened. It wasn't until 1946 that he got word that Aunt Sophie and Uncle Chester were killed by German soldiers when they tried to stop the invading soldiers from taking their cows. Aunt Sophie and Uncle Chester were shot near the barn when they refused to surrender the animals. One bullet each to the head was the response to their resistance.

After the German soldiers left that evening, the villagers came for the bodies and buried them on Bupchie's mother's farm. Bupchie's father had died of a heart attack shortly after the occupation, and our great-grandmother died (some said of a broken heart over the death of Sophie and Chester) a few months after her daughter and son-in-law were buried.

A friend of Uncle Steve went to Poland after the war to check on his family and, while there, went to see about Steve's as well. As soon as he pieced together the story of the deaths of Sophie and Chester over the cows, he wrote to Steve in America with the sad news. Immediately upon getting the wretched report, Steve raced to Bupchie's house to tell her.

Listening to her brother rattle off the appalling account, our grandmother said nothing regarding the death of Sophie and Chester or her father or about the farm being taken over by the Communists after the war. But when he revealed that their mother had died, Bupchie walked out of the kitchen and locked herself in her bedroom for two days and cried. After emerging, she never spoke of her mother again. She was dead and buried and that was the end of it.

The '52 Election

Many people glance back at the early 1950s and tend to remember how everything was so peachy keen and rosy. Including me. Especially me. They were not for those people Senator Joseph McCarthy accused of being Communists. From day one, when he first started pointing his chubby finger at eggheads, bleeding hearts, do-gooders, and fellow-travelers, my mother despised him.

Most East Vandergrifters were Democrats, and many were liberals. Eggheads were smart, educated people, and our teachers and the principal, Mr. Mathews, wanted children to be smart and educated. Did McCarthy only admire stupid, ignorant dolts? The bald-headed senator sure had one heck of a nerve putting down people who did good work, like the women of the Ladies Auxiliary.

"How could anyone listen to that vile man?" Mom commented often. Then, when President Truman decided not to run for re-election in 1952, she surmised, "Harry has had enough of those damn Republicans, always trying to stir up trouble."

The presidential field in both parties was thrown wide open, and the televised nominating conventions let our family observe the political process in action. Kenny and I could not believe that television could be so exciting, with delegates wearing silly hats, waving signs and banners, yelling, brawling, huddling in groups, whispering conspiratorially, and acting like idiots. If we had not seen with our own eyes those important people looking so stupid, we would not have believed it. No wonder our folks loved politics.

All activity in the house stopped during those two conventions. Kenny and I stayed up late and skipped school the next days, because "it was such an important part of American history," as Mrs. Dell explained in notes to Mr. Mathews.

The term "liberal Democrat" to Mom meant fairness for the little guy, strong unions for the hardworking man who labored in the steel mills, and justice for the underdog. The Republican party represented to her the rich getting richer and the poor becoming poorer.

Daddy, who fought overseas in World War II, owned a business, and was crazy about Ike, disagreed. He believed the Republicans were good for business, and what was good for business was good for the country.

The household revolved around the election. As a staunch Democrat, Mommy threw her infinite energy into getting the liberal governor from Illinois elected. Everyone, including our mom, liked Ike, but the Democrats would have to choose the Devil himself as their Presidential nominee for her to vote Republican.

Mommy and Eleanor Roosevelt gave their all to Adlai. Immediately following the Democratic National Convention, Mom phoned the mayor of East Vandergrift, the highest ranking Democrat she personally knew, and offered herself, heart and soul, to help Adlai Stevenson become the next President of the United States. She had nothing bad to say about Eisenhower, except that he was a Republican, but she could not stand his vice-presidential running mate.

When Senator Nixon cunningly went before the television cameras to explain the infamous slush fund, the Welkons and our parents laughed so hard you would have thought they were watching Red Skelton instead of Ike's running mate. When he mentioned his daughter's dog and wife's coat, I thought they were going to fling their coffee cups at the screen. Obviously, though, the rest of the television-viewing nation bought his sorry explanation.

Mommy was fairly sure that if Daddy were going to change his mind and vote for Stevenson, Nixon's shift-eyed speech would be the reason.

A GOP win would put Tricky Dick a single heartbeat away from the oval office.

As the campaign heated up, our excited mother did too. Mayor Kallock placed her in charge of the volunteers for Stevenson in East Vandergrift. She and other Ladies Auxiliary buddies pounded the pavement and doors passing out campaign literature. There was even a Stevenson placard in our front yard. Swept up by the momentum, she vowed to the Democratic Party Chairman for Westmoreland County that every one of the 546 registered voters in East Vandergrift would cast his and her vote for Adlai.

East Vandergrift's registered voters were predominantly Democrat, but General Eisenhower's war experience made him a folk hero to the men of America, our townsmen included. Many lifetime Democrats liked Ike, and Mom's pledge of carrying the whole town for Stevenson was quite a risky vow.

Besides working the phones, she and her volunteers had coffee klatches and on the day of the election carried signs for their witty hero in front of the polling place in town, the fire department, connected to the jail. The Democratic leaders from the surrounding towns called her night and day to ask advice, and the word around town was that she was a shoo-in if she tossed her bonnet in the ring for mayor. Mr. Kallock was worried. To put his mind at ease, she assured him there was no time in her busy schedule of wife, mother, and Auxiliary president to also run the town.

Stevenson was divorced and the Catholic Church came out against him. There was no question of our mother's quitting the Church in protest, but she was pretty steamed: "The Pope better mind his own damn business in Rome and stay the hell out of American politics."

On election day, her volunteers marched, drove old people to the polls, and dragged men just home from the mills out of the clubs and escorted them to the fire station to vote. Election fever spread to the school, where teachers held a mock election. Stevenson received all the

East Vandergrift school children's votes, an indication of how the parents would cast their ballots. It looked like a Stevenson landslide, at least in East Vandergrift. Few believed the experts' predictions of a hands-down win for Eisenhower. People clearly remembered the picture of Truman holding a copy of a newspaper proclaiming Dewey's win the morning Harry beat him in the 1948 election.

"It's not over till the fat lady sings," remarked Daddy again.

Daddy had not said much since Nixon's televised plea of innocence, and his campaigning wife assumed she had his vote. He even stopped wearing the "I Like Ike" button and quietly went with the flow as union leaders and politicos met and plotted and planned in our kitchen. The most repeated phrase in our house during the weeks preceding the election was, "Put on a fresh pot of coffee, someone's knocking at the door."

Stevenson got all but one vote in East Vandergrift. Yep, Daddy confessed, rather stupidly, that he cast his ballot for Ike, never dreaming in a million years, he kept protesting, that Stevenson would possibly get 545, all but one vote in the entire town. Not his intention to spoil the little woman's dream of handing the complete town to Stevenson, he merely preferred the general to the governor and hoped Eisenhower would not die in office. Anyway, he argued, it was a free country and he had every right to vote any way he chose.

As the family watched election returns on television that November night, tension filled the air. Refusing to speak to her repentant hubby, Mom would not even look at him. Taking the blame for Stevenson's loss, Daddy was handed a blanket and a pillow and relegated to the couch as punishment. It sure seemed as if they were going to get a divorce. They did not speak or sleep together for two weeks following the election. Finally, though, after swearing on a Bible that he would never vote for another Republican as long as he lived, Daddy again was allowed to share the marital bed.

To my surprise a few months later, some drunk at a wedding criticized President Eisenhower, and it looked like our angry mother was going to punch his lights out.

"He's our President!" Mommy yelled, with eyes blazing under her neatly trimmed Mamie bangs.

Mom Relives 1945

On the porch, at the kitchen table, or taking a Sunday drive, Mom's narratives of that sorrowful April and joyful August in 1945 were always the same. Here's what she remembered:

"When Franklin Delano Roosevelt died, the country mourned together. Businesses were closed, and churches stayed open for 24 hours a day, from the moment we heard of the President's death until the burial. The stained-glass windows of the Polish Church were draped in black, and there was an empty coffin at the foot of the altar. People cried in the streets, no music played, and the clubs officially closed. Every single person in East Vandergrift attended one of the three funeral Masses observed in town. The immigrants and their grown children prayed for the soul of the man who, by betraying his class, became the protector of the poor.

"F.D.R. died before the war ended. A few months later, President Truman made that world-shaking decision. When we dropped the bombs on Hiroshima and Nagasaki, I did not realize how bad it was. I thought, as everybody else in America, that we just had to win the war. Our boys kept dying and the Japanese kept fighting. They would not give up. When the Emperor finally surrendered, Americans danced in the streets. The fighting was over at last. Our men were coming home. People went wild with excitement. Places were jiving.

"Barbara thought the celebration and festivities were for her. You see, the war ended on August 15, 1945, her third birthday. She was thrilled watching people dance in the streets, honk their car horns, and kiss each other. I'm sure your sister will never have another birthday quite like her third one."

Timmy's Loss

The first time I had any feelings of loss was in the second grade. I noticed Timmy staring out a large window in the classroom with his hands in his pockets. Cindy, Francis, and I were sitting in the back of the room coloring and laughing; but I kept glancing over at Timmy, whose head barely reached the window ledge. Bathed in sunshine, he gazed out the window, lost in his own small world. It was his first day back to school since his mother had died of leukemia a week earlier. Her death came six months after the doctor discovered that she had this strange-sounding disease.

I put the crayon down and observed Timmy, framed in the window. Imagining my own mother leaving me forever, I felt his pain.

Daddy Goes Bankrupt

In 1952 our safe world came crashing down when Daddy went bankrupt two days before Christmas. Only six months earlier it seemed as though he really was on his way to that first million when he jumped with both feet into the vending machine business. After seeing the potential in the growing customer service, he sold the idea of placing his vending machines in various facilities where large groups of people congregated and wanted a place close by to get a snack.

All the gut work was Daddy's responsibility: filling the machines, repairing them if they broke, and counting and rolling all the coins. Of the total take, 25 percent went directly to the facilities that housed the machines. It was the easiest sell in the world to surrounding towns' school principals, gas station owners, and motel chain proprietors, who loved the extra income without doing any of the work.

The vending machine was a new idea and quite a gamble, but the bank thought Daddy was worth the risk and loaned him the money for all the equipment needed for all those new customers. Almost immediately the candy machines started doing really well. Daddy and his kids obviously weren't the only ones with a sweet tooth. Calculating that within a year he would recoup the investment, he poured the profits back into the business and bought more machines.

Aunt Veronica worked the phones, setting up appointments for new outlets. Besides her regular duties as secretary-bookkeeper-confidant, she serviced the machinery as well.

There was no stopping our pop, who donated to charities and spoke at Chamber of Commerce and civic luncheons. Town leaders asked his opinion on just about everything to do with the Vandergrift business community. Everyone took notice of him, including the Mafia.

The Don from the Family's headquarters in New Kensington sent a lackey, the Vandergrift chief of police, to ask for a cut of Daddy's profit. The Western Pennsylvania Mafia, with connections in Cuba's gambling casinos and later gunrunning for Batista, had the pinball, slot machine, and keyboard enterprises tied up. Vending machines, the Mafia bosses felt, also fit into their domain, now that Daddy had shown how lucrative they were.

Daddy handed the uptown police chief a 5-pound box of candy with refusal of "protection" and laughed while telling Aunt Veronica about the top cop's proposal. She did not think it was amusing. Neither did my dad when unknown assailants vandalized half the machines beyond repair the next day.

Within hours of the destruction, this time not removing his hat, Chief Guido made another social call. After Daddy kicked the crooked flatfoot out, without a parting gift-box, he got word that unidentified hoods had demolished the rest of the vending machines, almost everything he owned.

Deciding to fight back, he borrowed money from Bupchie and Uncle Caz to make loan payments and begin from scratch. Without any questioning of how or when he could repay them, Bupchie and Uncle Caz generously lent him the money.

Bookkeeper Aunt Veronica selflessly stopped drawing a salary. She said months later that she didn't mention it to Daddy at the time because, "I didn't want to burden him with mundane office procedures. He had enough on his mind. Besides, I had money saved and free room and board at home."

With five new vending machines standing tall in the office, Daddy was ready to begin again, this time deeply in debt but more determined than ever.

The candy machines were barely out of crates when an anonymous caller gave Daddy the final ultimatum, "Pay us, or get out of our way, or the next thing annihilated will be your family." The sinister stranger on the phone rattled off our names and ages. Our dad knew he was beaten when the gangsters discovered his Achilles' heel.

When Daddy lost heart, he hopelessly started to lose what was left of the business. Wanting to hang on till Christmas, he knew it would mean sacrificing the house, his castle, our home.

That Yuletide, with the magnanimous help of Uncle Caz's paycheck and loving support, Mommy made sure there were presents under the tree. In a bright green box with a big red bow was a neat Viewmaster for Jimmy. Thrilled when she tore open her presents, Barbara "indubitably" loved her Davega roller skates and skating skirt. Kenny's face lit up brighter than the 7-foot, decorated spruce tree when he unwrapped the coin and stamp collecting books. I followed the easy-to-understand booklet and grandly plunked out "Mary Had a Little Lamb" on my gift, a toy piano. Tears swelled in Daddy's eyes when Mommy kissed him and handed him the new best-seller by Norman Vincent Peale, *The Power of Positive Thinking*.

We kids pitched in the money Bupchie gave us for our parents' gifts. Future-lawyer Barbara bought our mom what they both loved most— a book, *Jefferson and the Rights of Man*, by Dumas Malone. Barbara was dying to read it when Mom was finished. Frustrated-artist Dad got a paint-by-number kit, depicting a colorful fall scene in the woods. Kenny and I helped Jimmy pick it out.

Tears streamed down the breadwinner of the family's face as he sat with his wife and soul mate on the couch contentedly watching us play with our toys while Gene Autry sang "Frosty the Snowman," his two-year-old hit, on the radio.

Then, out of the blue, Mom wistfully and softly said, more to herself than to any of us, "I'm the happiest woman alive."

Until New Year's, we celebrated what seemed like the best Christmas holiday in the world. The future looked bleak, but (as Daddy kept pointing out) the present was wonderful.

With more teardrops in his eyes, he proclaimed, "We have more than money can buy; we have each other. Nobody can ever take that away from us."

When the holidays were over, however, Daddy lost all hope. So depressed, he could barely get out of bed in the mornings. The only money coming in was from Jimmy's paper route; Bupchie and Uncle Caz provided our food and paid the utilities; Mommy bought nothing but the bare necessities with the little money she had secretly squirreled away. As poor as church mice for six months, that's what we were.

Then one day, while shooting the breeze with a business colleague, Daddy spotted a new piece of equipment on his friend's desk. Called a "checkwriter," it was a mechanical protection against forgeries. Writing down the company name and address, by the end of the day Daddy signed on with the sales force. As an independent distributor, again he was in business for himself, and within a year, he was the number-one salesperson for Pennsylvania and on top of the world again. The happy-go-lucky, whimsical Daddy we missed was back.

Aunt Veronica
Goes Away

While our dad was getting his life back on track after losing the candy business, Aunt Veronica went to Detroit to stay with her sister Helen and find work in the bustling motor vehicle industry. When people mentioned Motown then, they were referring to the auto (motor) town, not the soul capital of the world.

Armed with outstanding secretarial skills, Aunt Veronica left with one suitcase. Getting a job was easy; finding a place of her own was going to be somewhat more difficult. With its influx of workers drawn to the expanding economy, Detroit had a severe rental-housing short-age. Mom was to send Aunt Veronica's other possessions along after she was settled into her own place, if she were lucky enough to find one.

Fortunately for Aunt Veronica, she did not have most of her belong-ings, because within a week she returned home without even the one suitcase she did take. What she brought back was a bag of wrinkled, teenage boy's clothes and 15-year-old Cousin Tommy, Aunt Helen's son. When Daddy picked her up at the bus station, there she was, with the newest East Vandergrift resident. Surprised to see his sister-in-law return without warning, Daddy listened and tried to console Aunt Veronica. Tommy sat on the curb sobbing.

Tommy's stepfather had abused him almost nightly by tying him to a chair and beating him with a strap. The first night Aunt Veronica heard the commotion, she ran into the room and stopped Helen's hus-band, who drunkenly screamed at her then, like the bully he was, sulked off to bed. The next morning, Helen ordered her sister to either mind her own business or get out of the house.

That second night the same scene took place; but this time, after Aunt Veronica stopped the battering, she went to her room and waited, fully clothed, until 4:00 a.m. Then she slipped into Tommy's room, whispered for him to get dressed, tossed a few of his possessions in a paper bag, and grabbed her coat and purse. Together, frightened aunt and whimpering nephew hiked 10 miles to the Greyhound bus station, where she bought two one-way tickets to Pittsburgh and prayed that Helen's husband would not wake until they were safely on the bus heading east.

Bupchie cried while hearing the story; but her tears quickly dried and anger replaced them when Aunt Helen phoned to tell her to send Tommy back or else she was going to bring kidnapping charges against Aunt Veronica. Bupchie, not one easily intimidated by anyone, warned her daughter that if she or her husband tried in any way to get Tommy back, she would buy a gun and shoot both of them. From that moment on, Tommy had a new home in East Vandergrift safely under Bupchie's wing.

Cousin Tommy lived with our grandmother but spent most of his time at our house playing with Jimmy. Mommy helped him with his school work, Father Shezocki made him an altar boy, and at long last he received the loving support he craved but never had in Detroit with his abusive stepfather and cowering mother.

With Tommy safe at last, Aunt Veronica headed to Baltimore to look for work and stay with her brother, Uncle Joe. That journey was so successful that every time she called it seemed as if her life was getting better and better. She landed a secretarial position in the shipyards the first day searching for a job. The second week there she began dating her boss, a divorced man with a son almost her age. Her weekly phone calls were crammed with wonderful news concerning her new friends and Herb, Herb, Herb.

It was bad enough that Aunt Veronica went away, but now Kenny and I had to share her with some guy, besides Uncle Joe's three kids, Billy, Trixie, and Stevie. (Trixie's real name was Irene as her mother's, but everyone called her Trixie to eliminate any confusion. Go figure.)

Aunt Veronica's letters and phone calls made the Herb relationship sound quite serious; and within a few months of her leaving, they were engaged to be married. Our parents were ecstatic; Bupchie was angry that the chosen one was divorced; but Kenny and I were down in the dumps, because her marriage meant she really was gone for good and would never again be part of our daily lives. Feeling cheated, we envied our cousins in Baltimore who got to see Aunt Veronica all the time.

Besides being godmother to us both, she was the only adult we knew who acted like a kid. Although she may have teased unmercifully, she never talked down to us and invariably laughed at the same things we found hilarious. There was no replacing her, and it was hard for the two of us to get into the swing of the wedding planning. Mom was going to be the matron of honor, and Herb's son was to be the best man.

Two cars set off from East Vandergrift for the trek to Baltimore and the wedding. Daddy drove the lead one with Mommy, Bupchie, Jimmy, and Barbara. Uncle Caz, Kenny, and I trailed in the one driven by Uncle Caz's new girlfriend, Emily.

It sure seemed like wedding bells for Uncle Caz as well, judging by the looks Emily gave him the whole trip. I thought we were headed over some of those mountains during the day-long jaunt. The smitten driver never seemed to have her eyes on the road in front of her. In addition to loving her reckless driving, Kenny liked her a lot, but I needed time to see more of her before I decided how I felt. One thing I plainly saw, though, was that Uncle Caz was ga ga over her and practically speechless in her company.

We stopped for meals and snacks at Howard Johnson's and for Barbara to throw up. She always got car-sick. Kenny and I hated it when she upchucked on us on visits to Grandma Dell's. It was a relief not being in the same vehicle with her, especially on such a long junket.

The nine Pennsylvania pilgrims stayed at Uncle Joe's house, where the reception was also held. A cook in the Navy during the war, he did all the preparations for the feast-dinner. Extraordinary food, spirited conversations, plenty of pop, and loving relatives. What a remarkable wedding!

Cousin Trixie and I became good friends; so did Cousin Billy and Kenny. After dinner, our cousins let us watch the guy across the alley from their bathroom window expose himself, as he did at the same time every evening.

Aunt Veronica, the blushing bride, threw tradition out the window and ate at the pushed-together card tables with the kids. Uncle Herb was a living doll. Seated at the main table next to Bupchie, he blew kisses at his wife during the meal, nine whole courses.

Kenny and I shot most of the candid wedding pictures, and our favorite was of Bupchie in front of empty whiskey bottles. To this day, Barbara is still upset with that picture and has asked me hundreds of times why in the world we took it.

Our second best-liked photo was of Uncle (it was easy calling him that after the first moment we met him) Herb's sisters sitting on Big Jim's lap. The women were as much fun as Aunt Veronica, and we adopted them as our aunts. We also started referring to Emily as "aunt" after she caught Kenny and Billy sneaking a bottle of beer from the kitchen and didn't squeal.

Billy and Kenny became real pals. Four years older, Cousin Billy had Kenny's same reckless personality. They were twin, adorable devils when together. Most of their energy was expended harassing Trixie and me. After refueling with a handful of cookies, they played Civil War games. Billy was a Rebel and Kenny, the Yankee. The energized boys fought with water pistols; and one of Billy's friends, a colored boy, was the slave who Kenny finally freed.

What an astounding week that was! We stayed through the 4th of July. Good ole new Aunt Emily gave the boys firecrackers, and kept her mouth shut about who in the neighborhood was setting them off. How could any kid in his right mind not love that woman?

Uncle Joe, who owned a taxi cab that he won in a postwar raffle for returning GI's, took Kenny and Billy to work during the visit. It was amusing to watch the three of them in the front seat wearing cab driv- ers' hats. Of course,Kenny sat in the middle controlling the meter. After a week of gabbing with Marylander passengers, my brother decided that he fancied the way people from Baltimore talked; and he picked up the accent, then repeated to me, in the newly acquired affectation, swear- words and dirty jokes Billy taught him.

The newlyweds honeymooned at their new home four houses down from Uncle Joe's, and the path between the two was in continual use. There were duo pots of coffee going during the days and nights filled with nostalgic adult conversations, and there was a ton of remarkable eats cooked by Uncle Joe. Daddy could not get enough of those crab cakes and soft-shell crabs that he heaped on his plate.

It was a week-long party mostly held in the back yards. When the mosquitoes chased everyone indoors, the festivities switched to the playroom at Aunt Veronica and Uncle Herb's or around the dining room table at Uncle Joe and Aunt Irene's.

Not only did we celebrate a wedding and light up the sky with 4th of July sparklers, but Uncle Herb also ushered the kids to Washington, D.C. and conducted a tour while his bride and the matron of honor washed, hung, and ironed clothes. The trip to the nation's capital was really the women's idea to get rid of kids they knew would use the sheets on the clothesline as part of the game of hide-and-seek.

As we lingered for more smooches and fond embraces when it was time to head back to Pennsylvania, it was clear the Baltimore-East Vandergrift ties would never break. Not losing Aunt Veronica as Kenny and I had first imagined, we gained Uncle Herb, his sisters and son, Uncle Joe's whole family, and the complete city of Baltimore.

After Aunt Veronica's marriage, there were many pleasant excursions to Baltimore for holidays, Christenings, vacations, weddings, and impromptu family reunions, just because too much time had passed and everyone missed each other.

Romantic Daddy

No matter when or why Mom and Dad had a fight, he got over it in five minutes and spent hours or days trying to make her forgive him. He phoned. She hung up. He sent flowers. She returned them to the florist. Finally, he tossed his hat in the front door, and if she did not throw it back outside, he knew it was safe to enter.

Once, after a nasty argument concerning his mother, he flipped his fedora in and it was hurled back flat as a board. So mad, she stomped on it until she ruined it, but the old man was prepared. He pitched in, to Kenny's delight, toys from the five-and-ten: a fireman's, policeman's, cowboy's, straw, and top hat, followed by a derby and dunce cap. His coy wife tried not to laugh, but couldn't help herself. Opening the door, she put her hands on her hips and let him in. Daddy dropped to his knees. Wearing an Indian chief's bonnet, he kissed her from her toes up to her pursed lips.

Mommy had Daddy wrapped around her little finger, and she knew it. She could make him jump through hoops, and when she kiddingly said "jump," he asked, "How high, Babycakes?" After she forgave him, he claimed he was the happiest and luckiest man alive. Not able to keep his hands off her, he swore he worshipped the very ground she walked on.

Autumn Leaves

In the fall, Cindy, her brother Lenny, Kenny, and I gathered horsenuts that fell from the trees and made necklaces and bracelets from the hard brown seed inside the soft, green outer shell. Cindy and Lenny's grandparents, the Urbanskis, had one of the largest trees in town, across the street from our house to the right.

Kenny and I helped the grandkids sweep and gather their grandparents' leaves. What fun that was! We all loved playing with the rake, jumping in the dried leaves, and filling the wooden bushel baskets. After toting the baskets full of colored leaves to the back yard where Grandpa Urbanski burned them in a big metal barrel, we sat on their front porch glider and sipped steaming hot chocolate, waiting for the cookies to come out of the oven.

Number, Please?

Cindy's Aunt Tess was a telephone operator. Before the town had direct dialing, it was exciting to personally know the person behind the official voice, "Number, please?"

Everyone had party lines and had to be careful what they said on the phone, because it was very likely that someone in the neighborhood was listening in. If no one from the other five families who shared our phone line was eavesdropping, Mom was certain that Tess (snapping her gum in the phone company office uptown) was for sure, especially when someone sneezed and the two people who were having a supposedly private conversation simultaneously said, "Gesundheit," and then there was a click.

Any time there was a death, birth, scandal, or juicy tidbit of tabloidish news, Tess was the first to learn about it and would cut in on people's phone conversations to tell them the latest, scooping the town's main gossips, Cazzy (Cindy's uncle, no relation to Tess) and Sousha.

Vandergrift Lane

The only way in and out of town was via Vandergrift Lane, a very steep hill impossible to make up or down during snowstorms. That's when the teachers and principal, Mr. Mathews, parked their cars at the top and walked down. After school, kids used it for sled riding.

Miss Claypool, the first grade teacher, lived at the top of the Lane. Coming down into East Vandergrift proper, perched on the right, was the Italian cobbler's shop. Next to it sat an old beat-up house. It was vacant most of the time; but for a short period, a family on relief took up residence there.

Kathy Brown, a pretty blond girl in my first grade class, lived there with her mother and six brothers and sisters. The walls in their shabby home were bare, except for peeling wallpaper. When Daddy took me there to play with her, he dropped off baskets of clothes (some brand-new) and food for the family. They were very poor, and her mother always seemed sad. One day, without any good-byes, they left town. I never saw Kathy again.

In the middle of the incline was Lane Inn, a bar owned by the Zalenski family. Benny was in Kenny's class; Bonny, in mine; Chrissy, in Barbara's; and Danny, in Jimmy's. Mr. Zalenski was a union official and worked in the steel mill. His wife ran the beer garden, which had a bricked patio where the Zalenski kids had birthday parties.

Not quite 200 feet from Zalenski's bar, Vandergrift Lane twisted quickly to the left. The first sharp left after that was Quay Street, where we lived. There were several accidents at the point when the Lane abruptly changed course.

Once, some teenager was delivering cupcakes to a church bake sale and had the store-bought goodies on the passenger seat. The cupcakes slipped as she negotiated the bend; and instead of letting them drop to the car floor, she let go of the steering wheel and reached to save the desserts from falling off the seat. She smashed right into the rabbit hutch and vegetable garden in Louis Garleck's yard, which was in a direct line from the top of Vandergrift Lane. If someone rolled a boulder down the hill, it would have crashed right into their property. Those poor bunnies. Teenagers honked their horns and scared the crap out of them all the time.

The Lane went on past Quay Street and crossed over McKinley Avenue. This was the corner where the big boys hung out, gathering there at all hours of the day and night, smoking cigarettes and voicing lies about getting on base with their girlfriends. The truth was that the only place any of the guys scored was down the field during a baseball game. Their favorite meeting spot was in front of the Polish grocery store. People called it that because the owner was a woman from Poland. On the corner across the street was Bartow's, a variety store, where kids bought their comic books then sat on the porch steps to read them.

Mommy often sent Kenny to the corner to tell Jimmy to come home for dinner. If he wasn't there, he was usually shooting baskets in the Catholic school playground behind the Slovak Church across from their hangout.

Crossing over McKinley Avenue, Vandergrift Lane went past the Gulf gas station, the only one in town. It had the lone Coke machine in East Vandergrift. The Lane then ran smack dab into the tracks of the Pennsylvania Railroad on the far side of Railroad Street.

The Big Blue Bell

Christmas was three weeks away, and the fourth grade pupils were decorating the classroom. Mrs. Bell, our teacher, decided to cover the eight windows with students' holiday scenes on large brown paper treated with linseed oil so that the color-chalked pictures would stand out brightly with the help of classroom lights.

With 12 kids in the class and only eight windows, the fourth grade students would vote for the lucky designs to be hung in the windows. From those chosen and displayed, the entire school would then vote for the best three by standing across the street and looking up at the second floor classroom windows.

The only artistic ability I had was for tracing. I was a great outliner, big deal. Cindy, on the other hand, could draw anything, from faces and animals to buildings and landscapes.

Huddled in a corner, she and Francis Pluciennik were deciding what to depict. They were the best artists in the class, and everyone was positive they would win before we even opened the gallon tin cans of linseed oil. To prove us right, Cindy did a preliminary sketch on a piece of scrap paper, and her rough copy was as good as any Hallmark card I had ever seen. It made me realize how useless it was to even try. I even contemplated asking Mrs. Bell if I could do something else, maybe write a Christmas poem instead; but I knew she'd say "no" and then give me a pep talk about how we can't be good at everything, but we should never give up before we start and all that garbage teachers and other grownups pile on kids.

I must have looked down in the dumps compared to Cindy who was humming "Hernando's Hideaway" enthusiastically, because Mrs. Bell called me to her desk and asked what I was going to draw. Nonchalantly, I remarked that I couldn't think of anything that would look like it was supposed to be. Smiling, she suggested I pick out a small object and enlarge it; when people looked up from McKinley Avenue, they would know instantly what it was from that great distance.

Bingo! Students would not judge the window displays by how intricate they were, but by their simplicity. Purposefully walking back to my desk, I started contemplating Christmasy things. An enlarged tree ornament or anything that usually graced the front of a Christmas card seemed like just the ticket, as my pop used to say. At that moment, a funeral next door at the Lithuanian Church was ending with the bells slowly ringing. My inspiration. I glanced up at our homeroom teacher and grinned. This was going to be easy. For the first time I became excited about art, which I usually hated more than music class when we had to sing. I couldn't carry a tune to save my life and even mouthed the words to "Happy Birthday" at parties.

Vincent Gonka, the dumbest kid in class and a lousy artist, sauntered over to ask what he should do. I suggested that he sketch a snowman: three circles (little one for the head, larger one for the middle section, and the largest for the bottom), two black eyes, top hat, orange carrot nose, and red mouth. Drawing it quickly on scrap paper, I told him to do exactly that but to make it bigger to fit the window.

I decided to create my bell blue with snowflakes cascading around it. Piece of cake. After drawing the outline with a pencil, I soon finished and started filling it in with blue chalk.

Cindy, meanwhile, was doing the complete Nativity scene; everything was from her memory of manger scenes. In it were the three wise men, shepherds, sheep, angels overhead with trumpets, palm trees, cows, Mary, Joseph, and Jesus in a manger. All the animals and people had halos.

I whipped up the bell in record time and it looked really swell, if I do say so myself. Vincent was having difficulty with his snowman's nose. I went over to help him. White was such a boring color, but we were having fun filling the blank spaces and watching a snowman emerge. Sitting on the floor chatting about what we wanted for Christmas was enjoyable too. Mrs. Bell strolled over to praise Vincent's dandy snowman and to tell me how much she loved my bell. Everything we did was remarkable to our teacher.

Timmy was constructing a Christmas tree with colorful decorations and popcorn strung around it. He figured out the distance factor without Mrs. Bell's help. The other kids were busy as bees, drawing tiny designs and small figures on their large papers.

Still going strong and completely absorbed with her picture, Cindy didn't even notice that the rest of us had finished. Mrs. Bell and the whole class formed a circle around her on the floor and watched in awe as she drew complicated figures with detailed facial expressions. Maybe it was my imagination, but Mary looked a lot like Cindy and an angel appeared similar to me. Joseph resembled Francis with a beard, and baby Jesus had Timmy's face. Thank God Cindy covered the bottom half of the infant Savior with a white cloth. Timmy would have died of embarrassment if she had drawn a naked Timmy-Jesus.

Her stunning crèche was comparable to a photograph of that first Christmas morning, if cameras had been invented way, way back then. Every color of chalk dust covered Cindy, and sweat ran down her face, the drops enlarging her freckles. Knowing she had created a masterpiece, she signed it at the bottom. When Cindy dramatically dotted the last vowel in Petrouski, we burst into applause.

My other classmates produced some pretty impressive pictures. The scene of kids sledding down McKinley Avenue by Sandra McKee was really neat.

Francis drew the Polish Church: a procession of a fat priest (Father Shezocki would have been ticked off if he knew) and 25 altar boys, birds flying in the belfry, airplanes overhead, a paperboy at the corner, and a town drunk hanging onto a lamppost.

One ice skating scene was a superb idea, but Richie Kallock drew all the figures the same way, in the same pose, facing the same direction, as though they were the Rockettes on the frozen-over Kiskiminetas River.

His entry was sketched and colored well; however, he lost a window position, it was quite clear, to Irene Bliazes, who lived near the river and created a similar theme. In hers the skaters were Santa Clauses, all in different sizes and shapes: fat Santas, skinny ones, tall and short ones. Some had fallen and were sprawled on their bottoms with feet outstretched; others were doing figure 8's. Three Santas were on the mark and appeared to be ready to race. Two St. Nicks were ice fishing, and one was skating away, pursued by six wee elves with pointed ears, hats, and skates.

Bonny Zalenski conceived the Christmas party her parents threw for their regular customers and friends every year in the Lane Inn, the beer garden they owned. Stick figures perched on stools, clutching bottles of beer, while her mother, or a stick supposed to be Mrs. Zalenski, was behind the bar pulling a lever on a keg of beer. The best thing in the picture, though, was a juke box with a wreath on the top and music notes floating above it. One stick figure sat at a table with his head on his arms, obviously passed out, and another held on to the door while throwing up. The bar was decorated with mistletoe and multicolored crepe paper, and a blazing fire roared in the fireplace. In a corner was a festooned Christmas tree that reached the ceiling, making it about 14-foot tall. Dozens of Yuletide cards lined the door frames and edges of tables.

Deciding to add to the festivities, we kids gave names to some figures, people we knew who frequented Lane Inn and were known to drink a little too much. As we yelled out patrons' names, Mrs. Bell admonished us. "Now, now. No gossiping. It is not polite."

The lucky eight pieces of art were selected by secret ballot and taped to the windows. Before going outside, we trooped to the bathroom and water fountains, boys and girls segregated much the same as coloreds and whites in the South.

While waiting in line outside the girls' room, I spotted Frankie Poleski coming out of Miss Ceraso's second grade classroom and called him over to ask for his vote. Without any coaxing, he said, "Okay." He reminded me then, as well as now, of Baby Huey, big and gentle. I rustled up some more votes in the bathroom.

Then, Kenny came out of the classroom and paced over to the fountain, where I was getting ready to lean down for a quick gulp. I let him cut in front of me since no teacher was watching and asked him to vote for my picture. Bending down, he took a long deep drink, then raised his head, turned, and promised he would—for a dime, that is. I couldn't believe the gall and loudly protested. After shushing me (he was, after all, taking a sip from the girls' fountain), he dropped his offer to a nickel. We shook hands to cement the deal, and he swiftly walked—no running in the halls—to the second grade classroom.

Not a second later, Barbara strolled by on her way to the principal's office on an errand for Miss Kaib, the music teacher. I quickly whispered to her about the contest. Patting my head, she said she would vote for the best one. I knew she would vote for me and just said that to look impartial and fair-minded to classmates who were eavesdropping.

It was annoying sometimes to have a sister who acted like King Solomon and a brother who resembled an extortionist.

Hey, I wasn't the only one making deals in the hallway. Everybody in the fourth grade had a brother or a sister in the building and was trading favors for votes. The competitive spirit was alive and doing well in the East Vandergrift public school system. Winning was everything, in spite of what teachers said.

Cindy was behaving so blasé and cocky that when Judy, her sister in Barbara's seventh grade class, asked which illustration was hers, Cindy answered, with eyelashes fluttering, "You'll know the moment you look up at the windows." The best artist in the whole school, she won every contest in town starting from the time she first learned how to hold a pencil before she could crawl or talk.

The fourth grade class walked across the street, stood in line in front of Laura Beck's house, and looked up. Mrs. Beck came outside to find out which of the pictures was her daughter's. When Laura somberly told her that it hung inside the classroom, Mrs. Bell invited the slightly disappointed mom to come in and see how pretty it was, just like all the other runners-up. Mrs. Beck said she would, right before the end of school with cookies for the class. It was not in the least bit odd to have mothers visit the classrooms bearing gifts of baked goods, bringing their children umbrellas or sweaters because the weather looked threatening, or merely dropping in to say hello.

As we gaped up at the windows, I could not believe my eyes. Wait a minute. It was even better than I had imagined. The only pictures that resembled anything at all were my bell, Vincent's snowman, and Timmy's Christmas tree. The other chalk-covered, linseed-oiled paper pictures looked like mosaics; they were masses of bright colors.

Mrs. Bell chatted with Mrs. Beck while we 12 marched into school. Timmy, Vincent, and I held hands and smiled, walking ahead of the rest. Bringing up the caboose, Cindy dragged her body up the stairs as though she had just gotten word that her entire family had been murdered and her dog Snoopy was being held hostage. Knowing there was no way she would win the window art contest, her face was numb with shock.

The first order of business: We cleaned the room and ourselves. A while later, Mrs. Bell went from classroom to classroom, escorting each group downstairs and across the street in front of Laura Beck's house to vote. It took half an hour for the other seven grades to look at the afternoon's work and another 10 minutes for Mrs. Bell to tabulate votes.

Finally, Mrs. Bell walked in and announced the winners. Third place went to Vincent Gonka's snowman. He was so overjoyed that he cried.

Second prize was Timmy's Christmas tree, and I won first prize with my blue bell. It was the first and only art contest I had won in my life, and the first time Vincent ever won anything.

Cindy, my best and dearest girlfriend, yelled, "It's not fair. It's just not fair."

Listening to her complain, I understood her bitterness at not winning with her elaborate nativity scene, which was good enough to hang in an art gallery; but, as most wise people realize, sometimes life isn't fair. What's more, we learned an important lesson that day. You know how the old saying goes—all's fair in love and war and second floor window Christmas art contests.

The Fourth Grade
Teacher

Mrs. Bell, the fourth grade teacher since our mom's school days, had two claims to fame. After her 25th wedding anniversary, she wrote a letter to the Maytag Company to let them know that her washing machine, a wedding present, was still going strong. In response to her note of praise, the company featured her in a full-page magazine ad. There she was in her flowing white gown, with a copy of her letter at the bottom of the page, as a testament to the durability of their equipment and, I guess, her marriage as well.

The other thing that made Mrs. Bell a celebrity in our eyes was that her father had been a close friend of George McMurtry, one of the founders of the Apollo Iron and Steel Company and the town of Vandergrift. It just went to show what a plum teaching assignment the East Vandergrift school was since the illustrious McMurtry had a friend whose daughter chose to teach there.

The Polish Baron

Kids were first introduced to these moving words in Miss Ceraso's second grade classroom:

Here at our sea-washed, sunset gates shall stand
A mighty woman with a torch whose flame
Is the imprisoned lightning, and her name,
Mother of Exiles. From her beacon-hand
Glows world-wide welcome, and her mild eyes command
The air-bridged harbor that twin cities frame.
"Keep, ancient lands, your storied pomp," cries she
With silent lips. "Give me your tired, your poor,
Your huddled masses yearning to breathe free,
The Wretched refuse of your teeming shore,
Send these, the homeless, tempest-tossed, to me:
I lift my lamp beside the golden door."

Miss Ceraso's parents were immigrants from Italy, and she loved reciting Emma Lazarus's poignant poem that brought tears to even the most obstinate or apathetic second-graders.

Miss Adalgisa Ceraso, the second grade teacher, and her sister, Miss Evelyn Ceraso, the third grade teacher, were wild about the history of the immigrants. They especially appreciated hearing of the reasons people left their homelands and came to the new world.

Their father, Luigi, or Louis in English, left Italy because (it was rumored) he shot a man in a duel for the honor of woman. Sneaking out of Naples under cover of night, so the story went, he caught the first boat to America and made his way to Pittsburgh in 1880. Soon becoming a labor gang boss, he helped build hospitals and schools in the city. After a few years, he read in a newspaper about the new town of Vandergrift and decided to try his luck at steel-making. Within an hour of entering town, he had a job. Then, he got a room in a boarding house with 10 other Italian immigrant men in the heights' section of Vandergrift. As more Italians came to town, they too settled in the heights, which instead of forming its own community, stayed a part of Vandergrift.

Luigi Ceraso married, bought a house, and proceeded to have 12 children. All the kids went to college. Six became lawyers, four taught school, and two practiced medicine. The Ceraso sisters were the first two Italian-American women teachers in Western Pennsylvania and were extremely proud of their father's accomplishments.

Jealous people, however, gossiped that there was no way in blazes a guy working in the steel mill in the early 1900s could afford to later send 12 kids to college and beyond to law and medical schools without mob assistance. There, they swore, had to be some mob money involved; but our dad said that was mean and petty talk. Daddy had it on the highest authority that there was never a penny of Mafia loot that touched Luigi's hands. Too bad. Mafia connections would have certainly made Luigi Ceraso sound even more exciting than he already was, considering the duel and everything.

When Miss Ceraso, second grade, asked Kenny's class to do a family history to be presented in front of the students, Kenny wanted to make sure there was some thrilling stuff, so he asked his old man for the details. Even at an early age, my younger brother was well aware that our daddy-o tended to exaggerate a bit. Daddy didn't disappoint and disclosed the whole truth "may lightning strike me dead if I'm lying."

I'll let fanciful Father tell this story in his own way. I can still hear the twinkle in his voice: "First of all, Dell isn't our real name. It was changed by my father before I was born, and all I know is, you can't just say it, you sneeze it. Also, Dutch Schultz, the famous gangster, is my uncle. I met him in Chicago while I was out there working as a crime reporter.

Hail fellow, well met. Begged me to join his gang, but I wanted to return to college. That's about it for my family's history. Now, let me tell you about your mother's. Now there's an absorbing story. It seems that your mother's father, your real grandfather, who died before you were born, was the oldest son of a baron in Poland. The family had a castle, a stable of Arabian horses, and hundreds of people who worked their lands. He also had dozens of servants in the castle polishing all that silver and gold and chandeliers. The castle needed many servants because it had 20 bedrooms.

"Your great-grandfather, the baron, hung out with royalty from all over Europe. When he and the baroness, your great-grandmother, were in London shopping for diamonds, they'd stop by Windsor Castle to have tea with the queen and king.

"The baron and his sons (there were four younger than your grandfather) went hunting all the time and never had to work. One day your grandfather went duck stalking in the rain and caught a bad cold that turned into pneumonia. He was put to bed immediately, and a doctor from the village was called in. He was in really bad shape and it appeared to be a matter of days before he would croak.

"His poor mother, the baroness, who loved him the best, was grief-stricken and had to be put to bed with a sedative to calm her down. The baron, who also loved his oldest son the most, was determined to save him. Marching to the servants' quarters near the kitchen, he asked his chief cook if she knew of anyone who could nurse his son back to health. As luck would have it, her youngest daughter, your Bupchie, was resting in the kitchen warming herself near the fireplace and stood up and said she could. Only 15 years old and very, very pretty, she was as sexy as Betty Grable.

"The baron took her by the hand and led her upstairs to the bedroom next to his dying son, where she was to remain until the boy either got better or died. As ordered by the powerful aristocrat, your Bupchie stayed with the baron's son night and day, spoon feeding him cabbage soup, taking his temperature, bathing him, holding his hand, and singing to him. Slowly, day by day, week by week, his condition improved and he became stronger and stronger.

"Upon seeing his son get better, the baron decided to run over to Estonia and Latvia on a business trip and was gone three months. When he returned, his son was as good as new. He also discovered your grandmother still living in the castle, because she was too sick to get out of bed. As it turned out, she had a horrendous case of morning sickness and was in the family way with your Uncle Walter.

"Well, in short, the baron threw a fit and banished his son and your grandmother from the castle. Disowning your grandfather, the nobleman swore that the young man, and soon to be father, would never see a penny of any inheritance. The second son in line would take the baron's title and all the lands when the baron died.

"The baroness was grief-stricken again and again had to be put to bed with a sedative to calm her nerves, because she wasn't used to so much excitement. Meanwhile, your grandfather and grandmother quickly eloped to Warsaw, honeymooned at the Baltic Sea, and hopped on the first ship to America. They made their way to Morning Sun and lived happily ever after. Oh, yes, and one other thing. The baron's name was Kenny."

When Kenny sat down after telling the class his family history, Miss Ceraso, second grade, asked him who told him the things he had related and laughed when Kenny mentioned it was Daddy. Knowing our parents fairly well, she had been teased by Daddy at many parties and PTA meetings.

Kenny was crestfallen when Miss Ceraso laughed. Because of the reaction written all over his face, she quickly assured him that his history assignment had been wonderful. Furthermore, she remarked that his father should write a novel some day, preferably one that included more about the Polish baron Kenny and his castle. Sweetheart that she was, Miss Ceraso then turned to the class and said that Kenny deserved a round of applause for a fine history presentation.

Kenny was flushed with excitement when he ran home at lunchtime to tell what happened in school. I thought it was a great story. Barbara and Jimmy thought it was a scream. The official family historian, however, was not amused by Daddy's history lesson and clued us in (again) on the true story of Bupchie's trip to America and marriage.

Kenny was shattered, not by Daddy's tall tale, but that he wasn't the great-grandson and namesake of royalty and surely heir to the title. For years after knowing the truth, he still lorded it over the other kids in class who believed every word they heard.

I loved the line to girls he wanted to impress. "Someday we'll run away together to my ancestral castle in Krakow." He could shovel it as much as guess who?

Miss Kaib

Miss Kaib, the music teacher, wore somber dark clothes and low, thick-heeled shoes. Her brown hair, streaked with gray, was styled in a bun with wisps of hair falling around her face and neck. She peered through wire-rimmed glasses, and her lips, painted a bright red, never formed a smile.

Once a week was music class. I hated it when singing was involved, because I couldn't carry a tune in a bucket, no matter how hard I tried. While I hovered in Cindy's shadow mouthing the song, my best girl-friend trilled away like an opera singer, drowning out the complete soprano section and the boys who were the tenors.

God only knows why Miss Kaib selected some of the songs she did. "I Heard the Wild Geese Flying" could only be sung by Cindy or a diva from the Metropolitan Opera company, and "Cucaraacha" made us want to scratch. As Miss Kaib blew on her pitch pipe, away we sang and mouthed it, with the lucky ones playing the cymbals and triangles for maximum effect.

The times we listened to records were our preferred classes—no baby stuff like "Old McDonald" or "The Farmer in the Dell," one of Kenny's all-time favorites, but Chopin, Beethoven, or Mozart. Loving Beethoven's "Fifth," we rushed down the hall to our classroom after music class loudly humming "da da da daaa."

Miss Kaib, who started teaching when schoolmarms weren't allowed to marry, traveled around to and taught at the other public schools in the district. She wasn't a frightening figure, even though she never cracked a smile. We weren't fearful of any teacher who didn't give a grade. Music, art, and penmanship were judged by "satisfactory" or "unsatisfactory." You didn't have to be good to get an S, but you had to behave or else get a U. Miss Kaib must have been tempted more than once to give Cindy an S+ just to set her apart from the tone deaf S's.

The Shoes

Not only did Jimmy, Barbara, Kenny, and I have the same teachers as our mother, but we also had the same substitute teacher. Miss Grimm was her name; and her father had been the mayor of Vandergrift during the 1930s.

Since teachers rarely missed a day of school, unless they were deathly ill or had a family emergency out of town, Miss Grimm was the only substitute teacher for the East Vandergrift grade school as well as the three uptown in Vandergrift.

It was such an oddity for a teacher to be absent that our mom could recall specific dates when Miss Grimm taught her class. For instance, in the fall of 1931, Mom's fifth grade teacher and ours, Miss Miller, took a leave of absence for a week to attend her brother's funeral in Buffalo, New York. It was the second time Mommy had Miss Grimm as a pinch hitter. The first time was years earlier when Miss Claypool had pneumonia and was in the hospital for two weeks. Thank God Miss Grimm didn't need steady employment, because back then sub jobs were few and far between. Teachers did not casually take off Mondays or Fridays to extend weekends. As single women with no social life to speak of, school was their whole being and the reason for their existence.

When Miss Miller said good-bye to her children as she headed out the door on her way to her brother's funeral, she expected Miss Grimm to educate, not just baby-sit. School was serious business to those women, and nonsense in the classroom was not tolerated.

The next to the last day of Miss Grimm's tenure, she asked our mom to remain after school. Mommy wasn't worried that she had done something wrong, because she, and all the students and teachers, knew what a well-behaved, excellent student she was. Miss Grimm wanted Mom to go to Sophie Kaminsky's house to find out why she hadn't been in school for over a week. Before leaving, Miss Miller had pointed out that Sophie was the only absent student but probably had a cold or something. Now it was 10 days, and Miss Grimm was troubled that Sophie might be gravely ill.

As asked, young Mom went to Sophie Kaminsky's house to find out what the problem was. Sophie opened the door herself and said she wasn't going to school because she had no shoes to wear since outgrowing the only pair she had. Hearing her daughter give the explanation, Mrs. Kaminsky yelled from her bedroom that "school was stupid and useless for girls." In a drunken voice, she added, "Sophie don't need no shoes to clean the house and take care of her kid brothers and sisters."

Mommy wasn't shocked at what she heard. She knew full well that Mr. and Mrs. Kaminsky squandered most of their evenings at the clubs drinking and had no money left to buy clothes for their children. While Mr. Kaminsky worked, Mrs. Kaminsky continued boozing during the day. Sophie never invited kids over to play because her mother was always plastered.

The next day this was reported to Miss Grimm, who, after hearing the whole account, asked our mom and two girlfriends to accompany her home after school.

The four of them walked up Vandergrift Lane together, enjoying the fall air and colorful leaves crunching beneath their feet. The girls were ecstatic to be strolling home with Miss Grimm, because they heard that her family home was the most beautiful one uptown, and there were many lovely residences in Vandergrift owned by the richest people in town.

At the front door, the girls wiped their feet so hard that Miss Grimm laughed and declared they might take the rubber off their soles if they kept it up. As they walked into the living room, Mrs. Grimm was lounging on the divan embroidering a pillow cover. After shaking the girls' hands, she asked if they would like a spot of tea. Mommy was thrilled being treated the same as a grownup, especially by the mayor's wife, Miss Grimm's mother.

The maid went off to boil water while Miss Grimm took the girls to the attic, where she opened a cubbyhole and lugged out three boxes filled with ladies' shoes. The attic, Miss Grimm mentioned as she was looking through the cartons, was used as a guest bedroom. In it were many gorgeous objects including a four-poster bed and a roll-up desk, and the windows were stained glass. By far, it was the prettiest room the girls had ever seen, not counting the living room downstairs.

Miss Grimm chose 15 pairs of shoes in excellent condition but very old fashioned, high buttoned ones that well-to-do old ladies favored. After putting five each in three paper bags, she handed them to the kids and instructed them to take the footwear to Sophie Kaminsky and any other girl in East Vandergrift who needed shoes. Then they went downstairs and had tea and cookies with Mrs. Grimm while Miss Grimm played the piano for them in the parlor.

Sophie and Miss Miller returned to the classroom the next day. Mrs. Kaminsky reluctantly let her daughter go to school, because upon delivering the shoes, the girls warned Sophie that it was the law to go to school, and if she did not, her mother would go to jail. Miss Grimm had coached the students well, and Sophie showed up. As she clop clopped to her seat, the other kids began chortling. Suddenly, Miss Miller whacked a ruler against the blackboard and the class became silent. With all eyes on her, Miss Miller complimented Sophie on her handsome shoes then conveyed to the students that although Sophie had the prettiest shoes in the class, it did not make her any more special than anyone else.

"Clothes do not make a person better or worse," Miss Miller lectured. "What is inside a person's brain and heart, that is what matters." And, the teacher added, "if I hear anyone laughing at anyone else for the clothes they have on, that naughty student will be sent to the principal's office for a spanking."

Warning heeded, no one giggled at Sophie in or out of school. Students were afraid Miss Miller would find out from Mommy or one of Sophie's other girlfriends, who, by the way, started having tea parties after that. Pretending to be the mayor's wife and her affluent lady friends, the girls had a ball wearing those fancy shoes while politely ordering the invisible maid to boil some water and fetch more cookies.

Kennywood Park

A week before school let out for summer vacation, grade school and high school students got a day off to take a train trip to Kennywood Park, near Pittsburgh. The excitement was palatable. For one thing, it was thrilling riding on a train. The journey began uptown at the once-busy station next to the A & P. Trains by then were used mainly for freight, but passenger ones were still in service for special events, like transporting hundreds of screaming kids to the amusement park 30 miles away.

The big kids, per usual, were in charge of the little ones, which meant that Cindy and I had to keep our eyes on Frankie, Lenny, and Kenny to make sure they didn't get lost or fall off the train. We were ordered by parents, teachers, and older brothers and sisters not to let the three boys out of our sights for one minute. Sure. Try to stop three almost third-graders from joining other packs of little boys running up and down the connecting cars for an hour. If some scientist could have harnessed their energy, he would have generated enough to light up a city for a year. Cindy and I did not help matters by letting them eat cookies from the lunch basket we prepared the night before. The sugar hit their blood stream with incredible speed.

The Kennywood Park excursion had become a tradition, and the food we packed—fried chicken, potato salad, cookies—was part of the ritual. Neither of our families cared how many edibles in refrigerators we helped ourselves to, and that meant we could use the money for rides instead of sustenance. Well, we did allot some cash for cotton candy and popcorn, things you could eat even if you weren't hungry.

Kenny and Lenny, all skin and bones, ate half the basket of food before the train even left the station. One of the mysteries of the universe is, where did all that food go once they shoved it in their mouths? They were always starving and never gained an ounce. Frankie, who weighed more than both of them put together, only took cookies if they were offered.

As the train wound its way through tiny towns, Kenny, Lenny, Frankie, and their friends tossed rubber balls, shouted at the top of their lungs, and sat still long enough to stuff their mouths for the needed fuel their bodies required. Cindy and I were too busy waving at people along the tracks to bother trying to settle them down.

The moment the train stopped, hundreds of screaming kids ran to the entrance of the park to get a good place in line. It was an unwritten rule that family members could save you a spot, so Cindy and I took our leisurely time strolling to the front of the line where our speedy brothers and Frankie were waiting. Since we girls held the money, we were in charge of the boys' day's destiny. Oh, what power.

First stop was a picnic table under a shelter near a roller coaster. There was never a worry that anyone would steal the food, because everyone else at the picnic tables spread out their contents as we had and anyone could help themselves. Another unwritten law of this day was that grub was communal.

By the time the tablecloth and plates were set, other chums had joined us. Off we went to explore the park, which we all knew by heart. Part of the tradition was going around once to make mental notes of the rides we wanted to go on, and to see if some of the shorter kids had grown enough in a year to measure up to the cardboard Howdy Doody near the more grownup rides, like the roller coasters, which I refused to go on.

On my original Kennywood trip, Barbara took me on a roller coaster and I almost fell out. While it made its descent, I was pulled right out of the seat and would have fallen if Barbara hadn't hung on to me for dear life, mine. No more roller coasters for me; however, Kenny and Cindy loved them. The more dangerous, the better.

Clever Cindy had figured out a way for Kenny, a tad too short still, to measure up. When she detected an attendant yawning or reading a comic book as he guided kids through the line, she stood partially in front of Kenny who was on his tippy toes. Also, to add a few inches, he had on Cindy's straw hat that she wore on outings from June to the end of August. It looked great on her, but my sneaky brother resembled a mushroom, a total goof. The added few inches from the tip of his toes to the top of her hat allowed him to get on the ride, as long as the guy in charge wasn't paying much attention.

My heart beat overtime while I beheld Kenny and Cindy in the front car on the way up waving their arms in the air and yelling down at me. "Look, Ma, no hands." On their way down, I froze with fear as I heard them scream and watched as they clutched the bar in front of them for dear life. While they challenged death, the rest of our afternoon gang, which changed every few minutes as youngsters dropped off to go on rides and others joined it after enjoying one, knocked down milk bottles trying to win stuffed animals and had fortunes told in the penny arcade by the plastic Gypsy in the glass booth.

Kenny always won something at the lead milk-bottle stand or shooting baskets into hoops; his hand-eye coordination was unbelievable. After collecting the prize almost as big as he was, any girl in our group but me got to keep it. Usually, the lucky one was the girl who cheered him on the loudest and praised him the most. Cindy, the old con artist and accomplished *dupa* kisser, had a bedroomful of carnival prizes Kenny had nonchalantly pitched her way over the years.

After pairing with our brothers, we went into the tunnel of love. The boys, though we complained, made the winding trip a lot of fun. Making loud smacking sounds, they hooted, "We see what you're doing," if they spotted high school sweethearts taking the ride seriously.

Barbara and Jimmy and older brothers and sisters of our friends were in the park too. Arriving by carloads hours after the train had, they kept to themselves. None of us younger brothers and sisters cared anyway. The big kids strolled through the park, while the little ones ran. They talked quietly to each other; we screamed. They spent the whole day checking out the opposite sex, while we just had fun checking out the rides.

Cindy and I brought enough food along for our whole class and invited people to lunch as we bumped into them. Other mothers had also packed lunches, so we spread everything out together and dug in. Some kids didn't bring any food, but they were welcome to eat anything and everything and feasted as the rest.

For some reason, it always rained on the Kennywood outings. As kids raced to the shelter to get out of the rain, they too joined us for a snack. There was always enough food for everyone. When the shower stopped, or at least slowed, we headed for the rowboats.

Kenny and Frankie, and the duo boys in other boats, rowed as if they were at an Ivy League regatta. Cindy and I and the other girls let the boats merely drift. We argued about what the clouds were forming as they glided above the lake around the park, and the boys being boys had to splash whenever they passed. Going at such an incredible speed, they circled the manufactured pond at least 10 times to our one and almost capsized us in their wake. It was as though they were in a motor boat, and the energy from lunch gave them the added power.

The bumper cars followed the rowboats. When it was Kenny's lucky day, Barbara was in one already, not for the thrill of it but to get some practice driving a car. The look of panic on her face as Kenny headed toward her in a collision course was priceless. When contact was made and her head jerked backwards, she cried then threw up. She was the only person I knew who got car-sick in bumper cars.

Teachers also spent the day in the park, and it was thrilling walking and talking with them outside the classroom. I once saw Mrs. Bell slip a dollar to Vincent Gonka, just as she secretly bought him milk with her own money at school. I knew, because I was in charge of the milk money. As I collected the nickels, she gave me one for Vincent and said not to tell anyone. It was not necessary to tell me that, because we all were sensitive to his feelings and would never dream of embarrassing him. Kids in class treated him when we stopped by a candy store or got a cherry coke from Bartow's soda fountain. Sharsies was the name of the game.

Circling the park for the hundredth time and mimicking high-schoolers holding hands, our ears rang with the familiar refrain of "get lost." After walking and running the equivalent of a marathon, it was time to head to the train for the return trip home. The boys still had a reserve of energy and ran through the cars, jumped up and down in their seats, and recounted, ad nauseam, the day's activities.

Parents were waiting at the station to drive kids home, even though they never worried about us walking home on a dark June evening. They just knew that we would be tired and excited and wanted to tell all about the day.

As soon as Kenny and I walked in the house, our mother made us bathe, put on pajamas, and lie on the floor in front of the television to settle down. Within minutes we were asleep, and Daddy then carried us to bed, one in each arm. Predictably, I woke on the way up the steps, but Kenny, the whirling dervish, was conked out, colder than a mackerel.

After climbing out of my dad's arms at the top of the stairs, I watched as Kenny was laid on the bed. The folks loved to stare at him. And when he went into one of his famous deep sleeps, they stroked his head and kissed him repeatedly. Barbara said they did the same to me, but you had to be awake to appreciate how much love was expressed when our parents lingered at the door before turning out the light.

Summer Vacation

Although Kenny and I loved school, we could not wait for summer vacation to begin. It was the time to explore in the woods, walk the railroad tracks in both directions along the riverbank, play at the dump in the day and make berry stews and roast potatoes at night near a big boulder, race to the playground on foot and by bike, sleep on porches, crash weddings if not invited, pick tomatoes, dip in streams for tadpoles, and do a thousand and one other fun things with exuberance, the whole time not understanding what in the world grownups meant when they vocalized repeatedly, "Youth is wasted on the young." How silly they were. We did not waste a moment of valuable summer time.

Every Tuesday at six o'clock the firemen splashed streets. Kids on bikes congregated near the fire station right after supper then chased the fire truck to its destination. We'd race the truck by taking shortcuts through yards and alleys once the firefighters yelled where they were headed. The drama of the red truck with men hanging on the sides, wearing heavy, waterproof black coats, big hats, and high boots, was a sight to behold. Eagerly awaiting for one of the guys to shout the destination, Kenny and I sat with Cindy and a porch full of kids on her front steps, near the fire station. Widow Geeza Pampagoua's house stood between the jail-voting place-fire station and the Petrouski home.

The volunteers were men who worked in the steel mills on various shifts. There were always enough guys off work anytime in case of a fire. Although not one of them ever served in the military, most of them acted like heroes, ready to live out their fantasies of bravery. Men in town who fought in wars seemed quieter for some reason and didn't have that manly swagger and bravado attitude that the firemen had. Strange.

There were never any fires in East Vandergrift while we were children. The last one that anyone could remember was in 1933, when the old school house burned down. Once, though, there was a close call on Quay Street when Adam Adamchik and his mother's house started to smoke from an overheated coal furnace. It sure looked like a fire to the 10 housewives who called the fire department and the 20 kids who peddled their bikes the one block to the station to sound the alarm.

Before the truck arrived, five housewives, including our brave mom, ran into the smoke-filled house to save Mrs. Adamchik, who was taking her afternoon nap as she did every day at that time while her son was at work. When the volunteers finally arrived, they unfurled the hose and began spraying the house, smashing walls, shattering windows, and swinging axes in every direction. After watching this mayhem for a few minutes, a housewife raced past the men, went to check the basement, and threw a few buckets of water to deaden the blaze.

The smoke damage was minimal, but the ruin caused by the firemen was astronomical. There was water damage to everything, and walls, doors, and windows were demolished. What insurance didn't cover, the firefighters did from money raised at their annual carnival. Adam and his mother really made out on the deal, practically getting a new house thanks to the firemen's generosity (or guilt) following the fiasco.

While the firemen sprayed on the streets in the summer evenings, kids ran under the drizzle in their bathing suits and sat in puddles on the sidewalks. Women closed windows as though there were a summer cloudburst and rested on the porches watching the kids and the burly firemen frolic.

The fire hall was decorated with girlie pictures and sexy calendars; not nudes, but quite racy nonetheless. When the men weren't dousing the streets, they congregated at the station to play cards, swill beer, and gaze at the walls. Kids stopped by all the time to tell brothers or fathers to come home for dinner and, while there, checked out the lewd pin-ups.

The jail was attached to the fire department, where people voted on election days. During those days, whoever was in jail—usually a drunk sleeping it off—had to get up and help to get ready for when the poll opened. The overnight guest had to assist the church women set up for a bake sale and usually ate some of the profits; this was part of his punishment.

The fire station whistle blew at nine o'clock as a curfew for kids under 18 to go home. Children scattered like ants when it shrilled. No questions asked, they just went home. All games (30-more, hide-and-seek, baseball, kick-the-can) ceased when the whistle pierced. It also was heard loud and clear from one corner of town to the next during air-raid drills and on national holidays such as the 4th of July and Memorial Day.

The firemen's carnival once a year was held for a week on the playground behind the Slovak Church. There were games, penny pitch, dunk a firefighter, bingo, knock over bottom-heavy milk bottles. The prizes were the same as at any carnival: cheap glass, stuffed animals, coon skin hats, kewpie dolls, and lots of made in USA, Japan—crap that broke before you even got it home. It was just fun winning, even if it took a dollar to secure a prize worth 3 cents. "It's for charity," everyone announced.

All the people in town came and everyone spent money. There was a raffle nightly for a television and one on the final evening for a car donated by an auto dealership uptown. Well, it was sort of donated. He gave it to the firefighters for cost, and they paid for it after the tickets were sold. They always came out way ahead.

Besides games and raffles, the ladies of the town set up a food concession stand and sold hot dogs and sauerkraut, pierogis, kielbasa, French fries, and tons of fresh-baked goods. There were also cotton candy and popcorn booths and kiddy rides.

The carnivals used to be held down the field, but there were problems with that location. There was always too much drinking, and couples were seen sneaking off to the dumps to pet; therefore, the churches
put a stop to it being down there. Before it switched to the playground,
the field was large enough to accommodate elephants, horse rides, a
Ferris wheel, and a merry-go-round.

Circus folks ran it in the down-the-field days and gave the firemen a
cut, but they were a rough crowd. People in town did not relish "that
kind" of element floating around town, even for a week a year. That
group was thought of as a bad influence, and the women connected
with the carnival were said to be loose. It was deemed better for the
firemen to rent the equipment they needed to run their own carnival,
do the work, and keep all the money. More family-oriented on the playground, it was safer without those carny types. The women of East
Vandergrift did not appreciate "those kinds of women" carousing in the
clubs with their men. That just would not do at all, and they let everyone know it, including their men.

The only drawback with using the playground was that Father Cyril,
the shepherd of the Slovak Church, did not allow shorts on the church
property. The ban was not only on short shorts, but also on Bermuda
shorts. Girls had to wear dresses or slacks.

Few females dressed in slacks in those days, and hardly any kids wore
blue jeans, except farmers and high school trollops who wore them skin
tight, as though they were painted on. Because of Father Cyril's stupid
rule, we girls went to the playground in dresses that were extremely asi-
nine on a hot summer night. After tiring of the carnival, we would glide
down the sliding board or swing on the swings, and everyone could see
our "unmentionables," as we called our underpants.

The whistle didn't blow during the carnival week, and kids were permitted to stay out as long as their parents allowed.

Play Ball!

Summer would not have been summer without pickup baseball games.

Kenny and his boyfriends gathered on the front porch, strewn with bats, balls, and gloves. Frankie Poleski and Kenny, best friends, were captains of opposing teams. When any of the other boys argued that he wanted to be a captain for a change, my brother and his best friend refused to play and went off by themselves.

It was a well-rehearsed scene: They counted the guys on the porch, called up other boys and told them to run over, then recounted everyone as boys individually joined the group. If 18 boys didn't show up, they settled for the bases being covered, a pitcher, one outfielder, and someone from the team up at bat to act as the catcher.

However, it was difficult for the guy covering home plate to tag out a runner sliding in for a run; he was damned if he tagged the runner out and damned if he didn't.

Mainly, it was disorganized baseball, never the same time of day and never the same players.

Finally, realizing they couldn't round up 10 boys, Kenny and Frankie inevitably asked me, because I was quite good, if I do say so myself. Besides hitting and catching well, I was a swift runner.

Although asked to participate as a last resort, I was one of the first kids—boy or girl—picked for a team. Kenny, Frankie, and most of the other boys were third-graders; I was two years older with a slightly better sense of timing and precision in throwing.

Once asked to be included, I was delegated to call some of my girlfriends to join the game. Irene Bliazes was first. She was the fifth grade tomboy and a better baseball jock than all the boys on the front porch put together.

The next call went to Cindy Petrouski, the world's absolutely worst baseball player but the most fun to have in a game. She sang in the out-field, ran the bases backwards if she, by some miracle, actually hit the ball, and did headstands while waiting her turn at bat. Everyone wanted her to compete, but neither captain wanted her on his team.

One particular afternoon, we were about to play the final tiebreaker game in the World Series. Frankie and Kenny only played World Series games. Kenny won the toss of the bat, because he had little fingers and could grip a splinter remaining at the top. Frankie was a big boy with big fingers to match. Poor Frankie! He wasn't clever enough to realize that he would never win a bat toss with Kenny. If I suggested a coin toss, Kenny would turn to me in a rage, yelling for me to keep my big trap shut and mind my own bees' wax.

Kenny picked me first, as usual, and Frankie was ecstatic to get Irene. The final two remaining, as always, were Cindy and Frankie's little brother. Kenny chose Cindy, because Johnny Poleski never heeded his commands.

My captain sent me to first base since I could catch his throws. He directed Cindy to right field, but so far back that she whiled away most of the game picking buttercups and chasing her dog Snoopy until it was Kenny's team's turn at bat.

What a game! Kenny and I both hit homers—home runs right over the fence. This might seem rather far for kids our ages, but it really was-n't since we only used half the ball field and home plate was center field. If we had used the entire regulation field, no one would have hit home runs and that was what everyone wanted and tried to do. I trotted around the bases glowing with pride; and when Kenny hit his, he made it around by sliding into each base on his way into home. That kid loved to slide and felt that if he didn't become covered with dirt and grass stains from head to foot, he wasn't having fun.

The boys were aping older ball players by spitting, swearing, scratching their crotches, and bellowing, "Throw the bum out!" There was no umpire. We really didn't need one since the only way anyone struck out was to miss three swings. There were no walks because there were no ball calls. We swung at what we thought we could hit. The pitches were underhand, because no one had yet learned to throw overhand with any consistent accuracy. The fun of playing was hitting and catching the ball.

Cindy struck out every time and while in the outfield was never close enough to even try to catch a fly ball. Kenny, as pitcher for the Yankees and Willie Mays while he was up at bat, ran to right field when a ball was hit there, then leaped, caught the baseball, and fell into a slide. Meanwhile, Snoopy growled at him, and Cindy—gripping a fistful of flowers along with the glove—raced out of the way. Usually, if there were not enough gloves to go around, she did not get one. She really didn't need one.

In the bottom of the ninth inning, Kenny's team was ahead 57 to 56, and Frankie's team—the Brooklyn Dodgers—was last to bat.

Don Newcombe, alias Frankie Poleski, hit a bouncer directly to the pitcher's mound. It should have been an easy out, but instead of running to first and tagging him out or throwing the ball to me real easy, Kenny threw it overhand and hard, missing me by at least 40 feet. Frankie made it to second, and Kenny bawled me out for botching a ball that only Paul Bunyan could have caught.

Okay, so Frankie was at second, but he wasn't going anywhere. Big and slow, no matter what, he could never steal third while Kenny, small and fast, was pitching.

Joannie Welkon, who joined us when we bumped into her on the way to the field, was up next. She didn't start playing until the second inning, because she had to finish the cho cho, a treat sold nowhere but in our town, she just bought at Joe Stemplensky's candy store when we practically kidnapped her to make an even 10. It was iffy with her. She wasn't too bad a baseball player for a third grade girl and sometimes hit the ball when it was really slow and thrown right over the plate.

She cooled her heels patiently through 22 of Kenny's pitches before she lifted the bat and even considered swinging. He had to show off in front of her with spit balls dripping and a knuckle ball that was pathetic.

Joannie stubbornly waited and on the 23rd pitch swung and hit it to second base, where Joey Marhefka, covering second, wasn't expecting anything to happen for a while. He was slowly lacing his sneakers while waiting for Kenny to stop flirting with the batter and settle down. The ball went right over Joey's head, and by the time Kenny raced to the ball, Frankie was on third, and Joannie was safe at first.

Lenny Petrouski, Cindy's little brother, was up next. He kept rubbing his hands in the dirt and then rubbing them up and down the bat. His tongue was pressed against his cheek, pretending to chew tobacco. Swaying his hips, he fiercely looked down at the pitcher.

Trying to resemble a big league pitcher, Kenny went through elaborate windups, checked out the winning run at first, before releasing the ball underhand.

Winning-run Joannie sat on first base, trying on my shoes—white sandals—because she thought they were cute and wanted to see how she looked in them.

Cindy was lying on her back in right field getting a tan.

Cockily adjusting his Davy Crockett hat and pounding his fist into big brother Jimmy's oversized, well-worn glove, Kenny was in total control and alert. He struck out Lenny in three swings. One out.

While adjusting his eyepatch, Frankie yelled that the umpire needed glasses.

Johnny Poleski, up next, hit an easy foul ball, and Kenny ran behind the plate, caught it, then slid into home.

Timmy Ruzbacki, the smallest fifth-grader after me, was up next.

While Timmy waited for the first pitch, Kenny threw the ball repeatedly to me at first to keep Joannie from stealing second, which she had no intention of doing. She thought she had to slide into a stolen base since that was what the boys and Irene Bliazes always did. Because of that, Joannie had no desire of getting her dress any dirtier than it already was. The front of it was covered with cho cho stains.

Kenny was trying to get her attention because she and I were busy at first chewing bubble gum to see who could blow the largest bubble, and he felt that she was ignoring him.

Meanwhile, there was no problem with Frankie trying to steal home. No way could he outrun Kenny, whose fastest walk was faster than Frankie's fastest run.

Tension mounted.

Kenny shouted for Cindy to get up and look sharp. Then he called for a time-out for a team huddle.

I put on my shoes and sauntered to the pitcher's mound.

While Kenny proclaimed how proud he was of his teammates, Cindy mimicked him behind his back but stopped quickly when he turned around suddenly and caught her. She towered over him by 28 inches, but one of his stares put the fear of God in her. He had the classic Napoleonic leadership quality.

Quivering, Cindy prayed the loudest as Kenny led us in a "Hail Mary" and an "Our Father." Then, we gave the humble-looking captain three hip hip hoorays, leaped in the air, and returned to our positions.

Laughing during our dramatics on the pitcher's mound moments earlier, Timmy swung at the first pitch and missed. He nipped the second one. Strike two. On the third pitch, he hit a high and long drive out to right field, but way too far for a surprised Kenny to ever catch. Everyone (on both teams) yelled for Cindy to go back, way back, and watched as she raced backwards with the grace of the ballet dancer that she was.

Well aware of his owner's hand-eye klutziness, Snoopy growled and tugged at her pant leg, obviously trying to get her away from the ball which he knew could easily knock her out cold. This was one very smart pooch.

The sun was in her eyes, so Cindy closed them, covering her head with her left arm, holding out the glove in no particular direction, just up.

Always the sore loser, Kenny threw his glove down, kicked it, then walked, head down, toward home plate to congratulate Frankie who was jumping up and down, waving Joannie in as she rounded third barefooted.

Kenny extended his hand to Frankie. Just then, I screamed excitedly, "She caught it! Oh, my God, Cindy caught it!"

Everyone ran out to right field to see this miracle. Players on both teams believed in the Immaculate Conception and the Ascension into Heaven, but this we had to see with our own doubting Thomas' eyes.

There Cindy was, like a statue, left arm over her head, eyes closed, and ball resting securely in the pouch of her glove. Unbelievable.

Not one to be upstaged, Kenny pretended to faint on the spot at this miracle of miracles and was followed by the other boys.

None of us could ever remember Cindy catching a ball in a game, and we wanted to carry her off the field, but she was too heavy. Kenny suggested that we carry him instead, so we did.

Cindy led the procession, gloved hand clutching the ball, all the way to Joe Stemplensky's candy store, where the Brooklyn Dodgers bought the New York Yankees cho chos for winning another exciting World Series.

Going to Work with Daddy

Kenny loved going to work with Daddy; and Daddy treasured his company, as well as the luck his son brought him. At first, Kenny went along for the mere pleasure of riding in a car all day, stopping for treats, and having his dad to himself. The novelty wore off as Daddy had to compete with pickup baseball games.

He resorted to bribing Kenny with the offer of 5 percent commissions on the day's gross checkwriter sales. A good day meant $5; an excellent one, $10. Similar to a cat asleep on a window ledge who hears a flock of birds approaching in the distance, the mention of money perked Kenny's ears and interest. A born capitalist, he added and subtracted before he knew his ABC's; to boot, without pencil or paper, all in his head.

Nothing motivated Kenny more than cash, and he approached his pleasurable job like a general planning a military campaign. While other boys his age read about Horatio Alger, Kenny poured over the Dun and Bradstreet columns looking for leads. He figured the earlier they started, the more businesses they could contact; and the more customers they called on, the more sales they could make, thus the more money he would earn.

Not usually a morning person, Kenny was already dressed in his Sunday clothes—a sports jacket and bow tie. Sitting erect on the living room couch, grasping his miniature fedora, he waited for Daddy to finish shaving.

Kenny was raring to go forth and make his fortune, and his patience (what there was of it) was worn thin waiting for Daddy to eat breakfast, chat with the neighbors, and kiss the love of his life a thousand times good-bye. Those two were always necking, and we kids groaned loudly when they did.

Finally, the two salesmen took their places in the Oldsmobile. Daddy pushed his seat all the way back to adapt to his large girth. Kenny, perched on two pillows and a telephone book, stared straight ahead to a productive day's work. There was going to be none of Pop's lollygagging with Kenny along; they wouldn't even stop for lunch until the first machine was sold.

While eating their midday meal, a hot fudge sundae, the two salesmen read the local telephone directory and newspaper, checking out new businesses too young to be listed in their Bible, the D & B. As navigator, map reader, assistant, and Daddy's little helper, Kenny pushed for that second sale. If Daddy suggested an afternoon film, Kenny flatly refused, although he was the family's movie buff and could rattle off every flick every MGM and RKO star ever made.

Daddy called on customers, holding his briefcase in one hand and Kenny's hand in the other. When they met with a contractor near dinnertime, the wife, upon seeing Kenny, invited them to stay for the evening meal. Once the invitation was extended and accepted, Kenny knew the sale was in the bag.

His father told him to be extra nice to secretaries and wives, since they were the ones who ran the show and made the decisions for the men who professed to be the bosses. All Kenny had to do was think of our parents' relationship to see the wisdom in that statement.

The 36-inch assistant sales associate charmed the birds right out of the trees and wives in the kitchen as well. My younger brother, who never gave an inch with his siblings, was the perfect little gentleman with the customers' children. While Kenny flattered the mother and let boys his age beat him at games he could win blindfolded, Daddy was busy pitching the father in the living room.

After dinner and a second sale, our tired dad wanted to go home, but Kenny, invigorated by his growing commissions, insisted on one more stop, another sale.

They did well on night calls, while the businessmen were relaxing at home after a hard day's work at trucking companies or coal mines. The busy owner, reluctantly agreeing to see Daddy after he phoned for an appointment, opened the door to the dynamic duo. One look from the wife at Kenny standing in the door frame, hat in hand, blue eyes twinkling, clinched the sale.

If it appeared that Daddy had a tough customer, Kenny would sit in the kitchen eating another dessert, while the wife washed the supper dishes. There, he mentioned his brother and sisters waiting anxiously at home, praying that their father made some money for a change. He must have painted a grim Dickensian picture of home life, because the wife dried her hands and eyes on her apron, removed it, folded it neatly on the kitchen table, and marched into the living room holding Kenny's hand in hers, and gazed sternly at her husband. The firm look clearly stated, "Buy that damn checkwriter, so that this sweet little boy and his father can go home to their comfortable beds."

With the three checks resting safely in Kenny's sports jacket pocket, they headed back to East Vandergrift, stopping along the way to buy a new toy and some candy as a bonus for a job well done.

While Daddy parked the car in the garage, Kenny was in the kitchen telling Mommy how well they had done. Then, he found me to brag about everything they had eaten, whom they had met, and if they had been in Amish country, what covered bridges, horsedrawn buggies, and brightly colored farmhouses they had seen. He always felt like a sophisticated city slicker next to the little Amish children he met while on the road with Daddy.

After relating the day's events, Kenny reached into his pant's pocket, pulled out a wad of dollar bills, and laid them in a row on the coffee table. Then he leaned back on the couch, put his stocking feet on the marble table, and offered me a dollar to go 30 feet to the kitchen to get him a Pepsi. Later, Daddy joined him in the living room, flopped in his favorite chair beside the picture window, and the two of them discussed each sale, new strategies for the next time, and, proud as peacocks, remarked how bone-tired they were.

Betty Strips

At eight o'clock, Daddy was in the cellar cleaning checkwriters. Mom was in the kitchen having a cup of coffee with Mrs. Welkon. Barbara was doing homework at the dining room table with Priscilla Orkwis. I was in the bedroom studying for a spelling test. It was time for a break. I went down the hall to see if Kenny wanted to play a fast hand of "66," a card game we were addicted to.

The door to the boys' room was closed, and there was no light coming from the crack at the bottom of it. I put my ear to the keyhole in hopes of catching my brothers using swearwords, but only heard giggling. Not wanting to be left out, I opened the door quickly and yelled, "What's going on in here?" just like Mommy. The hall light came streaming into the room as they dove off the bed to either side of it. Kenny, crouching at my feet, reached up and pulled me down to the floor, covered his hand over my mouth, and with his free hand slammed the door shut.

Wiggling my body, I started to protest; but he had me pinned down with both knees on my chest and both hands over my mouth.

"I'll let you go if you promise to be quiet," he whispered, as he slowly removed his hand from my mouth.

"What's going on?" I responded.

He got off and helped me to my feet. "Jimmy and I are watching a show."

I couldn't imagine what he was talking about as I looked around the room in the dark. The only light was coming from the window facing Butch's house. There, framed in the neighbor's window, was Butch's sister Betty, our former baby-sitter and current high school senior.

"What's there to see?" I asked. "It's only Betty walking around her room." Bored, I stood up to leave.

Instantly, Kenny yanked me down on the bed. "Every night at this time she takes her clothes off." The words spilled out of him with the same enthusiasm I heard him express only for candy or money.

"I'm telling on both of you," I said. In simple translation that meant I wanted a favor to keep my mouth shut, although blabbermouthing was not one of my traits. Jimmy was sure I would never in a million years tell on him, but Kenny, who squealed quite often, wasn't too sure if I would or would not snitch. He knew I knew what they were doing was bad.

Instead of getting into lengthy negotiations, Kenny practically promised me the world, saying he would do my household jobs: dusting, drying the supper dishes, vacuuming, and sweeping the porch. Furthermore, he would run my errands, share his candy and money, and never, ever tattle on me as long as he lived, "so help me God."

As he was recklessly promising me the moon to keep silent, Betty, dressed in a tight sweater, was unzipping her gray felt skirt with poodle appliqués. Kenny shut up and squeezed my arm so tightly that he practically cut off the blood supply.

"Ouch, you're hurting me," I cried.

Putting his hand over my mouth, he hissed in my ear, "I'm sorry I hurt you. Now shut up or I'll kill you."

For a moment I forgot Jimmy was in the room; he was deathly quiet as Betty did some kind of dance, encircling her bedroom in a crinoline petticoat and padded bra. I blinked and her half-slip was on the floor as she stood in her bra and girdle facing the window. The two windows were 3 feet apart, and since she had baby-sat us as youngsters, she had to have known that her window faced the boys' room. I thought I detected a smile on her face as she leaned over, shook her hips from side to side, and pulled down the shade ending the show.

As promised, I kept my big trap shut and tried not to laugh while the folks discussed how delighted they were that Jimmy was finally studying every night in his room. Pretty soon Jimmy's boyfriends were doing homework at our house as well. Wanting to get his pal in on the fun, Kenny told Frankie about Betty's strip tease; but Frankie thought it sounded stupid and unexciting to watch an old lady take off her clothes.

Not wanting to be left out, I loved to open their door at a little past eight, turn on the light, and watch 10 high school sophomores plus one red-faced third-grader dive to the floor when I abruptly bellowed at the top of my lungs, just like Mommy, "What's going on in here?"

Saint Barbara and
Old Soul Daddy

"Oh, you two are so juvenile," huffed Barbara as she passed Kenny and me sprawled on the floor singing "M-I-C. K-E-Y. M-O-U-S-E" with black rodent ears on our heads. For full effect, we used coal to make mustaches and whiskers. As she slammed the door, Kenny yelled, "Har-dee-har."

Our older sister may have bugged us most of the time, but Kenny and I secretly admired her and her sensitivity. For example, when she found out James Dean had been killed in a car crash, Lord, you would have thought one of us croaked or something the way she carried on. Though, now that I think about it, I wonder if she would have shed as many tears. Besides treating us like lepers, she could be counted on to help us with homework, support us in a fib, and keep us enlightened with regard to what was happening in the teenage world of rock and roll.

We didn't see much of her, except in the hall at school occasionally and at bedtime, during her eighth grade year. At first Kenny and I didn't even notice she wasn't around much after school. Then, Mom brought up the subject of Barbara's disappearances at supper one evening. Kenny and I were speechless and had no comeback when we heard the story of Barbara's tutoring Marsha Kuruc, an eighth-grader at the Catholic school at the Slovak Church.

Marsha had contracted rheumatic fever and under doctor's orders was to stay home for months. When Barbara heard about Marsha's predicament, which could have meant repeating eighth grade, she went to talk to the Mother Superior at the convent, arranging to tutor Marsha until she was well enough to return to the classroom. Shocked that some little twerp was suggesting such a plan, the head nun called Mr. Mathews and found out she was dealing with the smartest young person who ever attended his school. Well, the little twerp changed into an angel of mercy in the sister-in-chief's eyes. Mother Superior met with Barbara every day to discuss lesson plans, and the numero uno nun even let Barbara give and grade Marsha's tests.

This arrangement had been going on for well over a month before Kenny and I finally got wind of it via Mommy. Boy, were we impressed. If we had done such a noble, selfless deed, the whole town would have been notified, and we would have expected medals, parades, and money. Barbara was on her way to sainthood, no doubt about it.

Not long after we had canonized big sis, our mom revealed a wonderful thing good ole Dad had done, too. Being the top distributor in the checkwriter company, he trained new sales staff. Then, the company paid him commissions for every machine the new employees sold for a year. Doing very well with this system, Daddy decided to scout out new personnel besides those who phoned the company directly. One such fellow Daddy had his eye on was a cop uptown who never gave our dad tickets when the meter expired while he was having coffee and donuts (after a full breakfast at home).

The policeman, Al Washington, and Big Jim really hit it off. Besides the absence of parking violations, Mr. Washington laughed at all of Daddy's jokes. Daddy spotted salesman-potential in his buddy and suggested that he try selling checkwriters. It seemed that Daddy kept running into businesses owned by Negroes and thought Mr. Washington could do very well seeking them out.

"I'm telling you, Al, things are starting to change," Pop announced to his pal, who was nervous about white owners' reactions to a Negro walking in their businesses. "I call on Negroes," Daddy countered.

Mr. Washington finally gave in, and Daddy completed the company paperwork to arrange for training. When management asked what he looked like, Daddy mentioned that he was a colored man.

"Sorry, Jim, you can't train him," was the response.

"Why not?" was Daddy's first question. His second was, "What would you say if I quit and went with another company?" Daddy won, and Mr. Washington started selling checkwriters, quickly becoming Daddy's stiffest competition.

"You have to stand up for what you believe in," proclaimed the matriarch, after recounting how our father almost quit his job over principle.

When Daddy walked in the door that evening, I swear, he looked 10 feet tall. Bursting with joy, he had more good news to share. Mr. and Mrs. Washington asked him to be the godfather of their new baby boy.

"But, Jim, you were never Christened. How could you be a godfather?" his concerned wife asked.

He smiled, "Oh, that. Al thought that God wouldn't mind, but to be on the safe side, I called Eddie." (Father Shezocki to the rest of the world.) "He told me to stick around after church this Sunday and he would make it official."

Mommy beamed. She had been trying to get her love to go through the ceremony for years, but he resisted. The only reason he even went to church was because of us and Father Shezocki, his good friend. After Mass, they liked to have coffee and donuts, exchange jokes, and basically hang out together, kibitzing about politics, business, movies, you name it, those two could discuss it in depth.

Mom didn't go to the Washington Christening, but Kenny and I did. Claiming she was too busy at the church or something, she felt uncomfortable, I think, about being the only white woman there. Our mother was a strong supporter of civil rights, except in matters of socialization. Too bad; she missed a swell party with tasty food.

I got a new dress for the occasion, and Kenny wore his new sports jacket and Snap-On bow tie. Chatting up a storm with the old ladies, he was also a hit with the kids, dazzling them with card tricks. Though, the cutest moment was when he first spotted Mr. Washington's daughter, who was the same age as Kenny and as short. It's hard for me to admit, but she was definitely the prettiest girl there.

Kenny noticed, too, and could not do enough for her. "Tara, can I get you some more cake?" "Tara, how about something to drink? Pepsi? Orange pop?" "Tara, want to see a card trick?"

I could not believe my eyes and ears. After all the harassment I had gotten over Timmy Ruzbacki and the redhead in the first grade who pestered me to death, here he was tripping over himself in front of everyone for the attention of Miss Tara Washington.

I heard small groups gush, "Aren't they cute together?"

"Oh, look at the two of them. How sweet."

"Isn't that the dearest picture you ever did see?"

All that aside, I wonder what the reaction would have been if they were both teenagers in high school. Liberal or no liberal, there would have been quite a ruckus at both the Dell and Washington households in those frumpy '50s.

The Washington baby was named after Daddy, and he was so moved he cried. I hated it when he blubbered, because I began as well and then Kenny started. It was comparable to Barbara puking on car trips— Daddy's tears caused a chain reaction.

When it was time to leave the pleasant green house in North Vandergrift, Kenny and I received hugs, kisses, bags of dessert, and candy. Open invitations to stop by any time we were in the neighborhood were also extended. Kenny's red face, which took on a crimson hue from Tara's kiss on his cheek, didn't return to its normal pale shade until Daddy's Oldsmobile pulled into the garage that evening.

Oh, I was dying to tease him with taunts of, "You have a girlfriend. You have a girlfriend," but Daddy whispered in my ear as we left the party, "How would you like to do something kind and special?" Daddy, the champion of the downtrodden, father of Saint Barbara (helper of rheumatic fever sufferers), asked me if I would like to be a virtuous person.

"You bet, Daddy, anything," I stood ready to join the ranks of angels.

"Well, then, don't tease Kenny about Tara." Geez, not fair of my dad to ask me something more difficult than running into a burning building to save people.

I looked up at Daddy, the strongest and best man alive, and gave him my answer. "Yes, Daddy, if it will make you happy." Oh, but let me tell you, I was chomping at the bit to get one little zinger in about Tara and that smooch as I ran after Kenny into the kitchen. He knew there had to be a reason I wasn't teasing him; but he never found out why I kept my big trap shut.

The Washing Machine
Repair Man

An era was over the moment the ragman carted away the wringer washing machine. Uncle Henry, new to the appliance business after selling radios and televisions after the war, installed the latest model automatic laundry equipment.

Daddy wanted to buy the dryer as well, but Mom dug in her heels and stubbornly refused to give up her clothespins and fresh-smelling sheets to a piece of housewifery apparatus she was sure would never catch on or be of any use to her.

The wringer washing machine, which we inherited when we bought the house before Kenny's birth, never broke down. The latest contraption, we soon discovered, was not as reliable.

Inevitably, Uncle Henry's appliance business was soon augmented by an even more profitable venture, the repair sideline. Appliance sales made him and his family comfortable; the repair afterthought made them rich.

Uncle Henry seemed surly to Kenny and me, but our mother's stories helped soften our image of him. When I close my eyes, I hear Mom tell us for the hundredth time, "When I was 12 years old, my mother remarried and the Yaschuk kids came to live at our house. Henry was 17 and worked driving a bakery truck. He never went to high school but was fascinated with radios and anything that was electrical. Such a nice boy, he built me a crystal set that I kept beside my bed. With it, I tried to pick up New York stations if the weather was clear, and when it wasn't, easily tuned into KDKA in Pittsburgh, the first radio station in America. Henry fixed electrical gadgets for people to make extra money for a home course in radio repair. Our house had radios in the living room, kitchen, and all the bedrooms. As he worked and studied in the attic, he dreamed some day of owning his own radio business."

Mom's stepbrother never charged her for repairs, even after the warranty expired. Uncle Henry, known as a skinflint and tightwad, was just the opposite with his stepsister and loyal-to-the-death customer. Her request for help sent one of his three part-time repairmen flying to our cellar, ahead of the 35 calls that preceded hers.

One such assistant, Ted Jastremski, sporting the familiar gray uniform, was a walking billboard. "Henry Yaschuk's New Appliance Sales and Repair Service" was stitched in red letters across the back of Uncle Henry's boyhood chum. Pals since first grade, they enlisted in the Army together during World War II and waved good-bye as Uncle Henry set sail on the Atlantic and Ted boarded the train west to begin his journey across the Pacific.

Mommy did other household chores while the popular and never-lonely repairman went about his work.

Kenny inspected his every move, handing him the appropriate pliers and screws. Usually, after spending a morning helping Mr. Jastremski fix the washing machine, Kenny gleamed with self-satisfaction at his much praised assistance.

One morning, however, after Uncle Henry's best employee and good friend had just left, I found Kenny sitting on the front porch swing being very quiet and deep in thought. For a kid who was constant motion from daybreak till sack time, this side of him came as quite a surprise. Suddenly, it dawned on me that maybe he had been a pest and Mr. Jastremski rudely told him to get lost or something almost as devastating.

I sat next to Kenny and felt sorry for him, although most of the time he really got on my nerves.

For instance, during a television program I loved, he leaped around the living room with a rolled-up pair of socks, using the lamp shades as basketball hoops and my head to bank shots. Or when he beat me at a race got my goat: Me on a bike peddling so hard that I thought my lungs would burst and him on foot, racing alongside me, keeping an even pace until the last few feet when he went into overdrive and practically flew over the finish line. But then, if I thought honestly about it, there were the spells when he stuck up for me and even lied for me. All in all, he was an okay brother, and I guess I could have done a lot worse. What if Mutsy Futsy, the neighborhood bully, were my brother? Ugh!

There Kenny sat on the swing, staring straight ahead at nothing in particular, with a strange expression on his face that I had never seen before. Seated quietly together, in unison we rocked the swing slowly.

After a few speechless moments, he turned and said, "Did you know that Mr. Jastremski was in the Bataan Death March during the war?" I shook my head "no." "He told me all about it this morning." Veering his face forward, my pensive pal gazed off into space. I did not know what to say.

I don't remember the precise moment we stopped using the potty, or went to bed without a bottle, or quit taking baths together, but I know it was that afternoon when Kenny ceased playing war. It was no longer fun and games once the washing machine repairman, Mr. Jastremski, revealed its horrors.

Where the Heart Is

Look-alike suburbs sprung up all over the place where family farms once stood. Riding on most Sundays to check out the carbon-copy suburban housing developments, the idea of moving brought cries of "I don't want to leave my friends" from all four of us kids, never imagining living any place but East Vandergrift, home.

Although Mom inspected the new, split-level, ranch-style houses with yearning, it was difficult to imagine her wanting to move away from Bupchie or the Polish Church, which she ran, it seemed, with the help of Father Shezocki. Besides, the burbs had no stores within walking distance, and Mommy didn't drive.

The beautiful houses seemed isolated from the good life where we walked to Hovanik's corner grocery store, Joe Stemplensky's candy store, the Polish Barber's shop, school, the Polish Church, and ball field. Why in the world would we want to leave East Vandergrift where our lives were so happy? It seemed as though we belonged exactly where we were.

Splish Splash

On Sunday outings, whether driving in farm country, visiting Grandma Dell and Grandpa Steve's house in Pittsburgh, or admiring suburban model homes, Kenny and I went along. Jimmy and Barbara were allowed to stay at home, while we, the two younger ones, roosted in the back seat, gazing at the bucolic country scenery and counting cows and out-of-state license plates.

The first time Kenny and I were permitted to stay at home, our parents went for a short business-pleasure jaunt to a housing development owned by one of Daddy's customers. For the few hours they were going to be gone, Barbara was in charge. That meant we had to obey her and do everything she said, no matter what.

As the three of us waved good-bye with promises of behaving ourselves, Jimmy was chalking a pool stick at the pool room behind Butch's family's candy store. Barbara turned to Kenny and me with one of her pretend-stern glares. "You two can do anything you want as long as you don't get me in trouble."

With that benevolent warning out of the way, she bounded into the house and phoned Roberta Adamik and the Vovaris twins—Henrietta and Harriet. Barbara invited the girls to come over and listen to records.

Roberta brought Judy Petrouski, and the twins brought their cousin, Priscilla Orkwis. The Big Bopper, Jerry Lee Lewis, Chuck Berry, and Buddy Holly entertained the group in turns on the hi fi as the girls jitterbugged to the deafening music. The volume was on 10, full force, lit cigarettes rested in the ashtray, and the six girls gabbed at once.

"Isn't Tab Hunter the cutest boy you've ever seen?"

"Priscilla, you should wear your hair like Grace Kelly."

"Debbie and Eddie's marriage is definitely made in Heaven."

"Barb, can't the hi fi go any louder?"

"Harriet, I think Tommy Chelko likes you."

Kenny and I decided to join the fun, lingering and listening on the couch for approximately two minutes before the girls sighed, "Do they have to be here, Barb?" Talk about being subtle.

Barbara handed us each a dime to get lost. Her exact word was, "Scram!" Faster than a speeding bullet, we were out the door headed to Joe's candy store for a bag of balloons.

At first we intended to just blow them up, but filling them with water appeared to be even more fun. As everybody who has ever been a kid knows, the purpose of water balloons is to throw them at somebody; and the somebody became each other. I ran; Kenny chased, then threw, and missed me, but not an open-windowed car. Water-filled balloon in hand, I raced toward my unarmed brother, lobbed, and got him in the chest.

The kitchen door opened and closed for over two hours as we filled the balloons from the kitchen sink, continuing the ritual of hunter and hunted. As we darted around cars, up and down Quay Street, and through the alley, I got silly, and Kenny—as always in a game—became serious. He had such a competitive streak that he kept count how many times we hit a bull's-eye, the two of us being the targets. The madder he got, the worse his aim became. At one point, I ducked as he threw, and he hit Cazzy, who was perched on his porch swing, pretending to read a newspaper, when in fact, he was really keeping an eye on us to report to the town the next day everything bad we did. Talk about a stool pigeon. When Cazzy bellowed, we ran to the back porch, with me laughing and Kenny warning that he was going to get even.

Walking into the kitchen and out, holding the chocolate cake Mom baked that morning, he threatened to throw it in my face. Knowing he meant business, I raced so fast down the alley that I knocked over two garbage cans. Contrary to Satchel Paige's wise advice, I kept looking over my shoulder to make sure he wasn't gaining on me.

There he was, charging down the alley, holding the cake plate as securely as his suspenders held up his pants. Quick-thinking I took a short cut through the Vovaris twins' back yard. Mr. Vovaris, cutting the grass, stopped to chat.

"Yes, yes, Mr. Vovaris," I replied. "My dress is pretty. Thank you." "No, no, not many people tell me I'm cute." Geez. Grownups babbled on about nothing all the time, saying every kid alive was adorable. Knowing their game, I complimented his lawn and hustled past the bird bath to Quay Street, scurrying as fast as my Mary Jane's could carry me back to the house. Only Barbara could save me from getting that cake in my face and all over my dress, which had just come back from the dry-cleaners. My neatnik mother would kill me if I got dirty.

I stopped dead in my tracks as I neared Frankie Poleski's house. There, hiding behind a bush, was Kenny. His knees were showing. Scuttling across the street, I tiptoed past the Poleski house; but when Kenny spotted me, he stood up and ran toward me, the whole time desperately trying to keep the cake from sliding off the platter.

Reaching our front porch, after slipping twice from the water on the street and sidewalk, I glanced up at Vandergrift Lane. What I saw turned my blood cold. Daddy's brand-new, green Edsel, the only one of its kind in East Vandergrift, was descending the hill.

Faster than a full-throttled locomotive, I shouted the alert to Kenny and rushed into the house to warn Barbara. Instantly, the music was turned down to one, the minimum volume. Harriet jumped two steps at a time upstairs to flush the butts down the toilet. The six young women and Kenny, after returning the cake to the kitchen, waved arms in the air to clear the room of smoke. Barbara and her girlfriends took seats on the couch and the two wing chairs, quickly passing sticks of gum around the room. Kenny and I, arms around each other's shoulders, positioned ourselves on the front porch top step as the long car glided to a stop. Mom got out, patted our heads, and trotted inside quickly to use the bathroom. It was common knowledge in the family that she had a small bladder, refusing to use rest rooms in gas stations, asserting they were too filthy and unsanitary. Yet, she didn't mind if we used them, or for that matter, the side of the road if none was in sight and there was a real emergency.

Daddy parked the car then reached for something in the back seat before he got out. Together, Kenny and I ran to him, arms outstretched for hugs and the candy we knew he brought us. Putting his hat on my head, he picked up Kenny. Holding the featherweight terror in his arms and my hand, he called "hello" to Cazzy, who was terrified of Daddy and afraid to speak. As Daddy negotiated around puddles, he mused how strange it was that it rained only on Quay Street and nowhere else they had been that day. Kenny agreed that it certainly was odd something like that happening.

As we reached the front door, that squeaky, unneighborly, well-known voice barked, "Jim! Diana and Kenny were bad all day, throwing water balloons, and Barbara's music was so loud it scared Fifi." Fifi was Mrs. Pinchek's vicious cocker spaniel that growled at everybody, including Pokey Dell and Snoopy Petrouski, two very friendly dogs who hung out with cats.

Daddy smiled at our crabby neighbor and answered, "Sure, sure, Mildred. Everything's fine now that Clara and I are home." To us, he whispered, "Keep away from your mother, your clothes are still damp." What a guy!

Mommy came to the door, looking relieved and relaxed, wanting to know what Daddy and Mrs. Pinchek were discussing. Cool Daddy-o answered, "The weather and music."

Sniffing the living room air, he winked at Barbara and her girlfriends, resembling cats with the canaries lodged in their throats, and whispered, "I see you burned popcorn again." Somehow he always detected the difference between his wife's smoke and anybody else's.

Mommy poked her head into the living room and announced, "Anyone for cake?" Kenny froze in his spot then turned to check out my reaction.

"Oh, do we have cake? Yeah, I'd love some," I answered, grabbing Kenny's hand and leading him into the kitchen.

Number Seven

Everybody we knew had big families in the '50s, and I begged our mom to have another baby. "I'll take care of it. I'll change all the diapers. I'll feed it." There was nothing in the whole wide world I wanted more than a baby in the house.

Bursting with excitement, Daddy finally announced that Mommy was pregnant. The good news came as a birthday present the night of my 10th birthday party-family dinner. Mom cooked my favorite meal, city chickens. Nothing to do with poultry, they are pieces of veal and pork on skewers, dipped in egg and corn meal, fried till a golden brown, then baked.

Kenny's gifts were 10 *Classic Illustrated* comic books. Barbara and Jimmy pitched in together for a Brownie camera. Since there was no visible present from my folks, I knew it had to be too big to wrap. Because there was nothing I was dying for, I couldn't imagine what it was. They made me guess. I didn't want to hurt their feelings so I started on the low end of my wish list. "A sweater?" "A coat?" "New shoes?" "A record player?" " I give up. What is it?"

When Daddy asked, "If you could have anything in the entire world, what would you pick?" I knew. Realizing what my 10th birthday present was, that split second was one of the happiest moments in my life.

Barbara, an eighth-grader, was shocked and embarrassed at the news, not only with regard to the baby, but also that our parents still did it, she voiced years later. Jimmy blushed and made a hasty retreat with some flimsy excuse about studying for a history test. I was ecstatic, and Kenny wasn't sure what to make of this new development. A baby would have been the last thing on earth he wanted. A new suit would have been better than that.

I guess my excitement, however, rubbed off on Kenny, because his enthusiasm grew in direct proportion to our mother's belly. By keeping us informed, she shared every phase of her pregnancy, even her morning sickness and swollen legs. We took turns rubbing her feet every night as she loafed on the couch; and Kenny touched her stomach often for any signs of life. Without a doubt, that first baby-kick was thrilling. From that moment until the infant's arrival, Kenny could hardly keep his little hands off her tummy for fear of missing a boot.

When we asked our pop what he wanted, he said that as long as the baby was healthy, he didn't care if it was a boy or a girl. Typical grownup answer. Kenny wished for a brother smaller than he was to boss around. I hoped for a sister I could take for strolls. Barbara and Jimmy did not even want to talk about it. The knowledge of how the baby got in a woman's stomach in the first place was just too much for them to even contemplate.

Kenny and I had trouble at first figuring out what a baby in Mommy's abdomen had to do with a stork. Then one night Barbara explained birth, not conception, to me. Feeling that Kenny was too young to know that gory stuff, I kept up the stork story with modifications.

Most of the time he didn't mention it, but at other moments he looked at me and started again with the questions. "Did the stork put the baby in Mommy? Where do storks live? How do they fly through the air without dropping the babies?" He had an analytical mind and the stork theory just didn't make sense. It was so illogical.

Finally, I related to him what Barbara divulged about the phony stork. Of course, I knew how the baby came out but didn't have the faintest idea how it got in.

Talk about innocent times. A fifth-and third-grader in 1956 actually believed that God gave married people babies any time they wanted them, similar to ordering a new car. It wasn't until the next year that Francis Pluciennik and Timmy Ruzbacki, armed with books and medical terminology, revealed to Cindy and me about the birds and the bees. Now that was hard to believe. What was the purpose of sex, the way the boys described it, besides having children? It sounded so stupid. Then.

After the big-bird fable flew out the window, Mommy prepared Kenny and me for the sequence of events before the birth (the water bag and labor pains). But no matter how knowledgeable we were, we both feared that our mother would die in childbirth, as other women had. "Poor Mr. Zablonsky. He raised those seven kids alone after his wife died in childbirth."

Naming the unborn baby became a daily game. Kenny and I wrote lists. He composed the boys' list and I did the girls'. Jotting down the familiar names of people in town, we quickly crossed off Sophie, Sousha, Cazzy, Lefty, Mutsy, Fudd, Modesta, and Geeza as too common. Movie stars were next: Burt, Natalie, Doris, Marlon, Gordon, Cyd, Humphrey, Tab, and Kim. Willie, Mickey, Babe, and Pee Wee were our favorite baseball names; and television supplied Lucy, Lone, Milton, Red, and Tonto. Dwight, Adlai, Winston, and Eleanor were our best-liked political and historical names. Trying out every one that came to mind, we realized it was easier naming pets than a baby who would be part of the family forever.

It was funny thinking of the times Mom would call out and become confused, as she did with just four kids. "Jimmy, er Barbara, er Diana, er Kenny, I mean Beulah, get over here right this minute and finish your dinner."

Daddy bought Kenny a book of names, and we bored everyone by telling of the origins. Finally, our pop said to give him our 50 selections, and he would pick out one at the hospital right after the baby was born.

Waiting an eternity for that baby to be born, Kenny and I resigned ourselves to the fact that Mommy was going to be pregnant for the rest of her life. Lent and Easter came and went. School ended and summer vacation fun began. Jimmy turned 16, and Daddy got him a used Hudson for his birthday. Barbara had a big picnic at Crooked Creek Park to celebrate becoming 14. Mom was treated to breakfast in bed and a Boston cream pie for her 34th birthday. Summer ended. Jimmy started his junior year. Barbara became a freshman. Kenny and I began the fourth and sixth grades. The leaves began to fall. Still that baby had not arrived.

The waiting ended on a chilly October evening, when Daddy, Mommy, Kenny, and I lounged in the living room, trying to see how smart we were while watching "The $64,000 Question." When Mom asked Kenny to help her to her feet, he yanked her up with a mighty eight-year-old tug. At that very moment her water bag broke. In a flash I knew what was happening. All hell broke loose. Kenny and I screamed and cried. Daddy ran around the house looking for his car keys, jacket, and hat. Calmly, Mom phoned Barbara, studying at the Vovaris twins' house, and told her to come home.

Sitting in the already-running Edsel, Daddy honked for his beloved, who was lolling in the bath tub shaving her legs. Kenny and I darted in and out of the bathroom, trying to hurry her up and down to the terrified, shirtless Daddy. The three of us were total wrecks while she was calm, cool as a cucumber, and collected. After all, this was her fifth child and easiest pregnancy. When she finally made it to the car and her fingernail-chewing husband, off they sped to the hospital.

The next morning, a very contented dad woke Barbara and me to say we had a new brother. I jumped up and down on the bed then raced to Kenny and Jimmy's room with the great news. Kenny bawled. He was convinced it was a lie and the baby was really a girl. After assuring him it was indeed a boy, he sat up and claimed ownership of the family's new possession.

With a pocketful of cigars, Daddy met the milkman on the porch to give him a stogie and a slap on the back. The milkman's smile turned into a frown when he was informed that the baby was named after him.

Later, when Daddy called the relatives in Baltimore to let them know about the baby's birth, I could tell by Aunt Veronica's loud laughter on the other end of the line that she thought naming the baby after the milkman was a scream.

Bupchie and we kids visited the hospital, where Kenny overheard Daddy whisper to the woman who shared Mom's room the origin of the baby's name. Nonplused, Kenny didn't understand what the joke was and why Mom was so upset. After all, Richard, the lion-hearted, was on his list.

Reserved Mom was even madder after she found out that Daddy had actually told the milkman "such a stupid thing." Claiming she could never face him again, she said we had to move out of town. Still in a frivolous mood, our pop replied that it would be a family secret; no one would know because we would call him Ricky, another name on Kenny's list.

After Mom calmed down, Daddy continued giving the milkman a wink when he left for work or ran out on the porch to order a quart of buttermilk, one of his weaknesses. Mr. Hunger grinned nervously as though Mr. Dell suspected foul play; and he started delivering milk to our house first to make sure Daddy was still at home. The shy Meadowgold Dairy's employee could not look Mrs. Dell in the eye after Mr. Dell's teasing. For the longest time, Mom sent Kenny outside with the extra orders because she blushed in the milkman's presence.

Years afterwards, whenever the origin of Ricky's name came up in conversation, Mom swiftly turned to Daddy, narrowed her eyelids, and firmly said, "Jim, don't even dare open your mouth."

Way Back Then

Kenny and I watched so many Superman programs, the ones with George Reeves, that without trying to do it, we memorized the introduction. "Faster than a speeding bullet, more powerful than a locomotive, able to leap...." Well, you know the rest. We could recite all the Presidents in order, too.

I guess after hearing something over and over it becomes engraved in your mind and nothing, but nothing, is ever going to make you forget it. The same is true of our mother's description of her brief high school year that she told and retold to make sure we knew how lucky we were to be second-generation Americans. I'll just press the play button in my mind and let my mom tell it herself. There she is at the kitchen table, smoking a Lucky Strike and drinking a cup of black Maxwell House coffee.

"I can't tell you too much about high school since I was only there for less than a year. But even for that short period, I loved it. My dream was to become a nurse, and my homeroom teacher told me what courses to take. One of the requirements was for a foreign language. I took German, my favorite class.

"The bad part about high school was that kids from East Vandergrift were not allowed to join clubs or become cheerleaders or be in plays. We were ostracized from the extracurricular activities, except football. The boys from East Vandergrift were the best football players and very popular with the girls uptown. How I envied those young women dressed so beautifully! They had that special air surrounding them, especially the banker's daughter, a senior who had a black chauffeur escorting her to school in the winter. In warm weather she drove herself and her girl-friends in a big yellow convertible. What snobs they were, always laughing and making fun of kids from East Vandergrift, who wore worn hand-me-downs that didn't quite fit.

"It was like the caste system in India. But the teachers were great. They were there to teach and were very fair with everyone. I was a very good student and got along really well with my teachers. When I quit high school, I thought for sure they would make my mother send me back, but in those days, during the Depression, a kid from East Vandergrift wasn't very important, no matter how well he or she did in school. Thank God, you children won't have to face that discrimination."

Changes

What a drastic change came over Barbara when she departed the East Vandergrift elementary school to become a freshman at Vandergrift High School. She and her girlfriends smoked and gossiped about boys, teachers, and girls they hated. Lounging in the girls' bedroom, they kept the window open and blew smoke out after first checking if Cindy's Uncle Cazzy was sitting on his porch swing looking up in their direction. When he was snooping, they opened the other window that faced Butch's house.

If I promised not to tell on them, sometimes they would let me sit on the floor and listen. Not often, though. Only if they needed a gopher. "Go get us a Pepsi." "Go see if Daddy's home yet." "Go answer the phone." When their needs were fulfilled, "Go away. Get lost!"

It was more fun hanging out in Jimmy and Kenny's room. Jimmy's friends liked me and allowed me watch while they played poker. Letting me look at their hands, they were very sweet, just as they were to their own little sisters. I loved running to the kitchen for their orders, especially for Eddie Lazinski who was soooooooooo handsome.

The high school boys talked about girls while they played poker, and Barbara and her freshman girlfriends talked about boys while they smoked. I was the proverbial fly on the wall and heard both conversations.

After becoming bored with the repetitiveness, I went to the front porch where Kenny, Frankie, and a bunch of their boyfriends were tossing baseball cards to see who could throw cardboard the farthest. They let me play because I always lost. When by some stroke of luck I won a toss, they loudly declared that I was out of the game and there was no room for girls on the porch. It was no skin off my back. Baseball cards were becoming very boring for me anyway.

If Bupchie had already beat me to the punch and kidnapped Ricky for an afternoon stroll, I ran over to Cindy's house to see what she was doing. Her mother was always sick and in bed with something or other and Cindy was usually doing housework. She and her sister Judy did the cooking, cleaning, washing, and ironing for their family of seven. Cindy was the only person I knew who made cleaning fun. Household chores I hated at home were a blast at Cindy's. Throughout the years, the only task I didn't help her with was whitewashing the picket fence, because the Petrouski family didn't have one.

The Hudson

The Hudson, nicknamed the "Half Moon" after Henry's ship, belonged to both Jimmy and Barbara; but once Barbara turned 16, she took complete possession of it. Lime green and boxy, it was always parked facing downhill because there was never enough gas in it to start when it was parked facing uphill. When it ran out of fuel, which was quite often, Kenny and I were summoned to help push it to a station where Barbara and her girlfriends chipped in for gas.

None of the girls found it odd when Barbara rolled down the window and told the attendant, "I'll have 15 cents worth of gasoline, please. And make sure to wash the windows."

Kenny and I rarely rode in it. Barbara swore that she didn't see us trying to flag her down as she cruised by. This, from our sister who could spot a dime on the street from 50 feet away.

Smart Daddy never permitted her take the Half Moon to buck-a-carload nights at the drive-in unless Kenny and I tagged along as chaperones. The second the car was parked downhill in the gigantic field, all nine teenage girls shoved Kenny and me out. While we found a comfortable spot on a patch of grass near a set of speakers attached to the car of a friendly family, teenage boys and girls roamed from group to group, breaking off into couples, taking turns necking in the back seat of the Hudson.

When the movies were over, the original occupants piled in for the drive home. That's when Kenny and I became quite popular with the girls, who quizzed us regarding the films they hadn't paid the least bit of attention to and were afraid their parents might suspiciously question them about. At first we were shocked, but then became accustomed to answering the teenage girls' initial inquiry on the way back to East Vandergrift: "What movies did we see?"

Melvin Sunderella

I wonder why some years stand out more than others. The year 1957 was one of those years. Jimmy became a senior and Barbara, a sophomore. She met, dated, and fell madly in love with Larry Facchine, the star football player, who was only a sophomore, but the first-string quarterback. Not the smartest guy in the world and very cocky, he was handsome and totally smitten with Barbara, who became the envy of every high school girl. Teachers loved her brains and Larry adored her body.

Meanwhile, Ricky celebrated his first birthday on October 3. Two days later, while Americans held their collective breath, *Sputnik* raced across the skies. Nearly everybody in the country was outside watching the Russian wonder travel around the earth that evening; however, I sat on a living room wing chair all dressed up for my first date.

I waited for two hours and finally gave in to Kenny's pleas of playing with him instead of waiting for "dumb and stupid Melvin Sunderella."

Kenny was great about my embarrassment; and, I think, we both somehow knew that our childhood days of togetherness were coming to a close. I was starting to grow up, and he was a little taken aback by the new me emerging. With teary nostalgia now, I glimpse back on childhood, but back then, all I wanted to be was more grownup. Ahh. Maybe youth is wasted on the young. But I digress in my middle-age. Let's return to that devastating night.

That evening Kenny taught me how to make chess moves; we searched the skies for *Sputnik* and settled for catching a glimpse of a falling star; we enjoyed his hula hoop and watched old movies until 4:00

a.m. Mommy didn't even object. She and Daddy were trying everything in the world to cheer me, but Kenny had them beat.

I can still hear him now. "He's ugly, anyway. You don't need a boyfriend, you have me. He's dumb. Timmy wants to be your honeybunch, and I like him. You're too young to get married. He has a stupid name. He smells. He's an ignoramus. You get germs if you smooch."

Daddy tried to convince me that I probably got the days mixed up.

Cindy's reaction the next day was, "Men! Who needs them anyhow?" as we made our way to church in the morning.

No matter what anybody said to try to cheer me up, I still couldn't get him out of my thoughts.

I first saw Melvin Sunderella outside the home ec room at the high school where seventh-graders from East Vandergrift went once a week. An eighth-grader from Vandergrift, he went to the high school full time with the other junior-highers uptown.

I clearly remember that initial glance. Cindy and I were discussing the potholders and aprons we were going to make when I saw him with his arm around Theresa Hojeski, a seventh-grader, who lived uptown but went to the Polish Church in East Vandergrift. I knew her since First Holy Communion days and suspected she was a little wild. It was rumored she went parking with high school boys, wore a bra since fifth grade, and used makeup.

Cindy was rattling on and on about how we could go into the potholder business to raise money for Christmas, but all I could think about was Melvin Sunderella's dark hair and green eyes, just like Daddy's.

Home ec was a double period, and we were allowed to walk through the halls during the change of classes. There was a five-minute break before returning to sewing machines and threading those stupid needles.

Cindy and I saw lots of kids from East Vandergrift who waved. Even though most of our sisters' friends were glad to see Cindy and me, Barbara and Judy seemed not to notice their younger siblings, no matter how emphatically we motioned at them while going up the stairs.

And when Cindy shouted their names, my God, if looks could kill, she would have been dead a hundred times.

I made the big mistake of confiding in Cindy about my huge crush on Melvin and pointed him out to her. I didn't know his name, so my friend took it upon herself to find Theresa at the end of home ec and ask her. Cindy learned that they were going steady. In the seventh grade? Wow! Theresa was wild.

The next day, back at the East Vandergrift elementary school, where we were the big kids, Cindy and I skipped lunch to play pinball at Carnegie's candy store next to the school. Regular patrons, we won free games all the time. Most of the time, the school bell rang while there were 10 freebies left. Cindy and I were the school champs, followed by kid brothers, Kenny and Lenny. The Dells and Petrouskis could not be beaten.

As Cindy sang "Jailhouse Rock" and thumped the sides of the machine, begging the little steel ball to go where she directed, I glanced at the door. In walked Melvin Sunderella. I almost fainted but instead bumped my pal and caused a tilt. Cindy was furious because she thought I did it on purpose. Quickly to shut her up, I told her to take my turn. She smiled at my sportsmanship then pressed the red free-game button for the five balls to slide into place.

I was trying to peek at Melvin without being noticeable. Cindy was oblivious to anything but that machine, playing with all her heart, as we both always did, and racking up the points. I whispered, "Don't turn around, but Melvin Sunderella just walked in." Suddenly she twisted around and shouted his name. I could have died or else killed her. But she wasn't being disloyal; she was just implementing an instant plan, Cindy informed me later.

He walked over and asked, "You're Diana and Cindy, right?" I couldn't believe he knew our names. Explaining softly, he said he had noticed us when we first arrived at the high school for the once-a-week classes there and asked Spike Vovaris (the twins' cousin) who we were.

Spike, who lived near the baseball field and dump, was a freshman. Thank God, Spike didn't know I had been mooning over him for two years, ever since that day he took Kenny and me for a friendly rowboat ride on the Kiskiminetas River. After that day, I could barely speak in Spike's company. Sometimes, though, I got the feeling he was flirting with me, but was pretty sure he was just being sociable to a little kid. After all, he dated girls older than he was. What would he see in me, someone who didn't even wear a bra? I knew having Spike as a boyfriend in the future was hopeless, but, still, it was nice to daydream about him. He was way cuter than Ricky Nelson.

Dreams were okay, but here was a living doll standing next to me at the pinball machine, and it seemed as if he was making eyes at me. Women instinctively know these kinds of things. My luck was too good to be true. As though reading my mind, Cindy, my pal, made an excuse about meeting Timmy and Francis outside and left us alone.

Alone at last, Melvin and I discussed the home ec teacher, shop class (he was making a bookcase), records (he revealed his favorite one was Paul Anka's "Diana"), his buddy Spike, and Barbara, of all people.

"I hear your sister's the most popular girl in high school." It was amazing how Barbara's popularity soared when she became a cheer-leader and started going steady with the star quarterback. "Are you two close?"

"Oh, yes, we're very close." I figured maybe a little of Barbara's luster might rub off on me and hoped that Melvin hadn't seen my older sister avoid me like I had the cooties. "Larry Facchine and I are good friends, too." What a bald-faced lie. When Larry sat in the living room with Barbara, he never saw anyone but her. The worst student in the sopho-more class was smitten with the brightest. What they did have in com-mon was jitterbugging and necking; they seemed to do both activities rather well.

Floating on cloud nine while impressing Melvin with the high school celebrities I knew, I was saved by the school bell before all the topics of conversation were exhausted. He had 10 minutes to make it back to the high school, but the path around the corner was a straight shot up that kids from East Vandergrift had been using for decades, since Mommy's time.

I ran to the seventh grade room; Cindy was waiting at the door with bated breath, wanting to know everything we chatted about. Walking in a fog into class, I barely heard what she was yapping about. I was in a blissful daze. I couldn't pay attention as Mr. Fantino discussed Christopher Columbus, or was it some city in Ohio? Instead of listening, I wrote Melvin's name in my notebook: in block letters, in script, inside a heart. I even tried out his name with mine in case we became serious. Diana Sunderella. I adored the sound of it.

Earth came back into focus when Richie Kallock tapped me on the shoulder and handed me a note from Cindy. "Are you in love? Do you want to marry him? Does he have a friend for me? Maybe we can double date. What's your mother fixing for dinner?"

As I read and pondered each question, Mr. Fantino asked what I was doing. Nothing I said made him mad; he liked me a lot for being a good student and the quietist person in class, one of those kids who never, ever causes trouble. I uttered the truth, since he obviously could see I was reading a note.

He wasn't used to kids telling the truth pertaining to reading or passing notes and got flustered. "Oh! Well, uh, uh, put it away and uh, uh, pay attention." I rarely got hollered at, but every once in a while my slight rebellions put me in a better standing in the class. Nobody appreciates a goody two-shoes in school.

At the change of class, Kenny spotted me in the hall and ran over. "Who's your boyfriend? I saw you talking to him." That was strange. I didn't see Kenny while I was with Melvin.

Because of Kenny and Cindy and their flapping jaws, everyone in school the next day knew about Melvin Sunderella and had us married off with a bunch of offspring. I swear, I don't know how I managed to make it through the morning classes, but I somehow did.

After a two-minute lunch, I hustled to Carnegie's candy store and sat alone at the counter sipping a Pepsi, trying to be cool as I waited for Melvin. Cindy, Kenny, and Frankie, pretending not to see me, sauntered in and headed for the pinball machine. They knew who I was waiting for, and I knew they were later going to razz me about it, but I didn't care. My sole concern was being with Melvin.

Within a brief time, the 5' 3" Italian hunk strode in and came right over to me. And, oh God, he had on the same cologne my dad splashed on after shaving, Old Spice. While I tried to keep from fainting with joy, the gang at the pinball machine laughed and peeked over at me. The jerks. They were making fun, but who cared?

As I attempted to play it cool and not let the jeering bother me, the door swung open and a tall red-headed boy I never saw before bounded in toward Melvin and me. His name was Barry Kerr, another eighth-grader and Melvin's best friend. He was awfully nice, and we instantly started discussing our many mutual acquaintances. The conversation switched to sports and his desire to be a basketball player.

While Barry and I chatted, Melvin eyed the activity at the pinball machine. "Hey, that little kid's good."

I turned to see who he was talking about. There was Kenny, gyrating as he performed to maneuver the steel ball where he wanted it to go. "Oh, that's my brother Kenny."

The three of us joined the spectators as Kenny was about to break the record on that machine, my record, but I didn't think Melvin would be impressed that I held the highest pinball score at Carnegie's candy store.

Melvin and I cheered for Kenny while Cindy kept giving me winks, her way of teasing. Then she noticed Barry Kerr and almost swooned when he smiled down at her. At 5' 9" in the seventh grade, Cindy rarely looked up to any boy in junior high. Barry Kerr was as tall as Jimmy, 6'

1" at least. I'm not sure if it was his height, red hair, smile, or freckles, but I could tell Cindy was in love.

From that momentous lunch break through September, Melvin and Barry spent their lunch time with Cindy and me. Cindy and I also started going to junior high hops uptown every Friday and danced with them, but they never walked us home, because Cindy's brother Skoozy picked us up and drove us home. Both of our parents didn't mind our being escorted by boys, but Skoozy took it upon himself to make sure we came straight to one house or the other.

Every Friday, Cindy and I slept over each other's house. After discussing the loves of our lives, we made Chef Boyardee pizzas and watched scary movies. If Cindy stayed with me, she joined in for Fred and Fran's burgers and '30s or '40s classic movies with the whole family. Whenever Barbara and Larry got in from a dance, everyone in the living room went upstairs and left them alone. After Larry left, Cindy, Kenny, and I went downstairs and watched the late, late movie.

The first month of seventh grade was pure Heaven. Then, at the end of September, Melvin asked me on a date for the first Saturday in October, but Barry didn't ask Cindy. I asked if she minded my going out with Melvin alone. I would have turned him down and waited for that double date Cindy and I always contemplated; but, no, she said she didn't mind. I accepted.

After planning a wardrobe, anticipating what to talk about, practicing kissing on the mirror, I got stood up! While I mulled it all over as Cindy and I walked to church, she kept rambling on about how I was better off without him.

After half genuflecting, we slid into a pew as Father Shezocki was saying, "In nomine Patris, et Filii, et Spiritus Sancti. Amen" and started to pick up purses and gloves while altar boys Cousin Tommy and Jimmy spoke the final response, "Deo gratias." Everything in between was a complete blur; it seemed as though I blinked and Mass was over.

As Cindy and I plodded down the church steps, there at the bottom facing up was Theresa Hojeski. In the six years since I had known her, only through the Polish Church, we probably exchanged a handful of words. "Pass the crayon, please." "May I borrow your handkerchief?" "Did you study your Catechism this week?"

Theresa smiled up at Cindy and me and waved. When we reached the bottom step, she came over and informed us that she and Melvin had gotten back together last night.

"Isn't that great news?" she rhetorically asked. Stunned, I didn't know how to play this game, the one she was obviously a master at.

Bewildered also, Cindy loudly, too loudly, said, "Sure! Sure!" and seemed to trip over her tongue. I knew she was searching for a biting comment but was lost for words.

Then, like that famous masked stranger, Spike Vovaris was behind me with his hand on my shoulder. He turned me around and started talking about what a great time he had with me last night and then asked if he could walk me home from church. I was too dumb to know he was rescuing me from a female barracuda.

Spike took my hand and shouted, "Come on Cindy, join us," without a word to Theresa. Then I knew what he was doing, but I wondered how he could have known. When I finally caught my breath, he explained that Kenny had mentioned what happened. Spike had also seen the reunited couple at the movies together and put two and two together. When he saw Theresa talking to me, he knew that she was trying to embarrass me.

Spike kept saying that Theresa was a fast girl, and if Melvin liked her, I shouldn't be seen with him. He felt that I could get a bad reputation being around him.

My savior stayed with us as far as Father Shezocki's house and when the Hojeski car drove up the street, he said good-bye and left to catch up with his boyfriends. Kenny caught up and challenged us to a race around the block. He won, I came in second, and Cindy dragged in third. Huffing and puffing, we went into Carnegie's candy store to buy Pepsis and play the pinball machine with money we didn't drop in the collection basket.

Kenny was trying to beat his own record, but I wasn't sure the numbers could go that high. As the machine pinged incessantly, in walked Spike with his cousin. They joined us at the pinball. And when Spike smiled at me, I forgot Melvin even existed.

Kenny tied his record score, and as the fifth ball made its exit, Spike touched Kenny's shoulder, looked at me, and said, "Your brother really loves you." Spike, I'm sure, wasn't making fun. As a mature freshman, he would say something charming like that after my devastating disappointment.

Kenny, though, was appalled of any talk of affection between us and became very defensive. Shrugging off Spike's hand, he darted to the door, and before skipping home, spun around, and shouted, "I do not. I love Theresa Hojeski. So there." So there, indeed.

Double Digit Day

"Happy birthday to you. Happy birthday to you. Happy birthday, dear Keeeennnnyyy. Happy birthday to you," the group gathered around the dining room table sang. It was Wednesday, October 30, 1957, and the second party for Kenny's 10th anniversary.

The first one was held the previous Saturday for his classmates and friends. And what a celebration that was! They played spin the bottle with Kenny claiming it was a practice twirl unless the empty Coke bottle ended up pointing at Joannie Welkon. He bugged her to death whenever it was her turn. If it did not aim at him, he screamed that she cheated and had to try again. His worried mom had to stop the game before Kenny got into a fist fight with the other boys when they accidentally spun toward Joannie. It was clear by the pained expressions on their faces that kissing her on the cheek was pure agony for every boy except Kenny.

The cellar was decked out with Halloween decorations: carved jack o' lanterns, paper skeletons, and witches on brooms. Besides the kissing game, they played records and danced, bobbed for apples, pinned the tail on the donkey, and stuffed themselves with cake and ice cream.

Later, Daddy and Jimmy took them trick-or-treating uptown. I have never heard of another place in America that ever celebrated Halloween for a week, but the kids of East Vandergrift did. They even branched out after covering the complete community and badgered fathers and older siblings to drive them to surrounding towns. Who knew the difference with masked and costumed kids?

Then, it was the middle of the week and Kenny's actual birth date. We had just finished dinner, Kenny's favorite—hamburgers, French fries, and yellow wax beans. The grownups and Barbara had steak. The rest of the menu included pumpkin and cherry pie and chocolate cake with chocolate icing and chocolate ice cream.

It was a family celebration except for Cindy and Frankie who observed holidays with the family as Kenny and I did with theirs. Bupchie and Ju Ju looked really cute in goofy party hats. Cousin Tommy was absent from the festivities because he had just left for Air Force training the week before; but Uncle Caz, Aunt Emily, and their one-and three-year-olds were present and accounted for. Shy Uncle Harry, Mom's stepbrother who still lived at home with Bupchie and Ju Ju, sat next to me, never speaking a word unless he needed something out of reach on the table.

Orange and black balloons were pinned to the drapes, and there were five spirited conversations going on at once. To add to the din, Frankie and Kenny blew their noise makers, and Cindy sang along with the album Daddy had on the hi fi in the living room—*Around the World in 80 Days.*

As Kenny admired the slinky Cindy presented to him, the phone rang. Hoping it was for her, Barbara jumped up to get it and raced back to inform Kenny it was for him. "Hurry up, it's long distance." What she really meant was "Hurry up and get off the phone. I'm waiting for a call." The telephone was practically an extension of her ear.

The Baltimore crowd on the other end of the line wanted to wish him the very best on his special day; and when he returned to the table smiling, Aunt Emily handed him a card from the gang on the phone. He ripped it open and out fluttered $20. He did not even read the message; he was intent on opening more presents. Grownups gave him what he liked best—money. Frankie was thrilled when Kenny exclaimed, "Just what I always wanted," when he saw the silly putty underneath the shredded paper that had wrapped it.

The noise was so loud that Father Shezocki and Mrs. Jarenski, after knocking on the front door and not being heard, opened it and proceeded in. They had been invited for dinner, but opted for cake and coffee for dessert.

After picking pieces of food off everyone's plates, Father Shezocki handed Kenny a beautifully wrapped box and commented that it was from both of them. Mrs. Jarenski added that she picked out the wrapping paper with Kenny in mind. It depicted a cartoon figure of a little devil with a pitchfork. Carefully undoing the paper, he folded it neatly on the table before removing the baseball glove inside. No kidding, he was sincerely overwhelmed, since he had never possessed his own glove, only hand-me-downs from Jimmy.

"One more present before we start eating the cake," announced Daddy as he tied a handkerchief over Kenny's eyes. Picking his son up, he pushed open the door to the cellar, which was off-limits all day because Jimmy had painted the floor. Wink. Wink. Daddy carried the birthday boy down the steps, and Cindy, Frankie, and I tagged behind.

When Daddy removed the blindfold, Kenny whooped with pure joy. Sitting in the middle of the basement was a regulation-size pool table. Cindy, Frankie, and I jumped up and down squealing. As far as we were concerned, it was a present for us too. With my trusty Brownie camera, I took a picture of Kenny alone beside the pool table as he racked the balls. After he complained dramatically that he was blinded for life by the flash, we trooped upstairs to rejoin the others.

Father Shezocki and Mom were in the kitchen scooping ice cream on top of the cake pieces. The babies, Ricky and Uncle Caz's two little ones (Caz, Jr. and Anthony), already were gobbling dessert with their fingers. Daddy, Aunt Emily, and Mrs. Jarenski were discussing what they were doing 10 years earlier when Kenny was born. Cindy was desperately trying to get a potholder order from Uncle Harry, who did not even know how to boil water and never cooked anything in his life. Frankie and Kenny were bragging to Jimmy that they could beat him at pool after only a week of practice. And Barbara was telling Bupchie and Ju Ju about her subjects at high school. The two grandparents did not speak English but understood it fairly well. What Barbara conveyed, though, was as mysterious to them as the sphinx, but they both smiled and kept nodding their heads with pleasure. Barbara had a captive and adoring audience in front of her. Meanwhile, I snapped away, taking great candid shots of the whole happy scene.

"Hey, Diana, let me take a picture of you and the other Dells," Father Shezocki yelled from the kitchen as he licked the ice cream scooper.

Mommy protested, then ran upstairs with Barbara to comb her hair and apply more lipstick. When they returned, we got in position for the family portrait on this important occasion. Kenny claimed it was a milestone turning 10, the beginning of the double-digit age. He and I sat on the chair at the head of the table, both pretending we had just blown out the candles. Crewcutted 17-year-old Jimmy, with Ricky on his shoulder, stood behind Daddy, who had on one of those ridiculous party hats. Ricky's face, hair, and "I Love Grandma" bib were covered with chocolate icing. Pretty Mom, looking stylish in her new sack dress, stood next to her loving husband with her arm encircling half his waist. Barbara, beaming in Larry Facchine's varsity sweater, thrust out her chest and showed her pearly whites for the camera.

Standing perfectly still, we posed as Father started the countdown. "One. Jimmy, stoop down a bit. You're too tall for me to get Ricky's head in. Two. Barbara, scoot closer to your mother. Kenny, Diana, sit still for Heaven's sake, or else you'll come out blurred. Everyone ready?"

When Kenny and I meet again and relive happy memories, I know one of the many will be the moment the Dell family, the seven of us, smiled at Father Shezocki when he shouted, "Okay, my beloved church mice, say cheese!"

Acknowledgments

Many people helped me in the writing of this memoir. Three I would particularly like to thank are Ruth Dell, my sister-in-law, who first suggested that I write about childhood; Barbara McPherson, my sister and trusted adviser; and Carol Dingle, a great friend, who edited this book. I am also grateful for many kindnesses to the following people: Linda Estes, Paula and Kathy Mahan, Christine Guido, Kay Kavanaugh Zarif, Susan and Andrew Reardon, Christina Dimock, Donald Hamilton, Heather Butts, Donna Alger, Mary Brodie, Gerard Leahy, George Sommers, Cindy Petrouski Green, Timmy Ruzbacki, Debbie Marshall, David McPherson, Jimmy Oscar Dell, Richard Ott, Meredith Kiger, Laura Beck Poskus, Zack Lombard, Bruce Guckert Jr.,Jean-Philip and Lorraine Rava, Maryann Hurley, Jacques Bargiel, Linda Kerr, Eddirland Duncan, Leigh Mason, Robert Szymczak, Rebecca Phillips Payne, Dorota Lotocka, Charles Milano, Melissa Hurley, Chris Batten, Lore Fields, my son Mark Clark, the love of Kenny's life: Beckie Peiples Thomas, and Mom.

About the Author

Diana Dell was born in 1946 in East Vandergrift, Pennsylvania, where she grew up, and graduated from West Virginia University with a degree in journalism. She worked as a journalist on a newspaper and also taught second and seventh grade classes. In 1970, after her brother Kenny was killed in the Mekong Delta, she went to Vietnam as a civilian with USO. There she was a program director in Cam Ranh Bay and director of public relations in Saigon, where she hosted "USO Showtime," a daily program on American Forces Vietnam Network (AFVN) radio. In addition, she set up "Feed the Children" programs in orphanages, coordinated programs and publicity for the 14 centers in-country, and escorted USO shows and visiting celebrities around Vietnam—from the Delta to the DMZ. Upon leaving Vietnam, following the Easter Offensive in 1972, she worked in Europe for a year as publicity director at the Frankfurt USO and two years as a freelance writer and photographer in Athens and Madrid. After owning an advertising agency in Massachusetts for 10 years, she taught Vietnam War history and journalism classes at Tampa College. Diana divides her writing time between Boston and Clearwater, Florida. She is also the author of *A Saigon Party*, a Vietnam War short story book.

5922567R0

Made in the USA
Lexington, KY
27 June 2010